SIGNS AND WONDERS

THE SOCIETY OF BIBLICAL LITERATURE
SEMEIA STUDIES
Edward L. Greenstein, Editor

SIGNS AND WONDERS
Biblical Texts in Literary Focus

J. Cheryl Exum, editor

Criticism is the pursuit of signs, in that critics, whatever their persuasion, are incited by the prospect of grasping, comprehending, capturing in their prose, evasive signifying structures.

Jonathan Culler

We can say that the sign...does not refer to a single unique reality, but *evokes* a collection of associated images and ideas....It harbours a principle of *transformation*: within its field, new structures are forever generated and transformed.

Julia Kristeva

SIGNS AND WONDERS
Biblical Texts in Literary Focus

Library of Congress Cataloging in Publication Data

Signs and wonders: Biblical texts in literary focus/ (edited by) J.
Cheryl Exum.
   p.   cm. -- (Semeia studies)
   ISBN 1-555-40249-6 (alk. paper). ISBN 1-555-40250-X (pbk. : alk.
paper)
   1. Bible. O.T.--Criticism, interpretation, etc. 2. Bible as
literature. I. Exum, J. Cheryl. II. Series.
BS1171.2.S55 1988   88-19169
221.6'6--dc19   CIP

Printed in the United States of America
on acid-free paper

CONTENTS

CONTRIBUTORS

Yairah Amit
Bible Department
Tel Aviv University
Ramat Aviv, Tel Aviv, Israel

David J. A. Clines
Department of Biblical Studies
University of Sheffield
Sheffield S10 2TN, England

Katheryn Pfisterer Darr
Boston University
    School of Theology
Boston, MA 02215

Ellen Frances Davis
Union Theological Seminary
New York, NY 10027

Tamara C. Eskenazi
Center for Judaic Studies
University of Denver
Denver, CO 80208-0292

J. Cheryl Exum
Department of Theology
Boston College
Chestnut Hill, MA 02167

Jan P. Fokkelman
State University of Leiden
2311 BZ Leiden
The Netherlands

David M. Gunn
Columbia Theological Seminary
Decatur, GA 30031-0520

W. Lee Humphreys
University of Tennessee
Knoxville, TN 37996-4350

David Jobling
St. Andrew's College
Saskatoon, Saskatchewan
S7N 0W3 Canada

Francis Landy
Department of Religious Studies
University of Alberta
Edmonton, Alberta
T6G 2E5 Canada

Peter D. Miscall
St. Thomas Seminary
Denver, CO 80210-2599

PREFACE

The essays and responses in this volume present readings of the biblical text from various literary perspectives. Though they focus on different texts and rely on different reading strategies, there are points of contact and overlap. Two of the essays deal with related stories, Francis Landy's analysis of the Akedah and my own study of Jephthah and his sacrifice of his daughter. Two essays treat related topics; both Tamara Eskenazi, in her study of Ezra–Nehemiah, and Ellen Davis, in her discussion of Ezekiel, explore issues of textuality specifically in relation to the formation of written documents. The essays span a considerable amount of biblical material. We begin with Landy's interpretive journey through a critical chapter of Genesis and its parallels. Yairah Amit's article on the Ehud story and mine on the Jephthah story utilize different approaches to examine two of the cycles that make up the book of Judges. David Gunn's essay and Peter Miscall's response take us through Samuel and Kings to Chronicles and Ezra–Nehemiah, and Eskenazi's article picks up with Ezra–Nehemiah, raising a different but related set of issues. Davis's study of Ezekiel moves us into the prophetic literature.

Essays and responses reveal the significant influence of recent literary critical theories on biblical interpretation. Discussion of gaps, ambiguities, and inconsistencies, and of theories of reading appear throughout the volume. The volume as a whole, by offering a variety of literary readings of biblical texts and critical responses to them, seeks to underscore the usefulness and importance of different literary approaches to the Bible and thereby to suggest that valuable insights would be lost were we to argue for the primacy of any one particular literary method.

I take this opportunity to express a special word of thanks to Alice Bach of Union Theological Seminary, New York, for expert editorial assistance.

J. Cheryl Exum

NARRATIVE TECHNIQUES AND
SYMBOLIC TRANSACTIONS IN THE AKEDAH

Francis Landy
University of Alberta

> R. Zera^c said: Going to sleep is a long journey.
> (*Pesahim* 109b)

ABSTRACT

We begin with the problematics of the split voice in
the Akedah that ever strives to reunite, in the ambivalent
context of paternal and divine envy and love. The range
of reference is expanded through a discussion of Job's
reworking of the Akedah motif and of Hugh White's
correlation of the Akedah with Greek myths of initiation. There follows a lengthy tracing of point of view in
the text, to show how every detail and especially redundancy focus attention on Abraham's unvoiced subjectivity; this is succeeded by an examination of spatial and
temporal modes, the subversion of narrative sequence
through anticipation and retardation, the mystification
of the place that thus attains a symbolic dimension. The
last section concerns the status of the Akedah as a symbolic transaction whereby contradictory narrative demands are mediated; it is set in the context of the theme
of child sacrifice throughout the Hebrew Bible and as an
inversion of the wife-sister stories in the Patriarchal narratives.

0. Introduction

0.1   A voice speaks to Abraham. It is ambiguous, both formally
and psychologically. Formally the voice is one of the many voices
that pass through the narrative, and yet it creates its world and

invents its history, and all the voices of its characters are inflections of it. The author enters the story and stands in an ambiguous relationship with the other implied, human author, whose voice is likewise heard in those of all its characters, including that of God, yet is almost self-effacing. As we will see, in our story the human author intervenes in his own right, subtly to comment upon and reverse one of his own statements.

0.2   The voice is experienced externally, as the voice of God, and yet is an inner voice, since the narrative has hypostatised in it its creative and questioning drive, and since every outer voice, especially a disembodied one, corresponds to some inner reality. Otherwise it could not be heard. People who hear "voices" listen to split-off parts of themselves. However, it would be fallacious to claim that the voice of God is purely an inner voice that legitimates what would otherwise be unacceptable. Abraham responds to something, an outer voice, speaking in the world, and an inner voice, that speaks also within himself.

0.3   Through this voice reality expresses and imagines itself and hence exists consciously. It is present in humanity, since humanity is part of creation, the indivisible universe, and because humanity has an especially intimate relationship with God: as creatures who create and imagine in their own right, who speak to God with their own refracted and reflected being, and who make God's words audible and legible. The definition of humanity as created in the image of God from the very beginning projects into the Bible a total framework of narration: a split voice that ever strives to unite. This shows itself, for example, in the complementary splicing of sources, such as Genesis 1 and Genesis 2–3, the confident external performative sequence and the tentative internal drama, whose syntactical interdependence Robert Alter examines in *The Art of Biblical Narrative* (142-145).

0.4   The voice has special authority here, in Gen 22:1, since it has guided Abraham throughout his life. It represents, in narrative terms, the deepest part of his consciousness, since he only exists in the narrative insofar as he responds to that voice. Abraham comes to life when he goes to Canaan, "as the Lord had said" (Gen 12:4). Likewise, it represents the deepest part of human consciousness, since Abraham is the archetypal human being, both as the primordial ancestor of the people whose tradition the narrator recounts, and the one on whom devolves the task of making humanity, fragmented at Babel, aware of its relationship, and of turning the curse of alienation into a blessing, since "through you shall all the families of the earth be blessed" (Gen 12:3). Abraham thus represents the collective consciousness of humanity, that which is archetypal in it.

0.5 What the voice says is then very strange. It tells Abraham to sacrifice his son to itself, that he should be reabsorbed into that voice. In the burnt offering the victim will be entirely consumed in the divine flame. So Isaac, the child of laughter, whose birth exemplifies being surprised by the joy whose precondition is incompleteness of knowledge, impotence to control events, and disbelief in destiny, also represents the corollary: the unexpectedness of death, the quenching of all laughter in time. It is very delicately communicated that the contagious laughter provoked by Isaac's birth has its bitter element. Sarah's scepticism, her sad old wives' wisdom, is, to all appearances, justified. Isaac himself does not match up to his hilarious birth, except in the sexual act (Gen 26:8). We feel in him the pity, the pathos, of adult sobriety.

0.6 Human sacrifice closes the distance between humanity and God: the creature feeds the divine flame, which throughout the Bible is a metaphor for God itself. That which is created dissolves in that which creates, the appearance with the source of being. Thereby history, the adventures of God in time, will come to an end. Or at least, in terms of the Bible, with the sacrifice of Isaac history will cease to have a meaning, and hence to be a narrative. Humanity will remain divided, quarrelsome, purposeless, without relation to God, in other words that which seeks to find itself in the world.

0.7 For Abraham, Isaac is the future. He is himself, projected in time. The text stresses his importance for Abraham through its list of affective epithets: את בנך את יחידך, "Your son, your only one." If it were not for Isaac, his entire life would be valueless. Abraham himself says, in Gen 15:2, "My Lord God, what will you give me, when I go childless?" What is noteworthy is the tone of intimacy and exasperation: אדני יהוה, "my Lord God," could well be translated "my dear God," an accusation of absurdity as well as a recognition of majesty. For מה תתן לי, "what will you give me," is not a straight question. It is more of a declaration of impossibility, "what *can* you give me?,," as part of the dramatic progression to the gift of a future. Abraham loves Isaac, as his sole meaningful possession, in which are invested all his hopes and his entire identity. He loves him both selflessly, as someone other, and narcissistically, as he loves himself. Hence the text in Gen 22:2 concludes: אשר אהבת את יצחק, "whom you love, Isaac."

0.8   For God, too, Abraham is the "only one," who comprises God's hope for the future. For God then the murder of Isaac, of Abraham projected in time, would mean the end of everything God values and loves. God and Abraham are exactly analogous.

0.9   The story introduces itself with a brief generic summary: "And God tested Abraham." Why did God test Abraham? What is the nature of the experiment? It may be, and this is how it is usually presented, that God is entirely disinterested, detached. If, for example, it is a parable against the practice of human sacrifice, the focus is on Abraham and his descendants, how they will receive the moral of the exemplary tale a didactic God has prescribed for them.[1] The text itself interprets its significance in terms of limitless obedience, though here the object of knowledge is God: עתה ידעתי כי ירא אלהים אתה 'Now I know that you are one who fears God" (v 12). God acquires knowledge, Abraham acquires blessing, in a curious reversal of the Genesis 2–3 story, in which humanity is cursed with divine knowledge.[2] The paradox of a God who lacks knowledge, hence the means of controlling God's own creation, puzzled Augustine (cf. Genesis 1–8) but is central to process hermeneutics, and, as James Williams has argued (130-131), is implicit in a narrative in which God is a character. On the structuralist actantial model, if God is the Sender of the narrative, God is also the Object, who obtains knowledge for itself, and, incidentally, for us. Thus the story is closed from the point of view of divine hermeneutics. On the human level it is open, since God sends blessing to Abraham, in other words an infinite fecundity. Likewise, the story is recorded for all generations to interpret.

---

[1] Most commentators confine the issue of child sacrifice to the narrative's prehistory; e.g. Westermann (398), Coats (396); the fullest exposition of the story as an etiology of pilgrimage and redemption from child sacrifice is to be found in Kilian (52-56); cf.Van Seter's harsh comments (237).

[2] This has been demonstrated through the excellent Greimasian analysis of Genest (esp. 158, 166).

0.10 But if God is simply curious, investigating Abraham's malleability, the ordeal does not essentially concern it. It is not the content of the experiment, but the fact of obedience, that is significant. The same could be said, even more cogently, with the prohibition of the fruit of the tree of knowledge in the garden of Eden. God is then precisely like an experimental psychologist who conditions his or her subject to obey every command, and then commands the subject to do evil. Then what is the status of the Bible as a history of resistance to unjust authority? Moreover, the supposition of a coldly curious God and the faithful automaton Abraham misses the metaphorical connection between the experiment that is devised and its object.[3] For absolute obedience turns humanity into a cipher and is the essential form of human sacrifice.

0.11 To look at it differently. According to familiar psychoanalytic theory, every fantasy has its latent content, motivated by desire or fear or both. The idea that comes into God's head, that Abraham should sacrifice his own son to God, does not appear out of nowhere. Further, since it is both an outer voice and an inner voice, and Abraham and God are parallel figures, we will have to study its meaning for both partners. In other words, why does Abraham acquiesce without protest? If the voice of God is also an inner voice, what part of the self does it articulate?

0.12 Conflict between generations, often linked with jealousy, is all-pervasive in Genesis. Straightforward Oedipal interpretation in terms of sexual rivalry and self-immolation is commonplace.[4] More to the point, in terms of Isaac's essential significance, is that Abraham has every reason to envy and fear his son, since he is his ultimate successor. He is thus the harbinger of his death. If the son possesses the future, he is invested with the father's rancor for his finitude.[5]

---

[3] For this problem cf. Coats (398 n. 11).

[4] The ambivalence of Abraham is explored in Zelig (32). Cf. Money-Kyrle (234), according to whom, in a rather desperate attempt to reconcile it with Freudian theory, the sacrifice of the son is unconsciously parricide, since the son is the reincarnation of his grandfather, as well as suicide, since the father identifies with his son.

[5] White (1979) adduces another factor: ambiguity arising from the hostility of father to son in a matrilineal society.

0.13   There is another aspect to this, however: if Isaac is Abraham projected in time, he loves him as himself, as we have seen. The lover seeks to identify with the beloved and draw the beloved into his/her orbit. Desire for the other threatens to destroy its otherness. The son, as the bearer of one's seed, is especially intimately related to oneself, and yet different. Abraham suffers the pain of every father who must relinquish his child. To pursue the divine analogy, it is the pain of God, who is possessive, jealous, and demands absolute obedience, yet who must allow the creature its freedom.

0.14   Rivalry, envy, and possessive love conspire to murder the child. Yet because the child is loved, as himself, he must be preserved. This is the basic tension in the story.

1. Amplification
1.1   There is an evident parallel with Job. God tests Job because God does not know whether Job fears God unconditionally, or merely through cupboard love. If God takes away all that Job has, except for his ambiguous נפש—life or soul—and in particular if God destroys his future, invested in his children, will Job continue to fear God? Like Abraham, Job is a paradigmatic figure, on whose virtue rests God's entire faith in humanity and hence in creation. God says to the Satan: "Have you seen my servant Job, for there is none like him on earth?" (Job 1:8). Like Abraham, Job is restored to progeny and prosperity. But there is a twofold difference. Abraham is brought to the brink; Job is taken over it. In Genesis we do not lose confidence in the narrator, that even this is one step in the unfolding of the divine promise; that knowledge will lead to blessing. In Job there is no future, no history, merely the realization that the world is and will continue to be a terrible place. None of Job's curses are contradicted. The book cannot be contained within a divine scheme. There is only the vision of creation that links God and humanity, and their communication. God is brought to knowledge, but not the comfortable knowledge of Genesis 22: "Now I know that you are one who fears God." It is more a questioning of the concept of fearing God, its meaning and desirability. An orthodox God who is quite sure of what it requires of humanity is suddenly made to confront what humanity really is and why God needs it, not to say "Blessed be the name of the Lord" in the face of every disaster, but to question it for the sake of truth. Job could be viewed then as an insidious commen-

tary on Genesis 22. Further, and this is the second difference, Abraham himself brings Isaac to the altar, and God in person tests him and intervenes. Abraham and God are in accord, both consciously and unconsciously. Job is passive, impotent to prevent his children's deaths, despite his prescience, with all his pious resources. Their murder is thus a rape of his will, his spiritual identity as well as his lineage; he is denied the choice that gives Abraham his moral dignity. Likewise, God is passive, totally susceptible to the suggestions of the Satan, to whom God abdicates power and moral responsibility. The only accord between Job and God is a parallel impotence and despair. The entire universe is in the grip of demonic forces.

1.2   Hugh C. White, in an impressive article (1979), postulates as the life-setting of the story of the Akedah a ritual of initiation, whereby the child symbolically dies, is sacrificed to the father, in order to enter the community at large. For parallels he draws upon a large number of Greek myths which turn on the narrowly averted death of the child by exposure or fire, and in particular that of Athamas and Phrixus, an extremely complex narrative with a number of astonishing similarities to our own. Athamas takes his son Phrixus to the top of a high mountain, to sacrifice him in obedience to a false oracle; Heracles appears, as the messenger of Zeus, to deliver him; Phrixus is then borne by a golden ram to Colchis, where he offers the ram up in thanksgiving. The golden fleece provides the occasion for another tale, also related to our theme. Moreover, Zeus is symbolically the father of Phrixus, since his mother, Nephele, is a phantom of Hera, Zeus' consort or other side. Athamas has two wives, one divinely given, the other terrestrial, whose intrigues complicate the action, just as Abraham has two jealous wives, one divinely given and endogamous, the other exogamous and excluded from the promise.

1.2.2   White believes that the story of the near-death by exposure of Ishmael through the jealousy of Sarah complements that of the near-death by fire of Isaac, and that somewhere in the traditiohistorical background may be discerned Hagar's revenge. Be that as it may, and much of White's argument is unconvincing (cf. e.g., Duhaime: 153),[6] the differences are surely crucial. For example,

_____

[6] In particular, his hypothesis for traditiohistorical development lacks cogency (cf. 25-26).

neither of Athamas' wives has any problem of fertility, although
one of them is a phantom, and Athamas seems quite unconscious
of her divine provenance. There is no correlation with Sarah's
barrenness, or her having procured Hagar for Abraham, which
gives our cycle an additional twist. The complexity of the myth
suggests a fusion and overdetermination of motifs that in turn
should make us wary of the form-critical and traditiohistorical
assumption that narratives were originally simple and one-dimen-
sional. Nevertheless the common basis of the two stories is undeniable. White claims, moreover, that the myths in which the child
is threatened with death by exposure are associated with abandonment by the mother, typically after she has been forced to flee
the paternal home with the child, and hence with the prohibition
of incest; myths of death by sacrificial fire are associated with the
father and entrance into the adult male community. These correspond to two stages in the initiation process, and to the tales of
Ishmael and Isaac, which thus have a common archetypal basis.
The combination of the two elements ensures that the child enters
the adult sexual community while not altogether losing what
White calls his narcissistic identification with his origins (8). In one
case, the Oedipus myth, the hero in fact consummates the union
with the mother; White speculates that this contributed to the
demise of the heroic tale (8). In another instance, that of Jason,
the hero is condemned to wander perpetually, so as not to return
to his origins. Moreover, Jason had set out on his travels to restore
the exiled and improperly buried soul of Phrixus to its home.

1.3 What White has shown, I think, is not that Genesis 22 orig-
inated in a rite of initiation, communicated through the Isaac
tribes, but that the same motifs and tension are pervasive in Greek
and Israelite literature and point, as well as to a possible shared
Eastern Mediterranean literary culture, to a common male experience: the experience of growing up, leaving the mother, being
initiated by the ambivalent father into the world, through the
ecstatic flame that draws on sexuality and death. One of the pro-
totypes of initiation to which White refers is Dionysius, reborn in
fire from his father; another name for Dionysius is Dithyrambos,
literally "He of the Twofold Door," whose music unites life and
death, childhood and adolescence.

1.4 It is as well to move briefly outside the intrabiblical world, for the sake of the contrast: Abraham and Isaac go back home,[7] history and the blessing are reaffirmed. They return without danger of incest, for Sarah is absent from the narrative. The elimination of the mother allows the text a certain formal perfection and completion. It may be explained either/both by the ambivalence of Abraham, his combination of love and narcissistic identification with destructive rivalry and envy, and hence his acquisition of an overall parental quality, and by repression, because absorption in or the danger of incest with the mother is too threatening. However, this repressed element is the subject of a number of stories of which, as I hope to show, ours is an inversion. These are the wife-sister stories, in which both our protagonists pretend that their wives are their sisters. Through its juxtaposition of the various stories, and the careful juggling of metaphor, displacement,and repression in a continuing narrative, the text ensures that the child/ancestor will remain in contact with, enfolded in, the matrix, while being free to pursue its independent existence in the world. The tragic quality of the Greek myths, of which White speaks, expressed in their episodic character, the irreconcilability of mother and father, leaving their heroes to wander perpetually pursued by their destiny, is thus resolved. The Bible has its confidence in history. But then there is Job, the only other point in the Bible where God tests humanity, which explodes this confidence. We perceive the biblical vision of a coherence in time, always questioned and redefined, from outside, from among the fragments, just as we see the Bible in and in contrast with its Mediterranean context.

2. Point of View

2.1 Let us look at the text. I wish to show how it concentrates almost unremittingly on the subjectivity of Abraham through an array of subtly combining poetic factors; how, in other words, we are invited to see what Abraham feels and understands. The way the text focuses on its hero's state of mind without rendering it explicit or even necessarily conscious is one of the elements that makes it "fraught with background," to use a term made famous by Auerbach's unsurpassed discussion of the Akedah in the first

---

[7] See, however, e.g., White (1979:24) for whom the singular, "And Abraham returned," marks the beginning of Isaac's independent life. On the other hand, the singular verb matches the singular of "he rose and went" in v 3.

chapter of *Mimesis*. Auerbach shows how through its elimination of all contingent detail, such as a description of Isaac's appearance, the text insists on its essential ethical, consequently subjective dilemma; speech leads to what is unspoken (10-11). Adele Berlin, in a fine essay on point of view in biblical narrative, in which she describes what she calls its film technique, delineates how the camera faithfully follows Abraham close-up, with one long shot when Abraham and Isaac leave their servants. She thinks this technique is responsible for the background effect that Auerbach made critical currency (Berlin, 1982: 72-73, 1983: 44-45). I hold, to elaborate on Berlin's position, that the camera eye is split, in the same way as the narrator's voice. We observe Abraham objectively, from without, as he moves unimpeded towards his goal, but also from within, seeing for example the mountain through his eyes, and feeling the pain with his heart.[8] In the next pages I propose to read the text closely to show how the text uses its rhetorical resources to develop this inner point of view, to evoke our imaginative sympathy. In particular, it uses redundancy, pronominal suffixes, emotive activities, paronomasia, and our reconstruction of language games; for example, how we would react if we were put into Abraham's position and our children asked us awkward questions. The process through the text will not be rigorously systematic, in part because I want to read it with a certain degree of freedom, to allow the reading to open up in unexpected directions, and in part because I do not want to dissociate technique from content.

2.2 Already the text suggests its affective focus through the opening dialogue: "Thus God tested Abraham and said to him, 'Abraham.' He said, 'Here I am.'" From the point of view of narrative, it is quite superfluous: the test begins with an overall framing summary that serves to isolate it as a paradigmatic event, a divine game, in the play of history, and continues with the most ordinary of trivial conversations, whose function is phatic, to open the channels of communication. On one level it functions as a stage direction that introduces the characters and allows us time to identify with the human actor. There is a background recognition of the special intimacy of Abraham and God into whose easy discourse the brutal command erupts. But primarily it also

---

[8] Cf. the very sensitive analysis of McEvenue (323-325), who regards this participant focus as characteristic of the Elohist.

invokes Abraham as a speaking subject. The abstract distanced
representation that encompasses the story (God—test—Abraham)
is replaced by an Abraham who declares his presence and a voice
that meets him. Thus we are enabled to hear God's command
through Abraham's ears and to wonder how he will respond.

2.3   God says קח נא, "take, נא." The particle נא further evokes the
addressee, whatever its connotation, whether of ironic politeness
or respect, as traditionally translated, or simply of softening the
blunt imperative; its function is conative, to compel the attention
of the listener. God says קח, "take," followed by the meaningless
particle נא, that introduces a moment, a syllable of suspense, before the phrase is finally resolved by the object את בנך, "your son."
God's message so far is an insistent "listen to me," suggesting both
the importance of what God has to communicate and a fundamental anxiety, which is indeed that Abraham, and his seed, will
not "hearken to God's voice" (Gen 2:18).

2.4   The voice continues, "your son, your only one, whom you
love, Isaac," a list of emotive epithets reinforced by second person suffixes, את בנך את יחידך, "*your* son, *your* only one," that give
Isaac a metonymic quality as an attribute of Abraham and trace
the new creature back to its source.[9] The grammatical object of
the sentence is thus attached to the ultimate object of the discourse: Abraham and Isaac belong to the same semantic field.

2.5   And then it passes on to the next magisterial imperative,
whose concentrated monosyllabic energy is projected first into
the immediate sentence and then into the narrative as a whole.
The two primary commands, קח, "take," and לך, "go," suggest
contrary movements, the one a retraction, of Isaac back into himself, the other a journey, from himself, the point where he says הנני,
"here am I," to an unknown place. The one is a tightening, a
grasping, the other a perilous adventure that implies a certain loss
of self. The story is a working out, to the point of exhaustion, of
the dynamic of the two commands.

---

[9] Cf. Coats (392), who notes also the repetition of the attributes in vv 12 and
16. Licht draws attention to the growing tension caused by the delay (120). For the
relational assimilation of son to father and father to God, see Genest (166). Davidson (57), quoting the well-known Talmudic interpretation, (Rashi, t.b. Sanhe-
drin 89b), emphasizes the focus on Isaac's significance.

2.6 The idiomatic indirect object לך לך is another poetic indicator that refers us back to Abraham, to the journey he is about to make and experience, which is in a sense also an inner journey, *to* himself. It would be anachronistic and fanciful, entirely midrashic, to interpret לך thus, except to underline the general point that every apparent redundancy has a connotative significance that makes us continually aware, for example, of Abraham as the emotional center, and the object, both direct and indirect, of the narrative.

2.7 But לך לך has another dimension. It recalls, paradigmatically, God's first command to Abraham, לך לך מארצך וממולדתך ומבית אביך, "Go from your land, and from your birthplace, and from your father's house" (Gen 12:1).[10] Thus the Abrahamic cycle will end with an evocation of the words with which it began, and hence look back and over the whole adventure, implicitly condemning it. Abraham would have done better to have stayed at home. The euphonious paronomasia, לך לך, that like קח נא softens the imperative, makes the phrase both memorable and beautiful, a civilized rhetoric that contrasts with the violence of its injunction. On one level, the decorous speech reflects God's status in the universal hierarchy; on the other, the mastery of language communicates the narrator's control over his formidable burden.

2.8 In Gen 12:1, the sentence ends, אל הארץ אשר אראך "to the land which I will show you." Here God concludes, על אחד ההרים אשר אמר אליך "upon one of the mountains that I will tell you of." In each case, then, the commission לך לך generates a parallel phrase to complete it. The land in which the promise of a blessing to all humanity will be fulfilled is echoed in that where it will be turned to ashes. The same voice and the same guidance bring Abraham to the land of Canaan and to the land of Moriah.

2.9 Abraham does not respond, despite our legitimate expectation; the voice that we heard earlier, and that brought him to life as a speaking subject, lapses. It is especially surprising given his fearlessness elsewhere. Abraham's passionate disinterested defense of Sodom against deserved destruction makes us wonder to

---

[10] The connection has often been pointed out; e.g., Crenshaw (15 n. 16). Miscall (12-14) sees in it a contrast of decidability; through its definitiveness Genesis 22 draws attention to the ambiguity of Abraham's motivation in Gen 12:1-3. Possibly the best treatment is that of Rosenberg (74).

what lengths he will go to save his own, unquestionably innocent, child.[11] Here truly the judge of the whole earth does not work justice. The test is only of interest because Abraham is not an obedient sheep. His puzzling acquiescence further suggests that it corresponds to an inner necessity, that an aspect of Abraham is in complicity with God.

2.10   In the next verse everything reinforces our sense of Abraham's consciousness. We imagine him waking early, almost too readily, saddling his ass, taking his servants; we glimpse the victim for a moment, "and he took . . . Isaac *his* son," before Abraham chops the wood for the burnt offering. Each of these actions is perceived, both visually, as directed by the objective and apparently impersonal lens of the narrator (Berlin, 1983:65), and emotionally, insofar as each has its weight of subjective significance, in the absence of which it would be utterly without interest. Moreover there is a gradual intensification of the sequence, that moves from the ass to the lads to Isaac, and then concentrates on the wood of the sacrifice. The disparity between the humbleness of the task and its gravity needs no critical ado. Further, it takes time to chop wood; each blow must be felt as compounding the murder. The displacement of this act, in which various critics see evidence of an inept welding of sources, is thus thematically and poetically justified (cf. Kilian: 88, van Seters: 235, Westermann: 358).

2.11   Then "he arose and went to the place which God had said to him." The fact of this journey is, I suggest, subordinated to its unerring quality. Abraham is perfectly attuned to the divine will and knows intuitively which is the place. Abraham's consciousness and God's consciousness are manifestly interconnected.[12]

2.12   From the point of view of plot the next verse is again entirely irrelevant; in fact it could be said that there is no plot, in any

[11] Cf. Crenshaw (20), whose suggestion that perhaps Abraham's silence was induced by having only one person for whom to plead does not seem very convincing. McEvenue (324) correctly shows that Abraham's silence solicits the reader to voice Abraham's protest for him.

[12] Gunkel's suggestion that a phrase identifying the place has been omitted is unnecessary; as Westermann remarks, it would destroy the parallelism with Gen 12:1-4.

conventional sense, until the crisis at the altar. Instead there are a series of incidents, each of which simply marks a moment in Abraham's unseen struggle. The real plot is the inner conflict, of which the narrator only speaks allusively, as if he himself were not a witness to it (Auerbach:11). In turn this suggests limits, whether or not ironic, to his omniscience.

2.13   The first incident is almost invisible from outside: "On the third day Abraham lifted up his eyes and saw the place from afar." We are aware that only Abraham recognizes the place and only for him does it have significance. Nevertheless it invites our participation; we see his vision and can only do so with his eyes and his thoughts. Thus the whole verse focuses our attention exclusively on the interiority of Abraham.

2.14   It is followed by a parting from the servants:

> And Abraham said to his lads: "Stay here with the ass, and
> I and the lad will go hither, and we will worship and return
> to you."

The servants are brought along to be left behind. This is their function, a very strange one in any narrative, characters who are introduced solely in order to take no part in it.[13] It compounds our sense of Abraham's isolation and provides an occasion for speech, in other words further evidence for his state of mind, an entirely enigmatic self-expression. We hear what Abraham says, but not how he says it. Is it a lie or a residual hope that induces him to say, "we shall return to you"? Assuming it to be a lie, with a touch of hope against hope, is it embarrassing? When he returns without the child, how will he explain himself? The very inadequacy of the deception indicates Abraham's confusion, heightened by his authority as their master. Moreover there is a barely comic, subversive undertone—the most dignified of the patriarchs has to resort to a crude, and what is worse clumsy, lie (as he does in the wife-sister stories). We sense the desperateness of the improvisation, and that God has put him into that situation.

---

[13] White raises, then assumes, the possibility that the young men are recent initiates (1979:14) to account for their redundancy. This in turn derives from White's hypothesis that the original context of the story was a rite of initiation. The evidence for this signification of נער seems doubtful (cf. Duhaime:152).

2.15   The servants with the ass represent the world that Abraham has to leave behind, the peaceful patriarchal household. Hence upon the dramatization of this farewell rests a turning point in the narrative. Until now the servants have interposed between Abraham and his son, and his fate. He has had a public as well as private persona. Now the text allows, or forces him, to be simply a father, whose intimacy with his son is tested in the next verses.

2.16   First there is a little detail:

> And Abraham took the wood for the burnt offering, and he
> placed it on Isaac his son.

Isaac takes the place of the beast of burden and is already bound to the wood. The widespread motif of the victim bearing the instrument of his death is the more poignant because for him it is unconscious. He might well feel privileged to assist in this small way in the rite. There is thus a discord between the heavy symbolism of the act for Abraham, or for us, whereby Isaac already becomes sacrificial, and its natural import for Isaac, now that they have left the ass in the profane sphere. Again we watch and interpret Abraham doing this, wondering for example at his insensitivity or self-control. A small detail is the redundant word בנו, "Isaac, *his son,*" as if it were necessary to remind us of the relationship. As in vv 2 and 3, the epithet and suffix reinforce our consciousness of Isaac's meaning for Abraham. Then Abraham takes the fire and the knife in his hand. Gunkel sees in this act evidence of Abraham's tenderness, that he did not wish the child to harm himself. And the two of them walk together.[14]

2.17   There follows the one interruption of the narrative concentration on Abraham: Isaac speaks. Through entering into speech and thus the human and literary community, Isaac ceases to be simply an object of joy and anxiety and becomes a subject, with his own character and feelings, poignant, because so imminent is its extinction.

2.18   Every word shows us, moreover, that it is a child speaking. We project ourselves into that voice, as into every subject. Not

---

[14] It is unnecessary to contrast the two interpretations with Crenshaw (23). He attributes the former, disparagingly, to Rouiller (20).

only is the voice new to the narrative but also to the world, with a freshness that has not suffered wear and tear. The death, and even more the murder, of a child is an extreme exemplification of human transitoriness, and the grief we feel with all the Bible's victims, because the child is so new, and so beautiful.

2.19   He says אבי, "father," an unfraught statement of relationship, suggesting both a lack of communication and a connotative depth, everything a good father means to a son. There is a trust that Daddy is dependable and can answer all questions, which is inevitably eery in context. Furthermore it is the most particular, hence critical, instance of Abraham's universal function as the father of humanity, recalling his divinely given name and God's summons at the beginning of the passage. God speaks to him as Abraham, the father of the multitude of peoples; Isaac addresses him as his own unique and loving father. There is no discontinuity between these two functions but an apparent paradox: it is as the father of the multitude of peoples, as part of his divine mission, that he has to sacrifice his son.

2.20   As before, Abraham answers הנני, "Here am I," an expression that is both habitual and paradigmatic. We glimpse, through just three words (הנני בני אבי), Abraham and Isaac's customary mode of talking, and we grasp Abraham's attitude toward his son: ever ready to answer questions, at his disposal, kindly, attentive. The willingness is also protective: he will attempt to dispel doubt, satisfy curiosity and consequently anxiety, lend a tolerant and essentially comforting ear.

2.21   Then Isaac asks his famous question:

> Behold, the fire and the wood, but where is the lamb for the burnt offering?

It is a child's question, with no trace of foreboding. One may wonder why it has taken Isaac so long to notice that a requisite item is missing. The question is curious about a world where everything is still mysterious yet explicable. That there is no lamb for the burnt offering may not be more anomalous than many other things adults take for granted, and is susceptible to answer. Curiosity, wonder, guilelessness characterize the child.

2.22 And then, in contrast, there is the equally famous reply:

> The Lord will provide a lamb for the burnt offering, my
> son.

In essence it can be reduced to (i) I don't know; (ii) it will come out right in the end. Our attention is fixed on Abraham, how he says this, both to himself and Isaac.

2.23 But the irony also encompasses him. He gives an answer that is no answer, that conceals the real answer, and yet turns out to be the literal truth. Something prompts him, suggesting, as when he sees the mountain from afar, that he is in touch with the voice of God and the rhythm of the story. Thus there are many inflections to his voice: the desire to reassure, to be a kind and protective father for as long as possible, overlaying his despair and perhaps secret hope, and beyond this the mingled voices of God and the narrator, the first sending Abraham on his path, the second arranging the story. The ambivalence of the ironic voice, superficially gentle and reassuring and inwardly despairing, with its cruel undertone, whether it derives from the situation or from the unacknowledged homicidal inner voice, is expressed in the ambiguity of the answer. The "lamb" may be a metaphor for Isaac, and thus truth is disguised as falsehood. If so, the substitution of human being for animal, the inversion of the usual sacrifical metaphor, is both anguished and defensive. Abraham dehumanizes the son, as when he loads him with the wood, both to distance himself from the relationship and not to communicate the truth. Or it may be a real lamb, out of pretended (or self-pretended) or genuine hope and trust. It may waive responsibility, putting the onus on God, and be half-directed toward heaven.[15] The voice emerges in its brief, mysterious complexity, and the two weld together, in an apparent harmony, the habit of a lifetime, ironized however by the utter dissonance of consciousness.

2.24 The Midrash interprets the final בני, "my son," as being in apposition to שה, "a lamb," and the reply as a subtle hint to Isaac,

---

[15] "It throws the ball back into God's court, so to speak" (Westermann:359). The Targum Onkelos may express this through the passive "Before the Lord it is revealed."

which succeeded in communicating the truth to him (T. Neofiti and Genesis Rabbah 56:4-5). Yet the two of them were still in harmony, יחדו, literally "as one," united in their resolve to do God's will. The difference between the first and second "and the two of them walked together," between innocence and knowledge, serves to express an identity of purpose. For us too the repetition of the phrase, across the dialogue that gave Isaac a voice and Abraham a tortuous enigmatic reply, implies both a sameness, an uninterrupted continuation of the journey, and a difference of awareness, as if we have been initiated.

2.25   But thereby it also indicates the pathos that underlies the dialogue, that in the end it cannot evade the truth. From the point of view of narrative technique, Isaac's embarrassing question and Abraham's desperate recourse, through giving us an internal perspective, prepare us for and at least make us think about the shock that Isaac cannot but receive. Abraham may shield him from knowledge as long as possible but in the end is helpless; we thus realize his suffering. Isaac's trauma, that Daddy can do such a thing, is moreover a particular concentration, a prototype of the loss of innocence of every child, every human being, who discovers he or she is mortal; that life, which seems so bountiful, is in fact fatal. The loving father is suddenly murderous; the source of life represents the ancestors and comes to reclaim the child.

2.26   After the introductory and rhetorically unmarked "and they came to the place," following "and they both walked together," the narrative focuses once again on Abraham through its reiteration of the phrase, "which God had said to him," stressing once again their mysterious affinity. The phrase is, strictly speaking, redundant from the point of view of content; "And they came to the place, and Abraham built the altar" would have been quite clear. It reinforces our sense of divine manipulation and of a pattern in the story—hence the authorial manipulation that makes the story fit, that makes it beautiful. The focus on Abraham, reestablished, is sustained until the climax by a series of verbs: "And Abraham *built* there the altar, and he *arranged* the wood, and he *bound* Isaac his son, and *set* him on the altar above the wood. And Abraham *sent* forth his hand, and he *took* the knife, to kill his son." There is a flicker of attention to "Isaac, his son," bound and set upon the altar. But the subject is Abraham, both grammatically and actively, as the initiator of every movement, the one who sets the scene, makes it a sacred site, dominates and controls it.

2.27   At one point, that where our absorption in Abraham is greatest, he is even the object of himself, "And Abraham sent forth his hand," as if he were the entire field of action. It is then that we are most aware of the narrative as an inner drama, before the brief transition to the theophany. The sequence of verbs is again, strictly speaking, unnecessary; from the point of view of plot we do not need every harrowing detail. Their effect is, on the contrary, rhetorical; they make us wonder how Abraham did it, what he felt (cf. McEvenue: 324). As in v 3, each humdrum act is loaded with emotional significance. The very itemization and patience of the description, the way for example it pedantically specifies, "and Abraham built *there* the altar," is itself rhetorically indicative. Abraham does everything correctly, meticulously, all in good time, as he has from the beginning of the story. The intensity of repression, and conversely the temptation to make a mistake, is imaginable and increasingly intolerable. Abraham would then be acutely self-conscious, conscious of the pain and the need to stop it, and determined to keep it under control. But this points to another overwhelming yet extremely subtle feature of the narrative: its silence. Between the first הנני which he utters to God, and the second הנני in response to the voice from heaven, he cannot speak to express his feelings. The text makes us imagine and reconstruct his experience, without granting us the direct access of speech. Those few words he does say can only deepen the silence, since they cannot refer to it. It is what is not spoken that is heard. The horror is literally unspeakable and is only spoken of, alluded to, through the silence.

3. Time

3.1   The ambiguity of point of view is also that of time: not only between narrator, reader, and event, but between sequential time and its subversion. Time is experienced objectively as history. The narrative asserts itself as something that happened long ago to someone else and is thus rendered tolerable. It is also felt from within, as the same segment of time is repeated in the imagination, detached from its original context, to become a symbol of a perpetual trauma. Each moment is conceived as part of a temporal succession, filled with a multitude of synchronic events, without pattern or purposeful direction; but the inner perspective

that I outlined in the last section, our perceiving the drama
through Abraham's eyes, brings to each moment the intensity
with which he entered it, so that its apparent duration and significance fluctuates. Beyond this, there is the narrative's paradigmatic
quality, as the meeting point of the eternal and the evanescent.
This section will concentrate on the different stratagems the narrative uses to communicate the emotional variability of time and
its relationship to rhythm and recurrence, and secondly, to ensure
the interpretation of different temporal orders.

3.2   The time of the narration may be parallel to the story told;
the moments of greatest intensity and apparent duration are ver-
bally the most protracted. (cf. Licht: 119; McEvenue). These moments may be expanded, while others may be eliminated
altogether. The reduction of the narrative to a few key moments
gives it form and embodies the mimesis of the story time by
narrative time; only that is recorded which is memorable. But the
reverse can occur: consciously or unconsciously a significant event
may be omitted. This possibility is only activated, however, if the
narrative draws attention to its aporia. The three days' journey in
v 4 is an example.[16] Then we use our imaginative empathy to
interpret the silence. The reticence of the author, in other words,
encourages our participation, implicates us more deeply in the
story.

3.3   A third stratagem is the use of prolepsis and analepsis (cf.
Genette: 40). A moment may be prepared for, and preemptively
filled, by anticipatory speculation. On the other hand it may echo,
e.g., through quotation, a previous moment. One example which
we have seen is the reminiscence of the promise in Gen 12:1 in the
divine command in Gen 22:2. As there it may acquire an ironic
resonance; nevertheless it introduces us to a symbolic frame of
reference that serves to subsume its components in a paradigm in
which individual moments lose their uniqueness and borrow intensity from one another.

---

[16] Auerbach (11) has been criticized for this kind of gap-filling, e.g., by Miscall
(17-21), who is sceptical about the ethnocentric supposition of character and motivation in the biblical text. Nevertheless, "gap-filling," no matter how culturally
preconditioned, is an essential component of the process of reading, as pointed out
by Sternberg (188-190). See also *Semeia* 31.

3.4 A fourth technique is *contrast*. The text will juxtapose temporal indicators that draw attention to the inclusive chronological frame, and hence to its status as prose, with other indicators that assert timelessness and hence the story's transcendence of its context, to suggest both an interruption of the sequence—suddenly another reality intrudes—and a coexistence, time as continually interpenetrated by timelessness.

3.5 The narrative does not set out to expose the illusion of linear time; on the contrary, the equivalence and inevitability of moments give it its tension. We will eventually reach Mt. Moriah, flinching, and the world will continue, bereft of Isaac. Time is the subject as well as the medium of all narrative, written in the proleptic anxiety of death (cf. Hartman: 300). We have recourse to memory both for consolation and, retrospectively, to redeem it from death, to make the memory present and transmit it to the future. Thereby we intermittently redeem ourselves. The attempt to give meaning to the past, to salvage something from the catastrophe, involves the poetic function, a reality made by language, contradicting that which destroys us.

3.6 There is also the vacillation between prose and poetry. In an article on James Kugel's *The Idea of Biblical Poetry*, I argued that these are always relative terms, not only in the Bible, as he suggests, but in all literature, that they are the constantly interacting poles of a continuum. Prose is marked by a relation to sequential time, while poetry evokes the "illo tempore" of myth and dream, and the experience of timelessness. This is reflected in other oppositions, such as objective detachment and subjective participation, by different types of subject matter, and by the contrast between metonymy and metaphor. I used Genesis 22 as an example of a text which identifies itself as prose through such temporal markers as "and it happened after these things" and "on the third day," as well as other indications (narrative stance, reference to social convention, the development of metonymic configurations), under pressure from poetic features, such as parallelism, which serve to articulate heightened moments, when time seems to repeat itself, to stop, or a wish for it to do so, as when the angel says, "Do not stretch out your hand against the lad, do not do anything to him" (v 12). This may be compounded, as in "Abraham lifted up his eyes, and saw the place from afar" (v 4), by allusion to a conventional poetic idiom, and hence to a poetic or epic style on whose resources the narrative draws. But I also tried to show how parallelism is adapted to prose through such familiar couplings as "he rose and he went" (v 3), or "and he lifted . . . and he saw" (v 4), in that it serves to fill narrative space, to make it notionally seamless. Moreover this opposition between poetry and prose is the stylistic correlative of the subject of the narrative, in which a timeless moment in which history and hence all narrative is at stake becomes the guarantee of ceaseless succession, in which the father dies to be perpetuated in his seed, and in which a closed action, God's coming to self-knowledge, permits the openness of the human future.

3.7   The narrative begins, "Now after these things," a determination apparently fixed and yet, as all commentators have said, serving to emphasize discontinuity from its temporal context. In the midst of treaties with the Philistines and other events, it marks the advent of the inexplicable, free from the continuing flux of causation that, as Robert Alter has argued, is characteristic of Genesis. This freedom ensures that the ensuing narrative is both set in time and detached from it. The ambiguity is emphasized by the subject—God—who can only enter time through dissimulation, and as an experiment, implying both an enclosed trajectory within which it will take place and a paradigmatic quality, since every experiment is a play with human potentialities, is a testing of hypotheses, and is abstracted from the tangle of actuality. But the test does more than this: it implies a drama of divine doubt that intersects with the human drama, an introspective questioning of the mediator of the divine blessing and hence of God itself that imperils the human axis. Instead of the network of human causes there is an enigmatic divine cause unforeshadowed in the immediate context, but intermittently recurrent, that gives to the text its mysterious and ambivalent background. The time of this introspection thus underlies, frames, and produces that of the surface narrative; if Abraham's journey is a working out of a divine thought, the voice with which he is mysteriously in touch, it is also the locus of despair at the project.

3.8   Thus the introduction establishes two temporal coordinates: one sequential, the other paradigmatic. It looks back, through the formal conjunctive sequence "now after these events," and then anticipates and defines the action; the whole narrative is in apposition to "God tested Abraham," is a working out and elaboration of it. Thereafter it remains faithful to the sequence, limiting its focus meticulously to the step at hand. For example, from the unfathomable background and long perspective of "God tested Abraham," we are reduced to "and said to him, 'Abraham,'" Abraham's reply, and God's speech, in which the words are recorded in the order, presumably, in which they were spoken. God's command is succeeded by Abraham's fulfilment. Their contiguity is perhaps emphasized by the temporal indicator, "and Abraham arose early in the morning" (v 3). He saddles his ass, gets his lads and his son, chops wood, all everyday preparations for a journey in which the assumption of a sequence is not intrinsically disturbed. This concentration on linear time, on giving every moment its due, has two effects: it avoids preempting the conclusion and it confers an ironical intensity. Every routine act is transformed by the occasion into an assertion of normality in the face of the intolerable; likewise ordinary time is sustained for as long as possible. The narrative equivalent is the prosaic effort to maintain its rationality, to tell the story coolly and unhurriedly.

3.9   The stereotyped progression, however, is accompanied by other temporal references. In the divine speech in v 2, for example, we have (i) the programmed future, the journey to Moriah; (ii) a retardation, in the description of Isaac, that compounds suspense; (iii) references back such as לֶךְ לְךָ; (iv) the temporal ambiguity that characterizes every divine-human encounter, especially one that may be nocturnal,[17] experienced in a vision or a dream, and which thus contrasts with the daylight and social interactions of the next verse.

3.10   Conflicting projections of the future, in the dialogue with the servants and Isaac, continue to be attached to the sequence; they are the main form of temporal complication. They serve to insert different possible versions of the story, to act as wish fulfilments or escapes, and hence both to keep alive the question of the future and reflexively to heighten the anxiety of the present. Fear instills a recoil from the future perceived as perilous. The future as an enigma and a source of speculation is resolved by the

---

[17] For Rouiller (18), the detail that Abraham rose early in the morning suggests that the command came at night, and is in turn indicative of its origin in the E source; cf. however, Auerbach (10), who sees in the detail primarily evidence for Abraham's promptness.

climax, in which all three eventualities are paradoxically fulfilled;
it is the point of conjunction of the present, past, and future, of the
reprieve of time, beyond which the temporal constraints are
lifted. Thus the three predictions of the future are consummated
in the limitless blessing of vv 15-18; the vanishing horizon opens
infinitely; temporal complexity supervenes over strict adherence
to the sequence. The continuous present of the mountain's name
evokes the time of narration, a prolepsis repeated in the blessing.
There parallelism combines with quotation from and reference to
the past, with a formulaic quality, as well as with its continuing
performative efficacy, to diffuse all sense of temporal focus. Thus
a narrative that is intrinsically situated in and preoccupied with
linear time becomes in the end timeless.

3.11   The sole interruption in the temporal progression is the silent passing of the three days' journey, a chronological gesture
that distances the text from the reader and marks a passage of
time that is both empty and poignant. Erich Auerbach's remarks
are, I think, fully justified:

> Thus the journey is like a silent progress through the inde-
> terminate and contingent, a holding of the breath, a process
> which has no present, which is inserted, like a blank dura-
> tion, between what has passed and what lies ahead, and yet
> which is precisely measured: three days! Three such days
> positively demand the symbolic interpretation which they
> later received (Auerbach: 10).

As readers, we fleetingly fill in gaps, reconstruct imaginatively
what those days must have felt like. But the messages are contradictory: a very long time in narrative terms is a very short time
in the time of narration. The two extremes correspond to two
subjective states: boredom, the tedium of a journey without incident or distraction, whose interminability is compounded by
depression, and, on the contrary, the mercurial celerity of a journey whose end could never be postponed long enough. Then just
before the climactic intervention, the narrative goes into slow
motion: "And they came to the place that God had told him of;
and Abraham built there the altar, and arranged the wood, and
bound Isaac his son, and placed him on the altar above the wood.
And Abraham stretched forth his hand, and he took the knife to
slay his son" (vv 9-10). The detail increases tension and our imaginative participation in the scene; one of its effects is to evade the

consummation, as if, by concentrating on the preparations, we will never reach the final moment. This way the narrative could be likened to Zeno's paradox of Achilles and the tortoise.

3.12 Finally the narrative is recapitulated and evaluated as blessing, "Indeed, because you have done this thing, and have not withheld your son, your only one." This is the principal instance of analepsis, whereby the narrative goes back on itself and preserves itself for all generations. Thus the sequence is duplicated and becomes an archetypal memory, aided by repetition, the circularity that typifies the narrative structure. For instance, God's blessing, with its allusion to "your son, your only one" (v 12), recalls the commission in v 2; God's summons at the crisis in v 11 recollects that at the beginning of v 2 Abraham's attentiveness, communicated through the word הנני, is unwavering. Hence the sequence contains equivalences that unify it, that enable us to perceive it synchronically as pattern as well as diachronically, that ensure that within each moment others are heard, and that being present—הנני—is a perpetual recurrence.

4. Place

4.1 The ambiguity of time corresponds to the enigma of the place. It is defined, as it were, in v 2 as being on a mountain, as yet unspecified, in the land of Moriah, an unknown region.[18] A future disclosure is promised—"on one of the mountains, which I will tell you"—but the next we hear of it, immediately afterwards, is in retrospect—"and he rose and he went to the place which God had told him." Prolepsis, the prospective anticipation, merges with analepsis, the backward glance, to obscure entirely the actual saying. The only apparent omission in the narrative is a word of God.[19] Its place is taken by an act of perception: "And Abraham . . . saw the place from afar" (v 4), conforming to the idiom in the parallel passage in Gen 12:1: "to the land which I will show you" (אראך). It is left in doubt whether there was a specific revelation, and if so when, or a continuous directing, and what is the interval between God's locution and Abraham's recognition, between

---

[18] Cf. Westermann (357): "There is no land known by this name." The late identification with Jerusalem (2 Chron 3:1) is taken seriously by Rosenberg (86, 235-236 n. 61).

[19] Gunkel (237) supposes that it has dropped out; on the improbability of this, see Westermann (358).

sight and speech. The ellipsis of this voice renders uncertain the boundary between Abraham's consciousness and God's, between his seeing and God's dictate, whether there was an actual interjection or merely an instinctual awareness corresponding to the congruity between Abraham and God that I discussed in my introduction.

4.2   The place recurs through unobtrusive adverbial particles in the narrative, to sharpen our sense of its contrast with our space, emphasized by rhyme; Abraham says to his lads, "Stay *here* (פה) with the ass, and I and the lad will go *thither* (עד כה)" (v 5). Isaac says, "*Here* (הנה) are the fire and the wood, but *where* (איה) is the lamb for the burnt offering?" (v 7). The place is unspecified, beyond in the first case, a mystery in the second; Abraham, as we have seen, in parting from his servants is leaving the normal world. In Isaac's question the mystery of the answer is compounded by ambiguity, for it is both the destination, other than "here," where God will provide the lamb, the ram is caught in the thicket, and it is "here," Isaac. Isaac then is unwittingly the destination of this three-day journey, whose culmination is the coincidence and sudden divergence of there and here, the passage of time and the end of time, the fusion of the participants in sacrifice and their guaranteed independence.

4.3   Once more the text stresses "the place that God had told him of" (v 9), closing the travel sequence with the same phrase with which it began: "and they came to the place" completes "and he rose and went to the place" in v 3. The lengthy paraphrase both distinguishes the chosen place and occludes it; only after the sacrifice is it identified by Abraham, and its location confirmed by the narrator as public knowledge.

4.4   Except that we do not possess this knowledge, and all attempts to guess at the locality have proved illusory. No mountain is known addressed by the improbable construction *YHWH yir³eh*. The narrator's intervention is puzzling, since usually his function is metalingual, to explain a word or a historical change. Here it merely duplicates what the narrative has just said. This strongly marked disruptive feature, rare in biblical narrative, is then apparently redundant.

4.5   It is often suggested that even for the narrator the place was unknown or forgotten (von Rad:237-238; van Seters:232). In that case the statement is extraordinarily ironic. It declares to be common knowledge that which all listeners will know to be concealed, even from the narrator. The solution to the mystery thus reproduces it, and, further, jeopardizes the narrator's role as communicator of the truth. That he goes out of his way to incur this suspicion suggests that it is not an innocent self-betrayal. It raises the question of the relation of fact and parable that pervades our thinking about the Bible, as part of its self-reflection; the narrative advertises itself as fiction, while maintaining its stance as history. This is also evidenced by the name: "the mountain on which YHWH sees/is seen" suggests a visibility (and a seeing) that can only be a manner of representation. It contrasts, on an intrabiblical framework, with the Deuteronomic insistence that on the mountain of revelation God was not seen.

4.6   In any case, even if the name was in current use, e.g., as an epithet, it does not thereby lose its symbolic value. The narrator's comment becomes an interpretation, whether ideologically motivated, as against those who ascribe it different etiologies, or to make the mountain a symbol of that which happened.

4.7   Framebreaks, authorial intrusions, especially one such as this which is apparently so unnecessary, abstract us from the narrative illusion and draw attention to the function of the narrator and the listener as those who recollect, live through, and transmit the story, who come to the same place and call it by the same name (cf. Polzin).

4.8   The place to which we come is the land of Moriah. Not only is the mountain unknown but so is its vicinity, a fact that has generated much geographical speculation, e.g., that it is non-Israelite, and thus alien to the narrator (White, 1979:28). More important than the site is the name, ארץ המריה, that with its definite article and theophoric designation suggests an allegorical significance. Van Seters' proposal, that the name is a contraction of *mōrā' YHWH*, "the dread of YHWH," is entirely plausible (238). In that case Abraham's journey is to the land of the dread of YHWH, where he will prove that he is truly God-fearing. As we have seen in the introduction, this corresponds to that which is most fearful in ourselves, our latent homicidal impulses, and which is most destructive in God. Thus the outer perspective is matched by an inner one. At all points, while not abandoning its external referent, the narrative forces us to consider it on a symbolic plane. God's voice cannot be localized in time or in space, the mountain cannot be identified, was perhaps obscure to or deliberately obscured by the narrator; the setting, in contrast to the land of Canaan to which Abraham confidently ventured in Gen 12:4, is allegorical. Abraham's three-day journey is thus to a part of himself that he most fears and is a symbol of that encounter.[20] On the mountain converge the outer elements—time, space, characters—and the inner ones—love, hate, narcissistic possessiveness, and renunciation. And through facing the fear we come to knowledge.

5. Symbolic Transaction

5.1 In this section I will study (i) how contradictory demands are accommodated in the narrative through deception, through the ambiguity of the mediating term, Isaac; (ii) its relation to other symbolic transactions in Genesis.

5.2 Symbolic transaction is my term for a transaction between two or more parties in which one or both sides of the bargain is not fulfilled in practice but expressed symbolically. In this way the narrative achieves its end while remaining open. Symbolic transaction occurs when the narrative is faced with conflicting demands that cannot be resolved except by a logical sleight-of-hand, such as mediation. A mediating term, according to structuralist theory, intervenes between the poles of an irreconcilable opposition and partakes of the nature of both; for each it represents the other. Thus it is rendered ambiguous. Isaac, as the mediating term that communicates between Abraham and God, that serves to unite them, represents both the continued existence of humanity as bearers of the blessing and dissolution in God. For Abraham, in sacrifice, he will be absorbed in God; for God, through the blessing, he becomes the instrument of fecundity, of unassimilable diversity.

5.3 The ambiguity implicates also the action. Is Isaac given or not given? From God's point of view it appears that Abraham has

---

[20] Similarly Crenshaw (28-29) interprets it as a journey into God-forsakenness, and, on Isaac's part, into oblivion.

complied with his demand: "Because you have not spared your son, your only one." The intention counts for the deed.[21] This is possible because of the deception, whereby Abraham believes that God genuinely desires Isaac's sacrifice. Proleptically God's acceptance of the gift validates the narrative program that begins with God's command and ends with its performance. Abraham thinks that he will complete the action; God can see that he will; and this foresight and recognition accompany and motivate the interruption. The anticipated denouement coexists with the actual salvation to generate a narrative counterpoint; one technique for superimposing opposites is temporal displacement. Another is metaphor, an alternative resolution suggested by Abraham. He sees a ram and sacrifices it instead of his son. Thus the sacrificial expectation is satisfied but the object changes; the ram is symbolically identified with Isaac, who is its disguised content. Evan Zuesse argues that sacrifice is a system of metaphor, whereby one object substitutes for another and is held to be equivalent to it on the basis of likeness, the sharing of properties and thus identity.[22] Abraham is sacrificed in Isaac, who transmits his seed; he is identified with God, the created image with its source, through dissolution in the flame at the sacred place.

5.4   It is unclear whether the ram is supererogatory. Its offering is not commanded by God, who accepts Abraham's will for the deed; on the other hand God directs Abraham's gaze to a serendipity whose theophanic quality is reinforced by the parallel with Hagar's vision of the well in Gen 21:19. The surrogate offering of the ram precedes the communication of the blessing in vv 15-18, thus leaving open the possibility that it elicits it.[23] The two narrative programs—the test of Abraham and the sacrifice—con-

---

[21] Genest sees in this a potential criticism of the whole sacrificial system, deferred and obscured, however, by Abraham's superfluous sacrifice of the ram (167, 172).

[22] Zuesse argues that taboo and sacrifice are intimately related. Taboo separates the symbolically similar (e.g., game and women) to preserve the divine order; sacrifice celebrates the liminal and heals breaches in the divine order by simultaneously fusing human and divine realms and by restoring the harmony based on their separation (496-500). Cf. also Kristeva (95)

[23] Cf. Genest (172-173), who sees in the sacrifice of the ram either a ritualizing reinterpretation or a discordant element in the narrative. She does, however, point to a possible semiotic connection between the ram and Abraham (ram—sheep—progenitor).

verge and are deflected along different coordinates, through prolepsis and metaphor. They turn into agents of affirmation of the main narrative, resumed from Gen 21:1-7, that of the birth and viability of the promised child, despite every danger.

5.5   Through the sacrificial metaphor, René Girard proposes, society preserves itself through finding alternative victims for its violence (2-4). Sacrificial victims are ambiguous, part of society yet marginal to it, and in particular incapable of taking revenge. Children and domestic animals are examples; likewise the pharmakos. A lamb would be a perfectly appropriate metaphor, belonging to the order of domestic beasts, part of Abraham's extended household, and related to animal society as Isaac is to Abraham. New life is restored to the source of life to regenerate itself. From this point of view the ram is entirely anomalous. Genest's interpretation that it represents Abraham, who is symbolically sacrificed instead of his son, is possible, but not conclusive, since תחת בנו would mean primarily that the ram is a substitute for Isaac. Further the sacrifice is unconventional in that the ram is a wild animal, neither Abraham's property nor part of human material and symbolic economy.

5.6   The sacrifice of the ram then suggests an element of transformation. Abraham steps out of the realm of culture, the sacrificial commonplace; in the land of dread he meets and incinerates something procreative, both in himself and Isaac, untamed, with multiple associations with beauty, pathos, vulnerability. The frustrated, trapped ram is the victim of violence that is turned into blessing. Violence is linked to sexuality; the fire represents God's vitality as well as destructiveness. Hugh White has pointed to the connection between death by fire in rites of initiation and the threat of castration. On the mountain Abraham encounters and attempts to destroy potency, as incarnated in Isaac, and thereby acquires it for future generations. As a metaphor for Isaac, the ram is divinely provided, evoking in turn the miraculous dimension in the entire Abraham cycle. Isaac is a prodigy, the child whose life is borrowed, product of a paradoxical intervention. This will lead to a further point.

5.7   The joke is reversed in the deception. The paradox that gives the child to Abraham and Sarah, and provokes their incredulous laughter, is rejected and confirmed by God's cruel joke. The lie permits the fulfillment of both sides of the symbolic transaction. It thus generates ambiguity: the coexistence of contradictory narratives.

5.8   The deception is all-pervasive. God deceives Abraham that the promise, and the miracle that brought it about, was a lie. In turn Abraham deceives the servants and Isaac. Yet at the end nothing is exposed; every lie turns out to be truth. The promise remains operative. God provides a substitute offering; yet the child is sacrificed. Abraham is still not privy to the divine test. The ambiguity occasioned by the singular verb in the last verse, "And Abraham returned to Beersheba" (Gen 22:19),[24] and the provision of a lamb instead of a ram leaves residual points of tension.

5.9   The single authorized narrative (what really happened) is then constructed out of alternative possibilities (what characters thought, how they presented the truth to each other, etc.) that remain potentially centrifugal; this is enacted in the transformation of falsehood into truth, the expression/repression of the concealed wish, to create a narrative texture in which truth and falsehood interplay, are both integrated and irreconcilable. Truth—the official story—distances and falsifies the lie, when it was perceived as truth; it removes it from history into nightmare. It imputes the truth that the lie unfolds, e.g., the unconscious desire. Thus it has a parabolic function, to be one story—a master-story—among others.

5.10   The menstrual cycle, the "way of women," is the condition of the rhythm of conjunction and disjunction through which life continues. By leaving that way, Sarah becomes the bearer of divine seed. The miracle breaks through the illusion of created order and difference and is acknowledged, beyond linguistic order, by laughter. The lie, I have suggested, reverses the transaction; language is used to communicate surreptitiously an unacceptable truth; conjunction in play permits disjunction in fact.

[24] White (1979:24) reads this as evidence of Isaac's initiated independence; Genest (165) remarks on the accompanying disappearance of the ass; Crenshaw (27) cites the Jewish tradition that Isaac was actually sacrificed and went to Paradise. Westermann suggests that יחדו, "together," in v 19 includes all members of the party; it alludes to the previous references (vv 6 and 8).

5.11 "The face of God disappears forever in showing itself" (Derrida:120). When God dissimulates, allowing characters to speak and interpret, language becomes ambiguous; it marks the partial withdrawal of the divine presence as well as its revelation. The divine ambivalence, the splitting of the voice in the command to Abraham, has its correlative in the relation of narrative to truth.

5.12 Let us look at the intertextual aspect. On the one hand the story is conspicuously isolated in its narrative context, unmotivated by preceding events and without influence on those subsequent to it. On the other hand it is part of a set of stories of various degrees of inclusiveness (e.g., the Abrahamic cycle, Genesis, etc.). One could treat these syntagmatically or paradigmatically, in accordance with their proximity or otherwise to the Akedah. Again we meet with an obstacle: its uniqueness in the Bible.

5.13 We have already amplified our text with Job and Ishmael, together with their correlates in Greek mythology. Let us look at the most obvious parallel: Jephthah's daughter. Jephthah's daughter is sacrificed because of a rash vow, made ambiguously under the influence of the *ruaḥ YHWH*. Clearly it is a sacrifice to narrative necessity and irony; Jephthah, the outsider, is incorporated into the family at the cost of personal extinction, while his daughter becomes the center of a cult. Likewise there is a symbolic transaction; God gives a saviour (מושיע) to Israel (cf. Polzin:177-181), whom God has sold into the hands of the Ammonites; the saviour redeems Israel, but at the cost of himself. God's promise, in Judg 10:16, never again to deliver Israel, is immediately broken; instead, Jephthah, the outsider or pharmakos, is the victim.

5.14 There are significant differences between this story and the Akedah. The child is actually sacrificed; there is no divine test or intervention; Jephthah is left with the desolation caused by his excessive speech, that literally bursts from his mouth (Judg 11:35). There is a contrast of gender, between sacrificed girl and spared boy, that participates in the sexual dialectic of the book of Judges. Intertextuality reinforces difference; the Jephthah story appears yet more macabre in the light of the Akedah.

5.15 1 Samuel 14 shares with the story of Jephthah the motif of the rash vow that inadvertently condemns a favoured child to death. Here, however, it is the people that acts as *deus ex machina*: the divine test that is operative in these chapters is designed to confirm Saul's fate; obedience to the people's will, rather than God's, anticipates 1 Samuel 15, and ultimately Jonathan dies.

5.16   The story of Elisha and the Shunammite woman (2 Kings 4) provides another parallel. Like Isaac, the child is of miraculous birth, heralded by annunciation; it dies and is resurrected. Thus the ambiguity whereby Isaac both is and is not sacrificed is replaced by the actual fulfillment of both possibilities. Of course there are also differences: the effacement of the biological father, the absence of a test.

5.17   A self-evident parallel is with the motif of the redemption of the firstborn.[25] Every firstborn son, like the firstborn of every animal and the firstborn of the crop and the trees, belongs to God. The substitution of money removes it from the sacrificial realm to the economic one, in which goods are exchanged and given notional value. Something incommensurable is signified by something commensurable. The transaction turns the trauma and finality of the actual sacrifice of the child, the terror and catharsis of the narrative, into the steady enrichment of the sanctuary.

5.18   The relationship between these texts is not so much aetiological as interpretative.[26] Halakhah performs the same duplicitous operation as Aggadah. An initial divine command, "All the firstborn of your sons you shall give to me" (Exod 22:31) is retracted twelve chapters later (Exod 34:20). In the meanwhile we are in the condition of Abraham in the story; many, evidently, remained there. The test, with its exegesis of God's command, elucidates the barely stated law in Exodus, granting it psychological background, in God's uncertainty, anxiety, curiosity, and thus absolves, through explanation, the imperative and the desire it expresses.

[25] Cf. Westermann (357-358), according to whom child sacrifice was already a phenomenon of the distant past. However it is clear that it was practiced at least until the destruction of the First Temple from references in Jeremiah and Ezekiel (cf. Green:173-174).

[26] Erling interprets Genesis 22 precisely as an aetiology, to explain the change from actual to surrogate victim, afterwards adapted to prohibit emergency human sacrifice (477-478). This function is not overt; more important, all aetiology is at the same time interpretation, exploring the meaning of a custom as much as its origin.

5.19   God's acquisition of the firstborn is attributed by the text to the exodus. This obfuscates the issue, since according to Exod 4:22 Israel was already God's firstborn. Liberation from Egypt then delivers them to himself. God is in the position of Abraham; sacrifice coincides with freedom. The text, however, is complicated by the substitution of both the Egyptians and the paschal lamb for Israel and its firstborn. The uncanny convergence of motifs, political and sacrificial, is beyond the horizon of the Genesis narrative; hinted at in the blessing and the narrator's toponymic comment, it is preceded—or explicated—by this exploratory existential encounter.

5.20   A last parallel I will adduce is the death of Aaron's firstborn sons at the consecration of the priests in Lev 10:1-3. Their act— bringing strange fire—is both sacrilege and sanctification; by coming too close to the divine flame they are absorbed in it. The closure is at the initiation of the hereditary priesthood that will maintain the sacred boundaries.[27] The distance between God and humanity at stake in the Akedah is perpetuated by the priests at the cost of an initial devotion; thereby God acquires/transmits holiness (אקדש) and glory (אכבד) (Lev 10:3). Both are liminal moments, governing Israel's history and ritual drama respectively and marked by an encounter with death. In Lev 10:3, however, the father does not interpose between the child and God; a sudden impulse meets with instantaneous visitation. The psychological focus and retardations of the narrative vanish. In a sense, then, the fate of Aaron's sons consummates the subversive wish in the Akedah and the displaced object of the sacrificial system.

5.21   Syntagmatically the Akedah would be studied in relation to other stories concerning Abraham, or to Genesis as a whole. The unity of both these corpora has been the subject of recent discussion, despite their episodic structure[28] and the fragmentation of the human race and the ancestral family that they recount.

---

[27] This would confirm the interconnection of taboo and sacrifice argued by Zuesse. For him the sacrificial victim is already part of the divine order.

[28] Cf. especially Miscall (though from a deconstructive perspective that denies the concept of ultimate unity); Rosenberg, for whom the unity of the Abraham cycle, as part of that of Genesis, is a political allegory, reciprocally implicating other texts (in particular, the story of David); and Cohn.

5.22 Disintegration, that makes the story more ramified, less capable of resolution, alternates with conjunction, that is a reunion of separated stories and hence a return to origins.[29] There is thus a double movement: sequential progression, the narrative unfolding in time, and reversion. For example, Isaac and Jacob in various ways return to the matrix for their wives. The future then reflects the past; the story's ultimate horizon, as in any quest narrative, is also its point of departure.

5.23 Symbolic transaction can be discerned most clearly in the wife-sister stories, in which the ancestral family is allied matrimonially with the foreign king without losing its exclusive identity. The marriage symbolizes political integration into the land, whose representative is the king; from vulnerable stranger Abraham turns into royal brother-in-law and receives riches. Thereby the danger of incest resulting from mandatory endogamy in a restricted family is averted. Whether metaphorically or actually, Sarah is Abraham's sister. The infertility of the marriage, reflected in that of the earth at the beginning of each wife-sister story, is a sign of its ambiguity as a relationship of siblings as well as of spouses.

5.24 The wife-sister story is in many respects the obverse of the Akedah; incestuous and homicidal desires polarize interfamilial possessiveness, love, hate, and jealousy. In both stories the patriarch gives up a loved person, and in both miraculously receives that person back. In the Akedah, surrender is also a reincorporation into the divine/human voice and a closure of the future; restoration grants the child freedom and is the precondition for dissemination. In the wife-sister story the patriarchal family is initially enclosed from the world. Appropriation by its ruler temporarily removes the wife from the divine aegis, aided by patriarchal deception; her return allies the alien people to the family, thus fulfilling Abraham's blessing, and secures fecundity, hence dissemination. Both the Akedah and the wife-sister story express the ambiguities of Israel's relations with the world, and with God.

5.25 The stories are sequentially interconnected. Isaac's birth follows the second wife-sister story and is the climax of the spate

---

[29] For the conjunction of the various isotopies in the story as the precondition for dissemination, cf. Genest (171).

of child-bearing at its conclusion. The Akedah threatens to retract the gift of that child, and thereby confirms the blessing. Similarly the Hagar-Ishmael ordeal relates to the first wife-sister story: among the benefits Abraham receives from Pharaoh are maidservants; his union with Hagar corresponds to his mésalliance with Sarai.

5.26 Another precondition for the birth of Isaac is circumcision.[30] In circumcision a wound to the organ of procreation permits potency. Like human sacrifice, ritual castration is attested in the ancient Near East and is linked to sacred celibacy. It represents a surrender of desire, hence the object of desire, and of masculine identity; it deprives the victim of the power to reproduce in his own right. Politically castration is an agent for subordination that creates a privileged caste of non-rivals. It is thus a sign of devotion, of self-negation; in relation to God, it relinquishes autonomy.

5.27 The correlation with the wife-sister story is evident; giving up the beautiful, i.e., desirable beloved, is both the extreme of subjugation to imagined rapaciousness and performs one aspect of Israel's task in the world. Giving up the capacity for potency (the internalized beloved) to God fulfills its other component.

5.28 The reduction from act to symbol is a sign of relationship and of difference. The exchange—promise for prepuce—formally subordinates Abraham to God and grants to every act of generation an element of divine blessing and concession. Thus Abraham is neither totally absorbed in God nor totally separated from it.

5.29 This involves also a change in the male human image that differentiates it from the state of nature, from its created perfection; thereby it becomes a symbol of culture.

5.30 This introduces us to the feminist problematic (e.g., to what extent does the superimposition of the male/female dichotomy on that of culture and nature distort male and female reality; to what extent does it construct it?).

---

[30] Alexander argues that Genesis 22, with its offering and covenant, is a sequel to the covenant of circumcision, parallel to the covenant with Noah in Genesis 6-9.

WORKS CONSULTED

Alexander, T. Desmond
1983　　"Genesis 22 and the Covenant of Circumcision."
　　　　JSOT 25: 17-22.

Alter, Robert
1981　　*The Art of Biblical Narrative*. New York: Basic Books.

Auerbach, Erich
1953　　*Mimesis*. Princeton: Princeton University Press.

Berlin, Adele
1982　　"Point of View in Biblical Narrative." Pp. 70-113 in *A
　　　　Sense of Text*. Ed. Stephen Geller. Winona Lake, IN:
　　　　Eisenbrauns.
1983　　*Poetics and Interpretation in Biblical Narrative*. Shef-
　　　　field: Almond Press.

Coats, George W.
1973　　"Abraham's Sacrifice of Faith: A Form-critical Study."
　　　　Int 27:389-400.

Cohn, Robert L.
1983　　"Narrative Structure and Canonical Perspective in
　　　　Genesis." *JSOT* 25:3-16.

Crenshaw, James L.
1983　　*A Whirlpool of Torment*. Philadelphia: Fortress
　　　　Press.

Davidson, Robert
1983　　*The Courage to Doubt*. London: SCM.

Derrida, Jacques
1978　　*Writing and Difference*. Tr. Alan Bass. London: Rout-
　　　　ledge and Kegan Paul.

Detweiler, Robert, ed.
1985　　*Reader Response Approaches to Biblical and Secular
　　　　Texts*. *Semeia* 31.

Duhaime, J. L.
1981　　"Le Sacrifice d'Isaac: L'héritage de Gunkel." *Science
　　　　et Esprit* 33: 157-77.

Erling, Bernhard
1986　　"Firstborn and Firstlings in the Covenant Code." *SBL
　　　　Seminar Papers* 470-478.

Genest, Olivette
1981　　"Analyse Sémiotique de Gen. 22.1-19." *Science et Es-
　　　　prit* 33:157-77.

Genette, Gérard
    1983   *Narrative Discourse: An Essay in Method.* Tr. Jane E.
                Lewin. Ithaca: Cornell University Press.
Girard, René
    1977   *Violence and the Sacred.* Tr. Patrick Gregory. Balti-
                more: Johns Hopkins University Press.
Green, A. R. W.
    1975   *The Role of Human Sacrifice in the Ancient Near
                East.* Missoula, MT: Scholars Press.
Gunkel, Hermann
    1906   *Genesis.* Göttingen: Vandenhoeck and Ruprecht.
Hartman, Geoffrey
    1980   *Criticism in the Wilderness.* New Haven: Yale Uni-
                versity Press.
Hunter, Alan
    1986   "Father Abraham." *JSOT* 35:3-27.
Kilian, R.
    1970   *Isaaksopferung.* Stuttgarter Bibelstudien.
Kristeva, Julia
    1982   *Powers of Horror.* New York: Columbia University
                Press.
Landy, Francis
    1984   "Poetics and Parallelism: Some Comments on James
                Kugel's *The Idea of Biblical Poetry." JSOT* 28: 61-87.
Licht, Jacob
    1978   *Storytelling in the Bible.* Jerusalem: Magnes.
Maccoby, Hyam
    1982   *The Sacred Executioner: Human Sacrifice and the
                Legacy of Guilt.* Thames and Hudson. London.
McEvenue, Sean
    1984   "The Elohist at Work." *ZAW* 96: 315-332.
Miscall, Peter
    1983   *The Workings of Old Testament Narrative.* Semeia
                Studies. Philadelphia: Fortress Press/Chico: Scholars
                Press.
Money-Kyrle, Roger
    1965   *The Meaning of Sacrifice.* 2nd ed. London: Hogarth.
North, Robert
    1985   "Violence and the Bible: the Girard Connection."
                CBQ 47:1-27.

Polzin, Robert
1980 *Moses and the Deuteronomist. A Literary Study of the Deuteronomic History*, Part 1. New York: Seabury.

von Rad, Gerhard
1972 *Genesis: A Commentary.* Rev. ed. Tr. John H. Marks. London: SCM Press.

Rosenberg, Joel
1986 *King and Kin: Political Allegory in the Hebrew Bible.* Bloomington: Indiana University Press.

Rouiller, Grégoire
1978 "The Sacrifice of Isaac." Pp. 13-42, 413-440 in *Exegesis: Problems of Method and Exercises in Reading (Genesis 22 and Luke 15)*. Ed. Francois Bovon and Grégoire Rouiller. Tr. Donald G. Miller. Pittsburgh Theological Monograph Series 21. Pittsburgh, PA: Pickwick Press.

Sternberg, Meir
1985 *The Poetics of Biblical Narrative: Ideology and the Drama of Reading*. Bloomington: Indiana University Press.

Turner, Victor
1967 *The Forest of Symbols: Aspects of Ndembu Ritual.* Ithaca: Cornell University Press.

Van Seters, John
1975 *Abraham in History and Tradition.* New Haven, CT: Yale University Press.

Westermann, Claus
1985 *Genesis 12-36*. Tr. John J. Scullion. Minneapolis, MN: Augsburg. [1981. Neukirchen-Vluyn: Neukirchener Verlag.]

White, Hugh C.
1979 "The Initiation Legend of Isaac." *ZAW* 91:1-30.
1982 "Word Reception as the Matrix of the Structure of the Genesis Narrative." Pp. 61-83 in *The Biblical Mosaic: Changing Perspectives*. Ed. Robert M. Polzin and Eugene Rothman. Semeia Studies. Philadelphia: Fortress Press.

Williams, James G.
     1982   *Women Recounted: Narrative Thinking and the God of Israel*. Sheffield: Almond Press.

Zeligs, Dorothy F.
     1974   *Psychoanalysis and the Bible*. New York: Bloch.

Zuesse, Evan
     1974   "Taboo and the Divine Order." *JAAR* 42: 482-501.

"ON THE MOUNT OF THE LORD
THERE IS VISION"
A Response to Francis Landy concerning the Akedah

Jan P. Fokkelman
State University of Leiden

It is the reader's attention that makes the text a work in the strict sense. A text has something to say as soon as it is heard, and not before, and it really can speak to the extent to which the reader listens to it adequately. A text that is neither heard nor read neither works nor blossoms. Without a reader all its meanings and values are latent. The text needs the ear or the sounding board of a good reader in order to express itself. Whether or not it can take full effect depends on whether we withhold our gifts of head and heart or use our talents to achieve good contact with the text. The true text is the properly read text. To the extent that we can claim or know something of a text as a result of such an interaction only, within that area of intersubjectivity, a good interpretation is the extension or even a part of the living text.

Genesis 22 has been received and interpreted by a sensitive critic. The account Landy gives us of his reading is highly personal and inimitable; these two qualities also make it profound and fascinating, as might be expected of the author of *Paradoxes of Paradise*, that book-length exploration of "the ecstatic flame that draws on sexuality and death" (§1.3).[1] There is no need for a respondent to compete with his interpretation, and equally I feel no need to criticize Landy. Landy's analysis covers practically everything essential in the Akedah story and I endorse it thoroughly. I particularly appreciate the fact that Landy shows the analogy between God and Abraham, their secret complicity; as a result, the fact that Abraham starts to perform his dreadful task without demur becomes much more understandable than in a

---

[1] See my review in *Bibliotheca Orientalis*.

9a ויבאו אל המקום אשר אמר לו האלהים
b ויבן שם אברהם את המזבח
c ויערך את העצים
d ויעקד את יצחק בנו
e וישם אתו על המזבח ממעל לעצים
10a וישלח אברהם את ידו
b ויקח את המאכלת לשחט את בנו
11a ויקרא אליו מלאך יהוה מן השמים
b ויאמר
c אברהם אברהם
d ויאמר
e הנני
12a ויאמר
b אל תשלח ידך אל הנער
c ואל תעש לו מאומה
d כי עתה ידעתי כי ירא אלהים אתה
e ולא חשכת את בנך את יחידך ממני
13a וישא אברהם את עיניו וירא
b והנה איל אחר נאחז בסבך בקרניו
c וילך אברהם
d ויקח את האיל
e ויעלהו לעלה תחת בנו
14a ויקרא אברהם שם המקום ההוא
b יהוה יראה
c אשר יאמר היום
d בהר יהוה יראה
15 ויקרא מלאך יהוה אל אברהם שנית מן השמים
16a ויאמר
b בי נשבעתי—נאם יהוה—
c כי יען אשר עשית את הדבר הזה
d ולא חשכת את בנך את יחידך
17a כי ברך אברכך
b והרבה ארבה את זרעך ככוכבי השמים וכחול אשר על שפת הים
c ויִרש זרעך את שער איביו
18a והתברכו בזרעך כל גויי הארץ
b עקב אשר שמעת בקלי
19a וישב אברהם אל נעריו
b ויקמו וילכו יחדו אל באר שבע
c וישב אברהם בבאר שבע

Genesis 22:1-19 in a colometric presentation

ויהי אחר הדברים האלה	1a
והאלהים נסה את אברהם	b
ויאמר אליו	c
אברהם	d
ויאמר	e
הנני	f
ויאמר	2a
קח נא את בנך את יחידך אשר אהבת את יצחק	b
ולך לך אל ארץ המריה	c
והעלהו שם לעלה על אחד ההרים אשר אמר אליך	d
וישכם אברהם בבקר	3a
ויחבש את חמרו	b
ויקח את שני נעריו אתו ואת יצחק בנו	c
ויבקע עצי עלה	d
ויקם וילך אל המקום אשר אמר לו האלהים	e
ביום השלישי וישא אברהם את עיניו	4a
וירא את המקום מרחק	b
ויאמר אברהם אל נעריו	5a
שבו לכם פה עם החמור	b
ואני והנער נלכה עד כה	c
ונשתחוה ונשובה אליכם	d
ויקח אברהם את עצי העלה	6a
וישם על יצחק בנו	b
ויקח בידו את האש ואת המאכלת	c
וילכו שניהם יחדו	d
ויאמר יצחק אל אברהם אביו ויאמר	7a
אבי	b
ויאמר	c
הנני בני	d
ויאמר	e
הנה האש והעצים	f
ואיה השה לעלה	g
ויאמר אברהם	8a
אלהים יראה לו השה לעלה בני	b
וילכו שניהם יחדו	c

traditional interpretation, in which God remains solely a force outside and facing humanity, the totally other. My appreciation is in no
way lessened by three details in Landy's study which I think need
correction.

Is there any response to be made? I start with the fact that
such a short text has elicited such a long text. My response will
consist primarily of a series of answers to the question of how that
is possible. I consider the story itself the substructure of the living
text and Landy's interpretation its superstructure. The original
Hebrew of Gen 22:1-19 contains only 306 words which I print here
in 74 lines, most of which are very short, and our modern translations thereof cover only one page on the average. Landy's interpretation requires more than 60 pages of typescript! Yet the
narrative does not break down. It is obviously strong enough to
bear a very large interpretative load. Wherein lies its force? If we
can show that, the textual underpinnings of Landy's close reading
will be illuminated more brightly.

Erich Auerbach has made us sensitive to the fact that the
Hebrew story is "fraught with background" and that view is fully
exploited by Landy. But the author of *Mimesis* has gone one step
further and has termed this narrative art *deutungsbedürftig*: it
requires interpretation. In the 40's, this one word revealed the
extent to which the process of the reader's allocating meanings is
necessary to the text. It legitimizes such activity by the reader.
The word accordingly contains the germ of what became an entire school of literary theory in the 70's: reception aesthetics in the
German-speaking world, reader-oriented criticism in the Anglo-
Saxon world.[2] It is one of the main aspects of Landy's work that
he meets the need for interpretation by regularly providing a
detailed gap-filling. The hermeneutics of intersubjectivity dealt
with in my first paragraph makes clear that such gap-filling is not
objectionably "subjective" but desirable, and even necessary.
Landy was invited, if not compelled, to fill gaps by a text full of
holes (see Sternberg; Perry); the art of economy has made Genesis
22 an ancient example of literary minimal art. What is actually
said in Genesis 22 is given life, radiation, and impact only by what
is unsaid and by the unsayable, both of which should be probed
by the reader.

---

[2] In his *Structuralist Poetics*, Jonathan Culler asks for a study of reading, the
allocation of meaning, and the rules of that game. For an example of reader-
oriented reading and attention to indeterminacy as the main characteristics of
Hebrew narration, see Miscall.

I repeat my main question in Landy's terms: can we show "the narrator's control over his formidable burden" (§2.7)? My answer is yes; the visible has the power to carry the invisible because the story is in the form of a fine-tuned system of balances and parallelisms. I will show this by reference to five points: the report/speech difference, word counts, an isotopy of numbers, the text as a binary/ternary fabric, a number of parallelisms and mutual homology.

The first characteristic I tend to look for in Hebrew prose is the distribution of narrator's text and character's text (or in short: *report and speech*). How much is there of the two and how do they alternate? That becomes immediately apparent in my colometric reproduction of the original by indenting all the spoken words (for a justification of colometric division, see Fokkelman, 1981:462-466). It will be immediately seen that report and speech alternate very regularly in Genesis 22. There are six units of both types of text:

speech		*report*	
		[A	heading v 1ab]
B	command: sacrifice (vv 1c–2d)	C	journey (vv 3-4)
D	instruction (v 5)	E	ingredients, climbing (v 6)
F	father-son conversation (vv 7-8)	G	arrival, altar etc. (vv 9-10)
H	prohibition: do not sacrifice (vv 11-12)	I	substitute sacrifice (v 13)
J	naming (v 14)		
K	blessing (vv 15-18)	L	return (v 19)

What is the meaning of this striking example of ordering? It is a first system of balances whereby the narrator demonstrates the complete control of his material. In the left-hand column, God speaks in B, H, and K.[3] Abraham is the speaker in D, F, and J, thus also three times. The speeches can be divided in another way: as three dialogues and three monologues. The monologues occur in D, J, and K. The dialogues come in B, F, and H (vv 1-2, 7-8, 11-12) and are approximately equal in length and structure. They start by calling to Abraham and he gives a sign of listening (3x הנני). The issue, the essence of the contact, then follows: the command to sacrifice in v 2, question and answer in v 7e-8b, prohibition and

---

[3] In this context Abraham's short הנני in 1f=7d=11e can be disregarded. A little later it does become important.

acknowledgement in v 12. It begins to become clear to us how the
differentiation of report and speech works here. Everything that
is thematically important, that starts or propels the plot and deep-
ens our experience of the story, comes in the speeches, while the
narrator's text is unassuming, is confined to practical acts and
reports virtually only details of performance by Abraham—with
an almost unbearable dryness. I have therefore put the speeches
in the first column above—and this is something that tallies with
the separate position of element A, which now starts the right-
hand column. The spoken word brings the terrible command that
starts the plot. The words of the character Abraham in v 5d and
8b contain an amazing mixture of hope, deceit, gamble, trust,
despair, and perplexity, while they touch-and-avoid uncanny
gaps. The spoken word of vv 11-12 brings the denouement, so
that opposition and balance are created between elements B and
H. The thesis/antithesis relationship of B and H is cancelled out
by the virtuoso solution that Providence offers Abraham in v 13:
the ram in the thicket. As a substitute, this sacrifice is a mediation,
a synthesis.

The naming in J forms an opposition to F. This fundamental
statement of faith in v 14 makes clear what was still the eerily
ambiguous and indeterminable content in Abraham's mouth in
v 8. The "a second time" (שנית) of v 15 and the identity 12e=16d
ensure that K forms a pair with H. The blessing of vv 16-18
broadly develops the acknowledgement of v 12 and has a peculiar syntax of comparable complexity. The two prohibitive clauses
of 12bc and the double motivation of 12de (a positive and a negative clause) together form a sentence which is continued and
developed chiastically in 16cd (again a double motivation, at the
front this time; a positive and a negative clause) + 17ab (two main
clauses with paronomasia of the predicate). This long period 16c-
17b is in turn chiastically summarized in the end pair 18ab
(blessing in the main clause + causal subordinate clause).

The continuing alternation of report and speech has ensured
that Abraham's journey and the uninterrupted series of his movements and preparations are cut into three parts: in C Abraham
prepares his journey and the horizontal movement takes place;
after the separation provided by v 5 the journey takes the father
and son up the mountain; and G finally contains the arrival (v 9a)
which immediately merges into busy final preparations.

The first lines (v 1ab) do not form part of the concatenation
of the *wyqtl*-forms which is the backbone of Hebrew narrative.

Landy perceives that they are an "overall framing summary."
They are in fact a separate *title*, a heading. The choice of the word
"tested" requires still more attention however. The narrator defines the core of the event, therefore, as נסיון[4] and all kinds of
meanings result. Firstly, in this way he gives the impression that
he is omniscient because he knows God's intention. Secondly, he
is already decisively guiding and defining our experience with the
narrative even before the plot has started. This cardinal word
imposes a powerful interpretative frame on the reader in advance. Thirdly, the narrator from the very beginning creates two
levels of knowledge by the heading. He lets the reader share in his
omniscience by revealing that it is "only" a test which awaits
Abraham. In this way, he takes in advance the worst sting from the
story of a son who is to be sacrificed, and our experience of the
events does not become intolerable. God, narrator, and reader
"know" that the principal will not go to the extreme with his
experiment now that it has been disclosed that the demand is only
a test. The only person who does not share this knowledge is
Abraham and this fact augments his trial. The difference in the
levels of knowledge creates somewhat more distance between
the reader and the hero; the reader cannot identify too greatly
with the patriarch, and that is psychologically desirable. The disclosure of the test characteristic is a safety valve. The reader
experiences the developments at two levels from the beginning:
the omniscient which regards the drudgery of the mortals from
heaven as it were, and the critical position of a father groping in
the dark. The reader's attention is divided in advance, and hence
to a certain degree also doubled, by the disclosure נסיון.

Different verses belong together in pairs and form short se-
quences: the conversation of vv 7-8, the last preparations of vv 9-
10, and the intervention of the angel in vv 11-12. We can continue
this throughout the text and then discover a high degree of *quan-
titative regularity*, again a sign of mastery and balance:

[4] This word is not biblical, but it is a good Hebrew substantive.

Verse	Description	No of words
1-2	definition נסה	37
	command	
3-4	journey	35 ⎫
		⎬ 70
5-6	men stay behind	35 ⎭
	father and son climb	
7-8	father and son conversation	28
9-10	final preparations	
	maximum tension	35 ⎫
		⎬ 70
11-12	intervention, denouement	35 ⎭
13-14	substitute sacrifice	
	naming	33
15-18	blessing	54
19	return	14

It is striking that the number 35 occurs four times, flanked by two numbers with the same sum 70, namely 37 and 33. There are almost as many words in vv 15-19: 54 + 14. The middle link is the climax of the tension which, after v 2, has risen rapidly and continuously. The fact that vv 9-10 really are central is apparent from these two counts which include the pair of verses first with the first half and then with the second. A striking symmetry of numbers is created:

vv 1-10 = 170 words   or   vv 1-8 = 135 words
+   +
vv 11-19 = 136 words   vv 9-19 = 171 words.

The central position of vv 9-10 becomes even more visible in this series: vv 1-8 = 135 words / vv 9-10 = 35 words / vv 11-19 = 136 words.

This working with counts is not as silly and superficial as it initially appears. The text itself exhibits an *isotopy of numbers* which is quite curious. Consider this part of the network:

—sacrifice your son on *one* of the mountains which I will point out to you

—he took with him *two* of his men, and his son Isaac

—on the *third* day Abraham looked up and saw the place in the distance

—and the *two* of them went on together.

Here we see a thread 1-2-3-2 developing and we now expect a one to follow. That number would appear if Abraham really had executed the command, i.e., if God had gone to the extreme. The "two of them going on together" would have become impossible, Abraham would have had to descend the mountain and return *on his own*. But that does not happen. The famous and very ambiguous "and the two of them went on together" of v 6d is repeated exactly in v 8c so that it becomes a refrain and a demarcation of two incidents (Landy's term) on the outward journey. Then there is the ordinal "a second time"; in v 15 the angel doubles his intervening speech. The actual series of numbers thus becomes asymmetrical: 1-2-3-2-2-2, and the sacred number of fullness and fortune, seven, finally terminates in a double Beᵓer Sheba ("the well of seven, spring of the oath, fountain of fortune"—all facets which the city acquired in the immediately preceding passage at the end of ch. 21). The designation "on the third day" is given a striking place at the beginning in v 4a.[5] Three is a sacred number, the number of completeness. The temporal climax "on the third day" here symbolizes the completion of the journey, a fact underlined by the spatial aspect, "Abraham saw the place [of the disaster?] in the distance." It is that same third day on which the climb and sacrifice itself take place—except that the victim is changed at the last moment.

The numbers acquire even more meaning and an intrinsic value if we see that they form a connection with a subtle and refined play on the root "one" which appears 3x in יחיד and 3x in יחדו. Once again there is a balance: "only" always comes in God's speeches, "together" only in report. This play of words contains the entire issue in a nutshell. The charged burden וילכו שניהם יחדו becomes an oxymoron: "two" and "one" stand side by side, but their meanings conflict. Are the two, father and son, really so united? Has not their יחדו (6d=8c) just become a semblance through God's command which sets the father against the son? Or, in terms of internal life, with Landy: is jealousy beating love? Isaac's level of knowledge is even lower than that of his father. The isolation of Isaac as the יחיד by God threatens to destroy the יחדו. Abraham himself goes through terrible loneliness, he is also isolated by the test, but the turn for the better comes: Abraham has not withheld "his only son" from God, and God reacts by not withholding or withdrawing "the only son" from Abraham. The

---

[5] The use of a complement before the *wyqtl* form is unusual but not wrong; the text does not therefore require "correction."

ambiguous יחדו, "united, together" of the outward journey and the climb becomes the relieved, unambiguous "together" of the return.

The play on words takes us on to other two's and three's. A text is a fabric in view of the Latin origin "textus". The text of the Akedah is a *fabric with a binary warp and a ternary weft*. The main factors or phenomena which obey the principle of two are as follows. The most important construction of the narrative, the plot itself, is in two parts. It is opened and propelled from v 1 to v 10 while the tension increases. The denouement starts with the intervention of vv 11-12; relaxation and relief spread rapidly. All kinds of elements which were extremely ambiguous and opaque before v 11 become unequivocal and simple from the denouement onwards. The gamble "God sees" becomes the solid confession "God sees"; the undermined "together" becomes a blessed "together"; while the white lie "we will come back" unexpectedly becomes true, and so on. The question "where is the beast for the sacrifice?" becomes the discovery of a ram as the sacrificial animal. The uncertain, painful, and loaded looking up becomes the relieved looking and finding; the identical clause וישא אברהם את עיניו וירא occurs in v 4 and 13. All these parallelisms or inversions are in the service of the rise and fall of the plot. Other important duplications are of course the refrain (6d=8c), the acknowledgement (12e=16d), and the angel's calling from heaven (11a=15).[6]

I would now return to the turning point in the intrigue, i.e. after v 10, and arrange eight elements around it. They form pairs and parallelisms which have mutual *homology*:

v 4 : 13ab = 7-8 : 13b//d = 8b : 14b//d = 5-6 : 13+19

Put into words, the uncertain and charged seeing is in the same relationship to the practical and discovering seeing as the ambiguous, desperate, and vague talk about a sacrificial animal is to the simple finding of an actual ram. And these contrasts continue: the perplexity and the gamble *whether* God will provide a sacrificial animal is in the same relationship to the finding that Providence really does work, as the words "we shall worship and come back" and the undermined unity of the climbing pair are to the simple cultic act of v 13 and the return of the father and son together in v 19.

---

[6] Important words that occur twice: mountain, ass, fire, knife, beast, altar, to stretch out (the hand), Beer-sheba, withhold, return, stay.

The action of the three principle is even more interesting. We find striking threes at various levels. There are three characters—father, son, and God—all of whom speak.[7] There are three monologues; there are three dialogues of similar structure. The narrated time, which covers approximately one week, has its climax on "the third day."[8] The presence of the spoken word in v 5 and vv 7-8 cuts Abraham's journey and acts of performance into three, vv 3-4, v 6, and v 9. The following occur three times:

—the vocative "Abraham!" (v 1d, 11c *bis*)
—the clause "they went together"
—the phrase "your son, your only son"
—the clause concerning "the mountain which I will point out to you" and "the place of which God had spoken to him" (2d, 3e, 9a)
—the key sentence "God sees" in 8a, 14b, 14d.

The uses of "three" appear to me to be the most characteristic of the texture and structure of the Sacrifice of Isaac.

Without being able to prove it, I feel that the sentence regarding seeing is the central or most important of the ternary phenomena, with *v 14d as the climax*. The use of this line as a saying "to this day" breaks through the frame of narrated time and draws the reader's today into the text—this in itself is an invitation to reader-oriented interpretation. The choice of the *nif'al* of ראה is striking after the transitive qal-forms of v 4b//13a and 8b//14b. The passive voice dissuades us from looking for an unambiguous interpretation and fixing on one specific agent (as the one who sees). I therefore appreciate the translation of the new JPS version here: "On the mount of the LORD there is vision." This translation has a very gnomic or proverbial ring and almost merits the label "enigma"—a genre designation which follows well on the mysterious *hintergründig* quality of this story as a whole. I interpret v 14d as the juncture where two trios are tied together: the series concerning Abraham's seeing (4-13a-14d) and the series of God's seeing (8b-14b-14d). Abraham's despair and faith tell us that God's seeing surrounds and leads to the mortal's seeing.

---

[7] The men are not important enough to be acknowledged as characters here. The sense of their appearance is their disappearance, so that we become aware of Abraham's solitude in v 6 et seq. Solitude means responsibility, and is well comparable to the loneliness = responsibility of Jacob in 32:22 when he is left alone in the night with another test ahead.

[8] Important words which occur three times: the root שבע, heaven, "God," seed, call.

The context supports this reading, for the "being seen" of God is characteristic of the whole cycle.[9] Seeing and being seen are part of a wider network in which the roots ירא and ירה also participate, due to alliteration. That network is crossed and partially borne by the series of *attributes* which are typical of the Abraham cycle. Just as the three acts or sections of Genesis 25-35 are marked by the stones which are given a sacred task by the hero Jacob (as a מצבה or heap of stones), so there are also markings in the landscape in Genesis 12-25: trees, altars, and wells are the beacons of the epic space. The first time Abraham builds an altar is inspired by God's appearance (ראה) and the place is by "the terebinth tree (of the) Moreh/Teacher" (12:6-7). The force field of the literary text causes that tree to change to the more frequently occurring "terebinth trees of Mamre." These two alliterative names create a framework in which the interpreter can place the name Moriah.

I should like to say three things about this famous name. The late identification of the books of the Chronicles, which interpret "Mount Moriah" as a name of Mount Zion, is not worthy of belief. Our text makes an appreciable difference between "one of the mountains," the anonymous place where Abraham must sacrifice, and the specifically mentioned "*land* of Moriah." I think it incorrect to try to fix Moriah on the map. To me the name comes across as a mythical designation intended precisely to defy localization. It points to a fictional space because that is the only place appropriate for something as unique and inconceivable as sacrificing one's only son. In that way the name Moriah fits the dimension of the timeless much better than the dimension of time. Without wishing to deny the connection with ירא, "to be afraid", which Van Seters and Landy make, I read the name Moriah as a literary-spiritual signal. I would not change one character or vowel and I interpret the name as the nominal sentence *mori Yah* = "the Lord (Jahu) is my teacher."

The story of the Akedah demonstrates a learning process by reference to the archetypical figure of Abraham. It is a growing process that is applicable to any parent, is often painful, and goes very deep: letting the child go. Abraham is given the lesson (or, in view of the name: the *torah*) that his child cannot become a

---

[9] God "appears" to Abraham (ראה *nifᶜal*) in 12:7; 17:1 // 18:1. Other important places with "seeing": 13:10, 14; 16:13-14; 21:16, 19; 24:62; and 25:11. And compare חזה in 15:1a.

man, independent, responsible, in his own right, until he symbolically returns him to the same power who had miraculously given him the child. That power is named God by the story in chs. 17 and 18 and by the faithful; others see it as life or nature or human destiny.

On this point a mystical reading of Abraham's journey is possible, a reading, incidentally, which does not consider other aspects invalid. His three day journey is then an internal quest of looking up shocked and uncertain in v 4 (very similar to the position of the person praying in Ps 121:1, "I lift my eyes to the mountains; where shall I find help?") via complete letting go or surrendering to a looking which is quite simple and practical but which also offers a surprising and new view of reality in v 13 (in the terms of the Psalm: "help comes only from the Lord, maker of heaven and earth").

In any case, the event is a growing process; for Abraham the limited time acts like a pressure cooker. A child is completely from oneself, one's own flesh and blood but at the same time completely not from oneself. A child is not a possession, and one's function as a parent is to become superfluous in some 15 to 20 years' time. Parents pass through thousands of forms of letting go. The first is childbirth and the cutting of the umbilical cord, and it is not only in the physical sense that that event is spectacular. Birth dramatically shows the starting process of letting go both emotionally and spiritually.

Identity and difference exhibit a particular dynamic between parent and child: they are very paradoxical in that relationship. The exact place to look at this is, for Abraham, a mountain. That mountain is a literary-spiritual vantage point. If we know that Gen 19:19 is the counterpart of Abraham's finding the ram, we can apply the words from that verse to the time Abraham looks around and we can say that Providence opens his eyes to reality; and that reality is different from what he might have expected. "On the Mount of the LORD there is vision."

To let a child go completely is a form of surrender which brings the parent's consciousness to a deeper level. The cycle also shows this by reference to a mother figure. That mother is Hagar, who experiences great distress in Genesis 16 and 21. At the time she thinks she must abandon her child to death, there is deliverance, there is living water, there is instruction. The water comes from "the Well of the Living One who sees me" (וראי); the instruction is based on reassurance and blessing. It is striking that

the Hagar stories have outstanding motifs and words in common
with Genesis 22,[10] and I had expected to find the development of
this in §5 of Landy's analysis, particularly since he also has an eye
for the male/female balance.

Like many predecessors, Landy too has referred to the
unique nature of the Akedah story. I would like to support this
claim by providing structural evidence. In a forthcoming issue of
Semeia, I examine *the structure of the entire cycle*. The key to the
correct division of the composition lies in the forms and functions
of time. A unique series of 13 age designations, three time thresh-
olds and two hiatuses in the narrated time divide the cycle into
five phases: I = Genesis 12-14, II = 15-16, III = 17-21, IV = 22:1-19,
and V = 22:20–25:18. Prologue and epilogue form a frame of תולדות
in 11:27-32 and 25:1-18, and we can also say that phase V is framed
with births: 22:20-24 and the details of ch. 25 stand around the
short story of ch. 23 and the very long story of ch. 24. The temporal sub-systems lead to the striking conclusion that the Akedah
(i.e., 22:1-19, no more) on its own occupies the entire phase IV. It
follows the central phase III (Genesis 17-21), which devotes a
considerable amount of narrative time to precisely the one hun-
dredth and cardinal year of Abraham's life. Phase II, Genesis 15-
16, precedes this center panel. By also narrating crises in the
waiting for a natural heir, those two stories are the counterpart of
Genesis 22. Thus the correct division of the cycle shows the separate place occupied by the Akedah in the whole.[11]

I end with three points of criticism pertaining to details. The
way in which Landy applies terms of Greimas' actantial model to
God's striving for knowledge is not completely correct. In that
model a vertical axis, that of the quest, connects the actantial
subject and the object. On the horizontal axis the sender (the
destinateur) grants that actantial object to the receiver (or *destinataire*). From this it follows that God occupies three actantial
positions in Genesis 22. Besides the hero Abraham, who is naturally the first subject, the deity is a second subject, because he,

---

[10] Some words in common: the וישכם אברהם בבקר as a start, שים על, הנער, דחק, the
name באר שבע. Motifs: finding the well // finding the ram; Hagar also receives the
blessing (numerous offspring); the naming of the well // the naming of the place
of sacrifice/the mountain; "the angel of the LORD called from heaven" also in
21:17, and God's command in 21:12 contrasts with that in 22:1-2, because Abraham
is informed in advance of the good outcome.

[11] The cycle itself is, in turn, part of the composition which is the book of
Genesis. See Fokkelman, 1987.

coming behind Abraham as it were, is just as curious as to the
outcome of the test. The actantial object is not God himself, as
Landy thinks in 0.9, but, strictly speaking, the knowledge for
which he strives. The reverse and a variant thereof is the widening
of consciousness which comes to Abraham at the supreme moment. On the mount of the LORD there is vision. God is not only
the *destinateur* who grants Abraham such insight, but on the horizontal axis he is also the *destinataire* to the extent that he himself
is curious as to the outcome on which the progress of history
completely depends, as Landy clearly shows.

In 5.4 and 5.7 Landy appears to work with a lamb/ram opposition as regards the sacrificial animal. But in actual fact that
relationship is different because the word שׂה is the counterpart of
the collective for sheep and goats, צאן, and as a *nomen unitatis* it
designates "a sheep or goat" without specifying young or old.
This general word is then replaced, filled in, or specified by איל,
ram. The symbolic meaning of the sacrifice of precisely a ram
appears to me to be that in that way Abraham is giving up the
natural ability of begetting children. That same natural course of
matters had not worked previously, and his son had accordingly
fallen to his lot miraculously. The whole of Genesis has as a motif
the infertility of the matriarchs: the forefathers of Israel do not
have first-born sons in the obvious natural manner. The ram in
Genesis 22 represents male natural procreative force and the patriarch relinquishes that.

The text 1 Samuel 14 is more relevant as a counterpart of
Genesis 22 than Landy recognizes in 5.14. The usual interpretation that the outcome of the religious ballot in 1 Sam 14:40-42 is
a surprise is incorrect. This reading has led to, and is thus always
supported afresh by, the incorrect translation of the oath that Saul
swears in v 39: "For as the Lord lives who brings victory to Israel,
even if it was through my son Jonathan, he shall be put to death!"
The translation of the second כי by "even" creates a concessive
clause and hence a father, Saul, who wants to consider Jonathan's
guilt and death as an extreme case but can hardly conceive it. This
parsing is wrong. Saul has himself organized the guilt and im-
pending execution of his son. He knows that his son was absent
when he made his men swear the foolish oath to refrain from food
during a day of pursuit, and thus he himself has prepared Jonathan's "guilt" in order to be able to kill him. In other words:
1 Samuel 14 is a case of a father organizing his son's murder with
malice aforethought (for the style and structure analysis which

forms the basis for this far-reaching interpretation, see Fokkelman, 1986). The correct translation of v 39 should render the second כי as an echo of the first and asseverative כי of the oath: "truly,"
exactly as properly translated in Gen 22:16-17.

This reading changes the relationship of 1 Samuel 14 to
Genesis 22. The one extreme situation now stands opposite the
other. Saul has been completely demolished by the conflict he had
with the prophet in ch. 13. To make matters worse, Jonathan replaces him as the hero and actantial subject in the war (14:1-14).
Jealousy, misery, deep despair, and the feeling of being left in the
lurch are the forces which now define him and paralyse his love
for Jonathan. Thus he comes to the decision to kill his son and in
that way even the score with a God and a prophet who at the time
(1 Samuel 9-10) wanted so badly to have him as king and
anointed him. The fact that the execution of this son, like Isaac's
sacrifice, does not take place is against the will of Saul. While
Abraham receives vision on the Mount, Saul proceeds in darkness
and religious fanaticism. The differences between the innocent
Isaac, who is silent (except for Gen 22:7), trusting his father and
rapidly disappearing from the picture, and the adult crown prince
exercising leadership are considerable. Jonathan is an important
agent, has his own opinions, and is a serious critic of his father.
And by his surprising attack on the Philistine sentry post he replaces his father as a charismatic leader. After the conflict with
Samuel, Saul finds matters very difficult. The pronounced personality of Jonathan represents challenges to him of a kind that
Abraham never knew from his son. But as a forerunner and prototype of the charismatic David, Jonathan ultimately has no (political) future while Isaac *is* the future.

WORKS CONSULTED

Culler, Jonathan
    1975   *Structuralist Poetics: Structuralism, Linguistics, and
            the Study of Literature.* London: Routledge and Ke-
            gan Paul.
Fokkelman, Jan
    1981   *King David.* Vol. I of *Narrative Art and Poetry in the
            Books of Samuel.* Assen: van Gorcum.
    1986   *The Crossing Fates.* Vol. II of *Narrative Art and Po-
            etry in the Books of Samuel.* Assen: van Gorcum.

1987   "Genesis." Pp. 36-55 in *Literary Guide to the Bible*. Ed. Robert Alter and Frank Kermode. Cambridge: Harvard University Press.

forth- Review of Francis Landy, *Paradoxes of Paradise. Bibli-*
coming *otheca Orientalis.*

forth- "Time and the Structure of the Abraham Cycle." Ed.
coming Kent H. Richards. *Semeia.*

Landy, Francis
  1983 *Paradoxes of Paradise: Identity and Difference in the Song of Songs*. Bible and Literature Series, 7. Sheffield: Almond Press.

Miscall, Peter D.
  1986 *1 Samuel: A Literary Reading*. Bloomington: Indiana University Press.

Perry, Menakhem
  1979 "Literary Dynamics: How the Order of a Text Creates Its Meanings." *Poetics Today* 1:35-61.

Sternberg, Meir
  1985 *The Poetics of Biblical Narrative: Ideological Literature and the Drama of Reading*. Bloomington: Indiana University Press.

Sternberg, Meir and Menakhem Perry
  1968 "The King through Ironic Eyes: the Narrator's Devices in the Story of David and Bathsheba and Two Excursuses on the Theory of the Narrative Text." *Hasifrut* 1:263-92.

THE TRAGIC VISION AND BIBLICAL NARRATIVE: THE CASE OF JEPHTHAH

J. Cheryl Exum
Boston College

> From the gods who sit in grandeur
> grace comes somehow violent.
> Aeschylus

ABSTRACT

To what extent can the story of Jephthah be considered tragic? Does Jephthah fulfill our expectations for a tragic hero? The paper begins with some general observations about tragedy and the tragic vision and proceeds inductively, letting the text itself shape our notion of the tragic. Jephthah acts against his will in taking the life of his only child, and yet he is unwittingly responsible for the terrible situation in which he finds himself. A vow made in ambiguous circumstances and in ignorance of its outcome forces his hand. The story does not call into question the underlying causes of Jephthah's misfortune. Its tragedy lies primarily in the conjunction of circumstances—in the chilling coincidence between the ill-chosen terms of Jephthah's vow and his daughter's appearance as the only "one coming forth" to meet him upon his victorious return from battle with the Ammonites—and in the divine silence, the refusal of the deity to take a position vis-à-vis these events.*

* Research for this study was supported by a grant from the Penrose Fund of the American Philosophical Society and by a fellowship from the Alexander von Humboldt Foundation.

1.1 My use of the terms "tragedy" and "the tragic vision" is heuristic and should not be taken as an attempt to force the biblical material into Aristotelian categories which are hardly applicable to it. Rather I am interested in exploring a particular dimension of biblical narrative, a dimension which reveals the dark side of existence, which knows anguish and despair, and which acknowledges the precarious lot of humanity in a world now and then bewildering and unaccommodating. One encounters it in various forms; e.g., in the "jealousy of God" in the Yahwist Epic, or in the sufferings of Jeremiah, or in the book of Job—unless one choose to side with the friends in maintaining that the suffering, the misery, the evil, and the unexplainable in the world are part of an inscrutable, larger plan for the good. Its clearest representation appears in the story of Saul, and here I want to consider to what extent it emerges in the story of Jephthah.

1.2 I shall not try to define tragedy (there is a great deal of literature on the subject and clearly no consensus), though I would like at the outset to describe what I take to be central ingredients of tragedy and the tragic vision. I shall then endeavor to develop and expand this notion of the tragic through analysis of the Jephthah story. In what sense does it share the tragic vision?

1.3 Tragedy is a literary form (see Krieger), which Northrop Frye has aptly described as exhibiting an inverted-U shaped structure (the rise and fall). Tragedy ends in catastrophe, and the catastrophic events which bring the tragic tale to closure are irreparable and irreversible. Tragic vision is a broader and more versatile concept (see Sewall; Krieger; Humphreys, 1985); it is a "sense of life" (Unamuno), a way of viewing reality, an attitude of negation, uncertainty, and doubt, a feeling of unease in an inhospitable world. What distinguishes this vision from the comic (or classic) vision is that it lacks comedy's restorative and palliative capacity. Comedy gives voice to a fundamental trust in life; in spite of obstacles, human foibles, miscalculations, and mistakes, life goes on. But tragedy, in contrast, confronts us with what Richard Sewall has called "the terror of the irrational." The tragic hero is the victim of forces she or he cannot control and cannot comprehend, encountering on all sides unresolved questions, doubts, and ambiguities. Comedy may also embrace questions, doubts, and ambiguities, but, as Sewall points out, it removes their terror. The tragic vision isolates the hero over against an arbitrary and capricious world, a world in which—to get to the crux of the matter—the problem of evil is irreducible and unresolvable into some larger, harmonious whole.

1.4   In spite of the sharp distinction between the comic and tragic visions, the two are by no means mutually exclusive; the great tragedies often offer a glimpse of the reassuring universe of comedy, and the great comedies reveal a tragic potential. Interplay is essential to the vitality of these visions. Tragedy without the tempering of a comic sensibility degenerates into melodrama, while comedy without a sense of tragic possibility becomes farce (Frye, 1965:50).

1.5   My posing the question in terms of "tragic vision" or "tragic themes" is likely to be judged a particularly modern preoccupation, a tragic world view being well-suited to our uncertain and troubled times. But after all, modern readings are what keep ancient literature alive for us, and without them, the Bible could well become a document purely of antiquarian interest or of concern only to the religious. I acknowledge my modern perspective, but I contend that the vision I call tragic is there—even if only implicitly—from ancient times, and my readings are an effort to demonstrate the enduring power of that vision. In this, I follow a kind of deconstructive approach, which seeks to disclose the repressed and unconscious dimension of texts. "Turn it and turn it again for everything is in it" (Avoth 5:22). My reading of the Jephthah story proceeds inductively, allowing the text itself to inform our understanding of the tragic. I have sought to respect the ancient character of the narrative and to recognize its cultural assumptions, and I do not think I have wrenched it wholly or violently out of its ancient context in order to make it fit my notion of the tragic. Fortunately texts do not yield readily to our efforts to categorize them and assign them a particular place within a conceptual system. Thus my analysis also seeks to show how the story resists interpretation along tragic lines and how it pushes against the boundaries of my description above and the features I shall very briefly draw out of the story of Saul.

2.1   Because it lends itself so well to interpretation along tragic lines (see especially the studies of Good, Gunn, Humphreys, Exum and Whedbee), the story of King Saul provides a good reference point from which to consider the tragic in the story of

Jephthah. Saul is thrust into a position of leadership he does not
seek only to have it torn from him and promised to another who
is better than he. His *hamartia* lies in his disobedience to Yhwh
(1 Samuel 13 and 15), though as David Gunn has pointed out,
Yhwh's instructions to Saul are open to misinterpretation. Though
Saul bears responsibility for the rejection of his house and the loss
of divine favor, his treatment at the hands of Yhwh seems somehow out of proportion to his guilt. Why is the deity so harsh and
unforgiving? Yhwh sends an evil spirit to torment Saul and though
sought out by Saul, refuses to respond. Under such circumstances,
Saul understandably wavers between sanity and madness, becoming increasingly alienated from those closest to him, and occasionally revealing an unexpectedly sinister side of his nature. He
is a victim both of his own unstable personality and of the an-
tagonism of God to the idea of human kingship. His tragic greatness arises out of his heroic struggle against his fate, his refusal to
acquiesce, as might a lesser man, one without hubris. To the very
end he strives to hold on to the kingship which he appeared initially not to want, and up until just before his death he seeks the
deity who has abandoned him. But to no avail; he dies in isolation
from Yhwh, perhaps the cruelest part of his fate. Saul's suicide is
his last heroic gesture, aimed at sparing himself abuse by the
Philistines. Though rejected by Yhwh, he still commands the respect of loyal subjects, such as the men of Jabesh-gilead, who
retrieve his mutilated body. But this act of human kindness, while
it meliorates Saul's tragedy, remains overshadowed by the fact of
divine rejection. There is no future for the house of Saul.[1]

3.1   When we turn to the story of Jephthah in Judges 11-12, we
find ourselves in a different atmosphere. Jephthah's human sacrifice appalls us more than any act Saul has committed, even the
wanton slaughter of the priests of Nob, for Jephthah acts against
his will in taking the life of his own child, yet he is unwittingly
responsible for the terrible situation in which he finds himself. A
vow made in ambiguous circumstances and in ignorance of its
outcome forces his hand. But unlike the case of Saul, there is no
apparent reason why this disaster befalls Jephthah, nothing of the
divine displeasure which drives Saul to despair and madness. Nor
does Jephthah suffer perceptibly as a result of his deed. Strangely,

---

[1] For a fuller discussion of my interpretation of Saul's tragedy, see Exum and
Whedbee.

we are not told how the act affects him; nor, for that matter, do we learn God's reaction. Jephthah's life does not end in disgrace; there is no outright rejection, no clear sense of alienation from God—central elements for Saul's tragedy.

3.2   Wherein, then, does the tragedy of Jephthah lie? Not in Jephthah's relationship to the deity per se nor in the character of Jephthah or his daughter, neither of which is sufficiently developed in terms of the struggle against fate that distinguishes the tragic hero—but in events themselves, in a certain ambiguity surrounding all that transpires, and finally, in the divine silence, the refusal of the deity to take a position vis-à-vis these events. Jephthah's sacrifice of his daughter to Yhwh is the preeminently tragic moment; it brings into relief an ambivalent quality associated with everything else about him.

3.3   The story of Jephthah opens, like that of Saul, at a point of crisis: Gilead, the home from which Jephthah has been expelled, comes under attack by the Ammonites. The deuteronomistic framework of Judg 10:6-18 forms the backdrop of the story, and portrays the Ammonite threat as affecting not only Gilead but also the tribes of Judah, Benjamin, and Ephraim. The book of Judges offers a pessimistic testimony to the deterioration of order and stability in Israel before the monarchy. Disorder is a fact of life, interrupted routinely by periods of respite. Even the judges who deliver Israel in times of need reveal unexpected shortcomings and serious faults. Consider, for example, before Jephthah, Gideon, who builds an ephod that becomes a snare to the people; and after him, Samson, who not only fails to live up to his Nazirite calling, but worse, fails to achieve Israel's deliverance from the Philistines. At this point in the Judges cycle, Israel's rebellion is nothing new, "And the Israelites again did evil in the eyes of Yhwh" (10:6), and punishment follows ineluctably upon sin. Yhwh sells them into the hand of their enemies (v 7) and they cry out in their distress. So far we have the usual deuteronomistic pattern, but vv 11-14 introduce a new element, the divine refusal to intervene, "therefore I will not continue to deliver you." The people implore divine assistance at any price, "We have sinned; do to us whatever is good in your eyes, only deliver us this day," and demonstrate their resolve by putting away their foreign gods and serving Yhwh. Interestingly, this is the only place in Judges where repentance is described, and yet, though plainly affected by Israel's response, Yhwh does not raise up a deliverer (cf. 2:16; 3:9, 15). In fact the deity's response is far from clear. Whereas 10:16 ותקצר נפשו בעמל ישראל is frequently understood as referring to divine compassion or concern for Israel's plight, Robert Polzin cautions us against an overly optimistic reading of the verse, correctly emphasizing its opacity. Polzin suggests reading, "and he grew annoyed [or impatient] with the troubled efforts of Israel" (177-78).

3.4   A crisis and a question set the stage for the appearance of Jephthah: "Who is the man who will be the first to fight the Ammonites? He will be head over all the inhabitants of Gilead" (10:18). Jephthah is selected by the elders of Gilead (11:4-5), who turn to him only in distress (11:5-8) just as the Israelites have repeatedly turned to Yhwh only in distress. If Saul is "kingship's scapegoat" (Gunn), Jephthah is the judge Israel deserves. "Do to us what is good in your eyes, only deliver us this day" (10:15). Yhwh grants them the deliverer they have chosen, a man who will win a great victory for them over the Ammonites, but at high personal cost, and who, though capable of providing effective leadership against an external threat, will prove unable to forestall internecine warfare.

3.5   The introduction to Jephthah in 11:1 alerts us from the beginning to an ambivalent quality about him. From the Gileadites' point of view, Jephthah combines the desirable with the unacceptable: "Jephthah the Gileadite was a mighty warrior and he was the son of a harlot."[2] The conjunction *waw* joins the two sides of this statement, giving them equal weight. This duality characterizes Jephthah's life: he will achieve desirable goals, victory for Gilead against Ammon, victory against Ephraim, but in both cases by what will strike us as unacceptable means. Even his name hints of his ill-fortune: יפתח, "he opens," perhaps a hypochoristic form of *yiphtah-el*, "God opens (the womb)," but, knowing what is in store for him, we cannot help connecting it to the fatal moment when he opens his mouth and out comes the vow that seals his tragic fate. The verbal root in his name is פתח and the verb used of the vow in 11:35 and 36 is פצה, but the association is not farfetched. Both פתח פה and פצה פה mean "to open the mouth,"and in Num 16:30 and 32 and Ezek 2:8 and 3:2 the verbs

---

[2] Y. Zakovitch (40, 45) proposes that *zonah* here refers to a divorced woman.

are used interchangeably. יפתח, "he (God) opens the womb"; יפתח, "he (Jephthah) opens his mouth." And may we not speculate on the possible implications of "he (God) opens his (Jephthah's) mouth," for is not Jephthah under the influence of the spirit of God when he makes his ill-fated vow?

3.6 Jephthah's unacceptable origins mark him as an outcast, a marginal figure who lives out his life in a marginal place, Mizpah, at the boundary between Israel and Ammon (see Landy). His brothers cast him out from the paternal household, and he flees to the land of Tov, perhaps for him a "good" land, from where he goes raiding with אנשים ריקים. The fact that he commands a following demonstrates his leadership abilities, but the nature of this company, worthless fellows, "empty men," again reminds us of Jephthah's unacceptable side.

3.7 If Jephthah's origins are questionable, so is his rise to power. Twice the text declares that the Ammonites attacked Israel (11:4 and 5). Only a crisis makes Jephthah's desirability as a mighty warrior outweigh his unacceptability as an outsider. Like Saul, who was first demanded by the people and then chosen by Yhwh, Jephthah is first sought out by the elders and only later affected by the spirit of Yhwh. Yhwh's attitude here is not so evident as in 1 Samuel 8, but may be hinted at in the absence of divine involvement in the elders' choice. Jephthah's retort in 11:7, "Why have you come to me now that you are in distress (צר)?," echoes Yhwh's response to the wayward people in 10:14, "Go and cry to the gods you have chosen; let them deliver you in your time of distress (צרתכם)." Both mock those who, having rejected them in the past, seek them out only as a last resort. Like the people in 10:15-16, the elders persist. But assistance granted under such conditions will have ambiguous repercussions.

3.8 Jephthah's rise to leadership occurs immediately, before his confrontation with the Ammonites. The people appoint him ראש and קצין, even though he had made becoming ראש conditional upon victory. In his newly attained position of authority, the former outcast speaks, through messengers, as the singular representative of his people, "What is between *me* and you that you have come against *me* to fight against *my* land?" Jephthah tries to resolve the differences between Israel and Ammon through diplomacy, but his attempt fails and fighting ensues. Israel achieves

a great victory over the Ammonites; the threat posed at the beginning of the story is resolved; the spirit of God with Jephthah
appears to signal the divine sanction of the people's choice of a
leader; and the elders' confidence that Jephthah could deliver
them is justified. We seem to have here all the ingredients for an
ideal conclusion—but not quite. Success has its price. Jephthah's
victory, won against the backdrop of his failed negotiations, is
Pyrrhic. The pinnacle of his career, his moment of greatest glory,
contains the seeds of his tragedy, for Jephthah has vowed a sacrifice to Yhwh, and victory demands it scandalous performance.

3.9   What provokes Jephthah's vow, which pops out of his mouth
(פציתי פי אל יהוה), bringing in its wake disastrous consequences? It
seems almost superfluous, excessive, since the obvious reason for
making a vow, to ensure success, would appear to be rendered
unnecessary by the fact that the spirit of Yhwh is with Jephthah.
Our speculations about what lies behind Jephthah's vow are efforts to resolve its un-reason, its sinister and seemingly unnecessary quality, its ultimately tragic dimension. Because the situation
lacks the urgency which calls for a vow, Phyllis Trible views Jephthah's vow as an act of unfaithfulness, an attempt to manipulate
Yhwh, who has already freely bestowed upon Jephthah the gift of
the spirit. But one could more plausibly argue that Jephthah
makes his vow under the influence of the spirit of Yhwh. "The
spirit of Yhwh was upon Jephthah, and he passed through Gilead
and Manasseh, and passed through Mizpah of Gilead, and from
Mizpah of Gilead he passed on to the Ammonites. And Jephthah
vowed a vow to Yhwh . . . " (11:29). Is the spirit of Yhwh the
driving force behind all of these activities or only some of them—
and if only some, which ones? On the basis of its role in inciting
other heroes to mighty, and sometimes curious deeds (cf.
Judg 6:34; 13:25; 14:6, 19; 1 Sam 10:10; 11:6; 16:13), we might assume that here, too, Yhwh's spirit inspires Jephthah's victory over
the Ammonites. The vow interferes, so to speak, with the logical
progression of cause and effect: does victory come as the result of
the spirit of Yhwh upon Jephthah or because of the vow? Can the
two, the spirit of Yhwh and the vow, now be distinguished with
regard to their function or to the outcome?[3]

---

[3] A similar ambiguity occurs in the story of Gideon. The spirit clothes him; he
sounds the trumpet and calls out the troops (6:34-35). He next asks for a sign, . . .
אם ישך מושיע בידי את ישראל (6:36; cf. Jephthah's אם נתון תתן את בני עמון בידי, 11:29-30). Is

3.10   More important, it is not the making of the vow itself which is so disturbing but its content. Had Jephthah said, "If God will be with me, and give me victory, so that I come again to my house in peace, then I shall set up an altar" (cf. Gen 28:20-22), we should probably not be troubled by the presence of a vow. Even the vowing of a person to the deity need not unduly upset us, as Hannah's vow to give Samuel to Yhwh "all the days of his life" shows. Thus it is not until Jephthah utters the last two words of his vow that we encounter anything particularly unusual, that we realize how dangerous, and scandalous, the vow is. Consider how the text lingers over details, postponing the crucial element of the vow until the very end, where it has maximum effect: "If you will only give the Ammonites into my hand, then the one coming forth who comes forth from the doors of my house to meet me, when I return in peace from the Ammonites, shall be Yhwh's and (now come only two words in the Hebrew) I will offer him (generic) up as a burnt offering (והעליתהו עולה)." Debates over whether he has in mind a person or possibly an animal are pointless.[4] The fact is היוצא could be—and *we know it will be*—a human sacrifice, and so we confront in Jephthah's vow a sinister dimension we are hardly prepared for, even from a former outcast and a companion of worthless men. Jephthah, however, seems blind to the implications of his vow. Interestingly he does not say, "the first one," but simply "the one coming forth" (היוצא), as if not considering the possibility of being met by more than one. It is odd that he speaks of only one and odder still that only one comes to greet him, and, as his response makes clear, he had not expected it to be his only child. The irony, the tragic irony, rests in the exact correspondence between the ill-chosen terms of Jephthah's vow and the subsequent events. We do not know what provokes Jephthah to set these particular terms or what determines this particular outcome, what accounts for the chilling coincidence between the vow and the daughter's appearance. The fact is their connection cannot be explained; it has no cause, at least not one we can name,

---

he no longer under the influence of the spirit when he asks for a sign or does the spirit not obviate the need for a sign?

    [4] Marcus lists the evidence for both positions. It seems to me on the basis of 1 Sam 18:6 and Exod 15:20 that Jephthah may well have expected a woman, who in the patriarchal society would have been more expendable than a man.

and that is the source of its terror. James Joyce called it the "secret cause" of suffering.[5]

3.11.1   Victory marks the height of Jephthah's fortune; the vow signals his descent into tragedy. It would be enough for us to hear, "and Yhwh gave them into his hand" (11:32), but the text elaborates, as if to leave no doubt about the scope and significance of the victory, "And they smote them from Aroer to the neighborhood of Minnith, twenty cities, and as far as Abel-keramim, an exceedingly great slaughter, and the Ammonites were subdued before the Israelites" (11:33). Unqualified victory demands performance of the vow, and we dread the recognition scene, for we know who will be the only one to greet Jephthah upon his return to his house. As noted above, the terror and the tragedy lie precisely in the coincidence between what is vowed and what occurs, a correspondence underscored on the verbal level by an almost exact repetition of terms. "If you will only give the Ammonites into my hand . . . and Yhwh gave them into his hand." "The one coming forth from the doors of my house to meet me . . . I will offer up . . . Jephthah came to Mizpah to his house and his daughter came forth to meet him" (literally, "and behold his daughter coming forth to meet him"). At this point the narrative pace becomes agonizingly slow, pausing over a poignant description of the relation of daughter and father: "and only she—alone— he did not have, except for her, son or daughter." The description inevitably reminds us of another sacrificial victim, "your son, your only son, whom you love, Isaac." But there, in a wonderful comic resolution, a ram was sacrificed instead of the child. The redundancy here emphasizes the daughter's singularity and, simultaneously, Jephthah's isolation. Jephthah, the outcast, the marginal

---

[5] I owe this reference to Sewall. In this analysis, I have tried to avoid implicating the deity too strongly, since the very ambiguity of the divine silence seems to me crucial to the story. It is not the case here, as in the story of Saul, that God is antagonistic. On the other hand, if we look at extra-biblical parallels where a father vows what turns out to be his own child, a chief feature is that the supernatural figure to whom the vow is made has something different in mind from the father; e.g., the frequently cited parallels of Idomenus, Maeander, and Agamemnon in Euripides' *Iphigenia in Tauris*, and many interesting examples and variations from Grimm's fairy tales ("Hans mein Igel," "Der König vom goldenen Berg," "Das singende springende Löweneckerchen," "Das Mädchen ohne Hände"). The rabbis did not shrink from implicating the deity and offered the interpretation that God punished Jephthah for his carelessly worded vow by causing his daughter to appear as its fulfillment (Bereshit Rabbah 60:3; Wayyiqra Rabbah 37:4).

figure, who tends to act independently even when representing others, faces his tragic moment alone. Where are all the Israelites who have returned with him victorious from battle? Jephthah's isolation is all the more striking when we perceive the contrast with his daughter, who has companions with whom to share her grief.

3.11.2   As in the case of the vow, vv 30-31, the text of v 34 delays until the last possible moment the crucial information that this daughter is Jephthah's only child, and thus only now makes clear that for Jephthah, her death means the tragic extinction of his family line. His tragedy—though not hers—would be lessened if he had other children. The moment he sees her, Jephthah realizes what will be required of him, and both his nonverbal response, rending his garments, and his outcry, "אהה, my daughter, etc.," convey a combination of grief, dismay, shock, and consternation.

3.12   In the entire narrative, only this scene furnishes any insight into Jephthah's emotional state, portrays an inner conflict, and thus it is the one scene in which his character approaches anything like tragic proportions. Unlike Saul, whose tortured personality finds ample expression, Jephthah faces an internal dilemma only briefly portrayed. But brief as it is, this "confrontation with extremity" (Krieger) is essential to a tragic presentation, for tragedy demands an awareness on the part of the protagonist that the situation is impossible, that there is no way out. Jephthah becomes a tragic figure insofar as he realizes that he has no alternative, that he is caught in a situation both of his own making and, paradoxically, an accident of fate. This helps illuminate, I think, the import of his words to his daughter. "I have opened my mouth" acknowledges his role in setting into motion this terrible course of events. "You have indeed brought me low, and have become my trouble" blames the victim, as others have pointed out, but it also, it seems to me, strives to convey his sense of being not wholly responsible for this horrible, unexpected result. It points beyond itself to the "secret cause." Oedipus did not intend to kill his father and marry his mother; he does so only because he does not know their identity. Jephthah did not intend to sacrifice his daughter; he speaks his vow without knowing the identity of היוצא. The experience of being trapped in an intolerable situation for which one is unintentionally, yet still somehow responsible gives rise to tragic awareness.

3.13   The vow is irrevocable and unalterable, and verbal allusions grimly underscore its tragic irony. Jephthah returns with the
elders as leader against the Ammonites (משיבים, 11:9) and subse-
quently returns victorious from battle (בשובי, 11:31); only his
words cannot be returned (לשוב, 11:35). They have gone forth
from his mouth (יצא מפיך, 11:36), claiming as their victim his daughter who came forth (יצאת) to meet him. After her brief period of
mourning, she returns to her father that the vow be fulfilled (ותשב
אל אביה, 11:39).

3.14.1   The narrative describes the sacrifice summarily, without
detail, a striking contrast to the story of Abraham's near sacrifice
of the young Isaac in Genesis 22. But there, because we know the
favorable outcome, know that Abraham will pass this test of faith,
we could tolerate the details—the building of the altar, the touch-
ing dialogue between father and child, the raising of the knife—
and the pathos they bring to the scene. Here we could not.
Though no *deus ex machina* saves the daughter, a contermove-
ment of resolution and repair serves to meliorate her tragedy: she
shares her last months in mourning with female companions, and
after her death is remembered by the women of Israel in a yearly
ritual.

3.14.2   Twice before in the narrative, in vv 30-31 (see par. 3.10)
and in v 34 (see par. 3.11.2), the tragic blow has fallen at the final
climactic moment. Now in v 37 the final word sounds a note of
relief.

> She said to him,
> "My father, you have opened your mouth to Yhwh,
> do to me according to what has gone forth from your
>   mouth,
> now that Yhwh has vindicated you against your enemies,
> the Ammonites."
>
> And she said to her father,
> "Let this thing be done for me,
> let me alone two months
> that I may go and wander upon the hills
> and bewail my virginity,
> I *and my companions*."

Immediately upon seeing his daughter (v 35), Jephthah comprehends the terrible tragic consequences of his vow; and in the encoun-

ter that follows between father and child, the daughter recognizes the awful fate awaiting her (vv 35-36). Only at the conclusion of her speech (vv 36-37) does she reveal that, unlike her father, she has companions with whom to share her grief. רעיתי, "my companions," is her last spoken word in the narrative; אבי, "my father," her first. Symbolically, through speech, she journeys from the domain of the father who will quench her life to that of the female companions who will preserve her memory.

4.1 I mentioned earlier (par. 1.3) the downward movement of tragedy and its irreversible catastrophic conclusion. Clearly Saul's story ends in catastrophe. Although acts of human kindness meliorate the tragedy (the medium at En-dor, 1 Samuel 28; the men of Jabesh-gilead, 1 Samuel 31), any relief remains overshadowed by the reality of divine rejection (see Exum and Whedbee). In the sacrifice of his daughter, Jephthah reaches his nadir. To what extent he rises above his personal catastrophe is difficult to decide. Can Israel's victory over Ammon compensate for the loss of his only child, the snuffing out of his one possibility of leaving behind descendants as a measure of his greatness? (Surely the large number of descendants attributed to Yair, Ibzan, and Abdon, judges before and after Jephthah—with an escalation that first includes daughters and daughters-in-law and then grandsons—draws attention to Jephthah's death without progeny.)[6]

4.2 Jephthah's story does not end with the tragic sacrifice. No attempt is made to smooth over the abrupt transition between the story of the sacrifice and that of the war with Ephraim which follows. We find, however, subtle ironic reminders of the tragic events, both in the words of the Ephraimites and those of Jephthah. The Ephraimites' threat to burn Jephthah's house over him with fire rings hollow now that his daughter, his "house" since he has no other children, has already been burned. In terms that have been forced to bear heavy weight, Jephthah reminds us, "Yhwh gave them into my hand" (12:3, cf. 11:30, 32) and perhaps "When I saw that you were not going to save me, I took my life in my hand" is a veiled reference to the vow and its consequences. (Note, too, that only the presence of one letter, the *kaph*, prevents

---

[6] This is not to discount possible oligarchic allusions in the information about the minor judges; see Jobling: 60, 77-78. There is no mention of Jephthah's wife or the possibility of further offspring.

our reading, "I took my life in my mouth.") Finally, the danger of uttering what turn out to be the wrong words is reflected in the deadly consequences of mispronouncing the word "shibboleth."

4.3 Jephthah fails to avert open conflict between Gilead and Ephraim, and we must ask ourselves how hard he tries. Gilead is victorious, but what meaning has victory when Israelite fights against Israelite? The Gileadites repeat Jephthah's sin on a tribal scale, slaughter of their own flesh and blood.[7] Human sacrifice and needless shedding of blood within Israel—hardly an impressive record for a judge. We are told that Jephthah judged Israel six years, died, and was buried in Gilead (or if we accept the MT, in the cities of Gilead, an uncertain burial for a former exile from his father's house, forced by events to destroy his own). That the end of his career leaves problems unresolved, that disorder reigns in spite of his military victories, that ambiguity surrounds his "successes"—all these things foster a tragic vision. Two important and related issues are left open: how, finally, to evaluate Jephthah, and—because it is the reason it is so difficult for us to do so—the silence of God.

4.4 Before addressing these issues, I propose to consider the characterization of Jephthah, for it is here more than anywhere else, I think, that Jephthah departs from our expectations of a tragic figure. What manner of man is Jephthah? Does he have the makings of a tragic hero? Like Saul, he holds a privileged position of leadership, which thrusts upon him the necessity of facing demanding decisions. We have already seen that he embraces contraries: as "the son of another woman," he is cast out (11:1-5); as a "mighty warrior," sought after (11:1-11). When his story begins, he appears as a fugitive, a marginal figure who lives over against his brothers, a man who demonstrates his leadership abilities by

_____

[7] I have not dealt in this paper specifically with Israel's attitude toward sacrifice (see Green, de Vaux) nor with the phenomenon of sacrifice. With regard to the latter, an analysis based on the theory of René Girard would prove particularly illuminating in my opinion. The hero returns from battle contaminated by violence. A cleansing rite is necessary, but something goes amiss. Violence is unleashed first in the hero's own family (his daughter) and then on another Israelite tribe (Ephraim). The pattern of escalating violence continues within the cyclical pattern of Judges, culminating in full-scale internecine war and mass rape and murder in chs. 20-21. The connection between women and sacrifice also calls for exploration; see Girard, pp. 119-42 *et passim*; see also Jay.

raiding with worthless followers. Against a background of crisis, he rises to a position of authority, in which he customarily appears in adversary situations. Disputation brings to light the trait that most clearly defines his character: he is a negotiator. But as a negotiator he has a curious record; there is something excessive about him, which disposes him to tragedy.

4.5   In his first speech, when the elders of Gilead approach him to enlist his aid, Jephthah reveals his penchant for negotiation. He aspires to more than what is first offered and succeeds in getting the elders to accept his terms. The negotiations develop along interesting lines and merit careful scrutiny. Initially the elders formulate their offer in a way that assures maximum benefit for themselves, while leaving their obligation to Jephthah somewhat vague.

> Come and be our leader
> that we may fight the Ammonites.

What's in it for Jephthah? He responds neither "yes" nor "no," but with a rhetorical question that reveals appropriate wariness, "Why do you come to me now when you are in distress?" Placed on the spot, the elders state their terms differently,

> . . . that you may fight the Ammonites
> and be our head over all the inhabitants of Gilead.

If קצין is a temporary military leadership and ראש a permanent civil one, the stakes are higher (see Rösel; note, too, that the fighting has been individualized, no longer ונלחמה but ונלחמת). But what remains unclarified is whether Jephthah will be ראש only during the conflict with the Ammonites or also after. Jephthah puts the proposition yet another way.

> *If* you are bringing me back to fight the Ammonites
> *and* Yhwh gives them to me,
> (then) I will be your head.

This response accomplishes two things with impressive economy. First it makes explicit that Jephthah will be head of the Gileadites after the battle, assuming he wins (if Israel loses to the Ammonites, the issue becomes a moot one anyway). Second, it lends divine sanction to the negotiations by making Jephthah's appointment as ראש contingent on divine favor. I shall return to this point later. The elders accept the terms, and the people make Jephthah ראש and קצין; i.e., he is appointed for the present crisis and for the future if he succeeds in ridding Israel of the Ammonite threat.

4.6   Jephthah's negotiating skills are soon put to another test, and this time they prove inadequate. His extensive negotiations with the king of the Ammonites (11:12-28) do not succeed in averting warfare. A long and contorted effort to present his case, with all sorts of appeals to history and divine intervention, Jephthah's argument is a curious example of rhetoric with a sense of *déjà vu* about it.[8] His appeal to the example of a failed attempt at negotiation and its outcome becomes yet another failed attempt at negotiation with the same outcome. Interestingly enough, neither the Ammonite king nor Jephthah benefits from the lesson in history Jephthah relates. Jephthah describes Israel's attempts to reason with earlier kings—the kings of Edom, Moab, and Sihon king of the Amorites—their failure to listen, and Yhwh's subsequent dispossession of them in favor of Israel. Like the kings before him, the king of Ammon also refuses to listen (cf. 11:17 with 11:28), and thus the Ammonites will soon meet the same fate: Yhwh gives them into Israel's hand (cf. 11:21 with 11:32). Jephthah's confidence in divine disposition, "all that Yhwh our God has dispossessed before us, we will possess," and his conviction that right and God are on his side ("I have not sinned against you, but you are doing me wrong to fight against me; Yhwh, the judge, judge today between the Israelites and the Ammonites," v 27) should suffice to convince him that Yhwh will give him victory in the upcoming battle, and thus from another angle point to something excessive about the vow.

4.7   Against this background of negotiation, Jephthah's vow does not appear out of character. Moreover, it is very much in context. When we compare the situation Jephthah refers to in his speech with the account of those events in Numbers 20-21, we find the Israelites vowing to God that they will put Canaanite cities to the ban in return for victory (Num 21:2). Israel's vow accords with the circumstances, and since Jephthah's situation so much resem-

---

[8] Jobling (128-31) analyzes interestingly the curious elements of this speech, suggesting that "Jephthah is dissatisfied with his case, and that he is disingenuously avoiding reference to the real basis of Ammon's claim" (129).

bles Israel's , a vow is not altogether unexpected. In fact, the two
vows are strikingly similar in their protases.

אם נתן תתן את העם הזה בידי   Num 21:2
אם נתון תתן את בני עמון בידי   Judg 11:30

Only with the apodoses do we note the dissonance in Jephthah's
vow. In the first case, Israel promises to devote to God through
destruction (חרם) what God gives them in battle. Jephthah, however, does the excessive; he vows a special offering to God, a
personal sacrifice from his own household. All too soon he will
discover that his vow demands the ultimate sacrifice on his part—
"you have indeed brought me low and have become my trouble"
(11:35, with pun on כרע and עכר emphasizing his individual misfortune). His is the only biblical instance of a vow where no apparent relation exists between the thing promised and the
condition of the vow (for discussion of the examples, see
Marcus: 18-21; Parker). The similar situations and similar language in Num 21:2 and Judg 11:30 make even more apparent that
Jephthah does not vow the obvious thing, an offering to God of
Ammonite spoil. That he vows the ultimate rather than the obvious (and perhaps even the logical?) lends further poignancy to
his tragedy.

4.8   By the end of the narrative, negotiation, if it can be called
that, completely breaks down. Again Jephthah fails to prevent the
outbreak of hostilities. Indeed, his exchange with the Ephraimites
(12:1-4) seems lame in comparison with his laborious reasoning
with the Ammonite king. The Ephraimites' anger at not having
been called to join Jephthah in fighting the Ammonites meets with
Jephthah's insistence that he sought their aid in vain, and thus we
have two different versions of events not reported in the narrative.
Surprisingly, Jephthah does not try reasoning with the Ephraimites. The Ephraimites threaten Jephthah's house, already de-
stroyed in the only sense that really matters, but do not announce
full-scale war with Gilead. Here particularly Jephthah reveals a
tendency towards excess. Without waiting for the Ephraimites'
response to his explanation (v 3), he calls together the men of
Gilead for battle. Not only is he less patient and less persistent
than with the Ammonites, where twice he sent messengers to
plead his part, but his dealings with the Ephraimites stand in
sharp contrast to the way an earlier judge handled the same sit-

uation. With some clever rhetoric, Gideon succeeded, where Jeph-thah does not, in averting the Ephraimites' wrath. Jephthah, the mighty warrior, is a man of bloodshed. His "diplomatic" failures result in fighting, and in one case needless slaughter; his faithful-ness to his vow costs his daughter's life.

4.9 The characterization of Jephthah as a negotiator whose vir-tue is also his weakness shows his potential for tragedy, but does not define him as a tragic figure. Jephthah, in contrast to a persona like Saul, fails to attain genuinely tragic proportions. To be sure, the makings are there: the *hamartia*, the incautious vow—but ex-cept for the scene when his daughter comes to meet him and he comprehends his destiny in one consuming and agonizing mo-ment, there is no inner struggle, no wrestling against his fate (see Ricoeur, Sewall). Unlike Saul, who knows he has lost the kingship yet multiplies his efforts to hold on to it, Jephthah does not grap-ple to find a way out of a situation for which there is no way out. I said of Saul that a lesser man might merely accept his fate. Jephthah does just that. He lacks hubris, therefore no significant tragic development occurs within his character. His would be a tragedy of a different order, of a greater magnitude, if, like Aga-memnon, he resisted; or, if like Jephthah in Amon Oz' short story "Upon This Evil Earth," he displayed a desperate clinging to the hope that God would intervene, "I have not withheld my only daughter from you. Grant me a sign, for surely you are tempting your servant."

5.1 No one knows exactly what Aristotle meant by catharsis, but is seems to have some connection to the satisfaction we experience in witnessing the strength of the human spirit as it rises to meet calamity (cf. Krutch). We admire in tragic heroes their ability to confront misfortune head-on, when, like Saul, they expend the full range of their human powers before they are broken by necessity. We pity Jephthah, but we do not at any point admire him.

5.2 The tragic hero's agony and gradeur lie in her or his isolation. Jephthah faces his cruel destiny essentially alone, for although his daughter accepts what he must do and urges him to carry out his vow, she does not share in his tragedy so much as she shares her own personal tragedy with her female companions—away from him and away from the company of men.[9] Nor do the people, exulting in victory, step in to ransom Jephthah's daughter, as the people ransomed Jonathan from the oath of his father Saul (1 Samuel 14). No solace comes from God either, no ram in the thicket.

5.3 The daughter, too, lacks the development that makes for a genuinely tragic personality. She accepts her fate so willingly and obediently that it is shocking (and the narrative does not tell us how she knows or surmises the terms of the vow). She places her communal importance—her role as sacrificial victim that the vow may be performed—over her individual life, and because she does not fight her fate, she does not attain the kind of tragic stature that we find, for example, in Iphigenia. Her tragedy lies in the sacrifice itself, an outrageous, violent act, and in life cut off in its promise, a doleful theme of "incompleteness" well established in literature from the Greek tradition of the young woman who dies on the eve of her wedding to Wordsworth's "Lucy Poems." In the pace of a few brief verses, she moves from mirth and celebration of her father's victory to mourning, and just as quickly she passes into death and celebration in communal memory. In particular the juxtaposition of her joy and Jephthah's dismay in the scene when she comes to meet him upon his return from battle is striking. A negotiator like her father, she asks for time to mourn her lack of fulfillment. Yet she is not isolated in sorrow; and as we have seen, the company and the yearly commemoration of women meliorate her tragedy.

5.4 The heart of Saul's tragedy may be located in what Paul Ricoeur describes as the Aeschylean paradox of human guilt and hostile transcendence (220). Saul is guilty and yet punished beyond measure by an unforgiving deity. In the story of Jephthah, ambiguity shrouds both sides of the paradox. Jephthah, too, is

[9] The patriarchal bias of the narrative is clear in the way it presents the tragedy both from Jephthah's perspective (his line comes to an end: "apart from her he had no son or daughter") and from his daughter's (she laments her virginity and by implication the denial to her of the role of motherhood, clearly a patriarchal concern). Her memory is kept alive because of the community of women and their ritual, but ultimately, of course, through the story; and her story keeps Jephthah's memory alive, with the remarkable irony that perhaps the most memorable thing about him is not the kind of thing one wants to be remembered for. Yet his name is remembered and hers is not.

guilty. His suffering is not imposed on him; he opens his mouth
(11:35, 36). But, like Saul, he is not really evil. His vow is not, I
think, a sign of insufficient faith (so Boling, Trible). Rather it illustrates his piety, his confidence in Yhwh, for he has consistently
invoked Yhwh in his other undertakings (11:9, 37). Ironically, his
piety precipitates his disaster, and again we see signs of the ex-
cessiveness which disposes Jephthah to tragedy, transforming his
virtue into *hamartia*. Jephthah's "guilt" remains particularly ambiguous. No negative judgement attends either the making of the
vow or its performance. The loss of his daughter is not presented
as punishment for a rash vow made either in overzealous piety or
lack of trust. The aftermath of the sacrifice, its effect on Jephthah's
inner life or his standing within the community, is passed over in
silence, and its effect upon his outward performance of his duties
is, at best, only hinted at in the account that follows, where he so
clearly fails to prevent tribal hostilities. Saul had the kingship torn
from him, experienced the terror of divine rejection, but still dies
a king. Jephthah dies a judge, but without suffering the indignity
of rejection or the curse of divine abandonment, and this absence
of censure not only makes us uncertain how to understand Jephthah's guilt, it also leaves us in doubt about the role of the deity.

5.5   The source of the tragic in the story of Jephthah is not divine
enmity, as in Saul's case, but divine silence. Beginning with the
refusal to continue to deliver the Israelites in their distress (10:13)
through the elders' choice of Jephthah and negotiations with him,
the deity remains strangely aloof from the affairs of Israel and
Jephthah. Jephthah, on the other hand, regularly refers matters to
the deity (and here we may recall Saul's constant seeking after the
divine will). He involves Yhwh in the decision to make him head
over Gilead, "if . . . Yhwh gives them to me" (11:9); in other
words, setting this condition may be Jephthah's way of seeking
divine affirmation: Jephthah will be head only if Yhwh shows it
should be so. The elders follow suit, binding themselves to Jephthah's words by an oath to Yhwh (11:10). Furthermore, Jephthah—and the narrator supplies this bit of information—speaks all
his words before Yhwh at Mizpah (note the play on מצפה and
פציתי). In his negotiations with the Ammonites, in addition to tes-
tifying to Yhwh's past action on Israel's behalf, Jephthah appeals
to Yhwh as the final judge of the conflict between Israel and Ammon. "May Yhwh, the judge, judge today between the Israelites
and the Ammonites" (11:27). Even his daughter brings the deity

into the picture, citing Yhwh's granting of victory to Jephthah as ground for observing the vow (11:36).

5.6   That the spirit of Yhwh affects Jephthah (11:29) offers a sign that Yhwh intends to come to Israel's aid through him. But we have already seen how the imposition of the vow raises questions about the role of the spirit. Apart from this curious animation of Jephthah, the only time Yhwh acts directly (as opposed to being spoken of) is to give the Ammonites into Jephthah's hand (11:32, 36; 12:3). If not a tacit acceptance of Jephthah's vow, this action nevertheless implicates the deity and helps determine Jephthah's tragic fate. That fate is sealed when Jephthah's daughter comes to meet him. He has opened his mouth to Yhwh (פציתי פי אל יהוה; פציתה את פיך אל יהוה)—thus he and his daughter accept the inevitability of the sacrifice. To speculate why Yhwh does not intervene at this point in the story gets us nowhere. The account of Abraham's near sacrifice of Isaac shows us one possible direction our narrative could have taken, a last minute intervention by the deity to save the child. Euripides' *Iphigenia in Aulis* shows us another, where the gods are without pity.[10] But in Judges 11, God neither requires nor rejects human sacrifice. Silent transcendence, if not a form of hostile transcendence, clearly raises questions about divine benevolence. Jephthah does not experience Saul's sense of separation from Yhwh, but, like Saul, he cannot depend on the goodness of Yhwh. He makes no final, urgent appeal to Yhwh which Yhwh refuses to answer, as in Saul's case. Rather as in Greek tragedy, Jephthah faces alone a fickle world, a world where seemingly unrelated events conspire to overwhelm, where a victorious warrior returning from battle can meet tragedy at the threshold of his house. His story does not call into question the underlying causes of his misfortune; its tragedy lies in that "secret cause."

---

[10] The ending which has Iphigenia spared is generally regarded as spurious, and I accept this view. In Euripides' *Iphigenia in Tauris*, Artemis substitutes a hind for the sacrifice and transports Iphigenia to Tauris. In Aeschylus' *Agamemnon*, Iphigenia is killed, an unwilling victim, at Aulis.

WORKS CONSULTED

Boling, Robert G.
1975   *Judges. Anchor Bible*, 6A. New York: Doubleday.

Burney, C. F.
1903,
repr. 1970 *The Book of Judges*. New York: Ktav.

Corrigan, Robert W., ed.
1981   *Tragedy: Vision and Form*. 2d ed. New York: Harper and Row.

Exum, J. Cheryl and J. William Whedbee
1984   "Isaac, Samson, and Saul: Reflections on the Comic and Tragic Visions." Pp. 5-40 in *Tragedy and Comedy in the Bible*. Ed. J. Cheryl Exum. *Semeia* 32. Decatur, GA: Scholars Press.

Fisher, Loren R.
1971   "Two Projects at Claremont." *Ugarit-Forschungen* 3:25-32.

Frye, Northrop
1965   *A Natural Perspective: The Development of Shakespearean Comedy and Romance*. New York: Harcourt, Brace & World.
1966   *Anatomy of Criticism*. New York: Atheneum.
1967   *Fools of Time: Studies in Shakespearean Tragedy*. University of Toronto Press.
1982   *The Great Code: The Bible and Literature*. New York: Harcourt Brace Jovanovich.

Girard, René
1977   *Violence and the Sacred*. Trans. Patrick Gregory. Baltimore: Johns Hopkins University Press.

Good, Edwin M.
1965   *Irony in the Old Testament*. Philadelphia: Westminster.

Gray, John
1986   *Joshua, Judges, Ruth*. The New Century Bible Commentary. Grand Rapids: Eerdmans.

Green, Alberto R. W.
1975   *The Role of Human Sacrifice in the Ancient Near East*. ASOR Dissertation Series, 1. Missoula, MT: Scholars Press.

Gunn, David M.
1980   *The Fate of King Saul: An Interpretation of a Biblical Story.* JSOT Supplement Series, 14. Sheffield: JSOT Press.
1981   "A Man Given Over to Trouble: The Story of King Saul." Pp. 89-112 in *Images of Man and God: Old Testament Short Stories in Literary Focus.* Ed. Burke O. Long. Sheffield: The Almond Press.

Hertzberg, H. W.
1969   *Die Bücher Josua, Richter, Ruth.* Das Alte Testament Deutsch, 9. Göttingen: Vandenhoeck & Ruprecht.

Humphreys, W. Lee
1978   "The Tragedy of King Saul: A Study of the Structure of 1 Samuel 9-31." *JSOT* 6:18-27.
1980   "The Rise and Fall of King Saul: A Study of an Ancient Narrative Stratum in 1 Samuel." *JSOT* 18:74-90.
1982   "From Tragic Hero to Villain: A Study of the Figure of Saul and the Development of 1 Samuel." *JSOT* 22:95-117.
1985   *The Tragic Vision and the Hebrew Tradition.* Philadelphia: Fortress.

Jay, Nancy
1985   "Sacrifice as Remedy for Having Been Born of Woman." Pp. 283-309 in *Immaculate and Powerful: The Female in Sacred Image and Social Reality.* Ed. Clarissa W. Atkinson, Constance H. Buchanan, and Margaret R. Miles. Boston: Beacon Press.

Jobling, David
1986   *The Sense of Biblical Narrative: Structural Analyses in the Hebrew Bible,* Vol. II. *JSOT* Supplement Series, 39. Sheffield: JSOT Press.

Krieger, Murray
1960   *The Tragic Vision: The Confrontation of Extremity,* Vol. I of *Visions of Extremity in Modern Literature.* Baltimore: Johns Hopkins University Press.
1971   *The Classic Vision: The Retreat from Extremity,* Vol. II of *Visions of Extremity in Modern Literature.* Baltimore: Johns Hopkins University Press.
1981   "*The Tragic Vision* Twenty Years After," in Corrigan: 42-46.

Krutch, Joseph Wood
    1981   "The Tragic Fallacy," in Corrigan: 227-37. Repr. from
                The Modern Temper. New York: Harcourt, Brace and
                World, 1957.

Landy, Francis
    1986   "Gilead and the Fatal Word." Pp. 39-44 in *Proceed-
                ings of the Ninth World Congress of Jewish Studies.*
                Jerusalem: World Union of Jewish Studies.

Marcus, David
    1986   *Jephthah and His Vow.* Lubbock, Texas: Texas Tech
                Press.

Moore, George F.
    1895   *A Critical and Exegetical Commentary on Judges.*
                The International Critical Commentary. Edinburgh:
                T. & T. Clark.

Oz, Amos
    1982   על האדמה הרעה הזאת. Pp. 200-243 in ארצות התן. Tel Aviv:
                Am Oved Publishers Ltd. ET = "Upon This Evil
                Earth." Pp. 185-239 in *Where the Jackals Howl and
                Other Stories.* Tr. Nicholas de Lange. Toronto: Ban-
                tam Books.

Parker, Simon B.
    1979   "The Vow in Ugaritic and Israelite Literature."
                Ugarit-Forschungen 11:693-700.

Pedersen, Johs.
    1914   *Der Eid bei den Semiten.* Strassburg: Karl J. Trübner.

Polzin, Robert
    1980   *Moses and the Deuteronomist. A Literary Study of
                the Deuteronomic History*, Part 1. New York: Sea-
                bury.

Ricoeur, Paul
    1967   *The Symbolism of Evil.* Tr. E. Buchanan. Boston:
                Beacon Press.

Rösel, Hartmut N.
    1980   "Jephtah und das Problem der Richter." *Biblica*
                61:251-55.

Sewall, Richard B.
    1980   *The Vision of Tragedy.* New Haven: Yale University
                Press.

Soggin, J. Alberto
    1981   *Judges.* The Old Testament Library. Tr. J. S. Bowden. Philadelphia: Westminster.

Steiner, George
    1980   *The Death of Tragedy.* New York: Oxford University Press.

Trible, Phyllis
    1984   *Texts of Terror: Literary-Feminist Readings of Biblical Narratives.* Philadelphia: Fortress.

de Unamuno, Miguel
    1954   *Tragic Sense of Life.* New York: Dover.

de Vaux, Roland
    1964   *Studies in Old Testament Sacrifice.* Cardiff: University of Wales Press.

Zakovitch, Yair
          "The Woman's Rights in the Biblical Law of Divorce." *The Jewish Law Annual* 4:28-46.

THE STORY OF JEPHTHAH
AND THE TRAGIC VISION
A Response to J. Cheryl Exum

W. Lee Humphreys
University of Tennessee, Knoxville

The terms "tragedy" and "tragic" seem much used and often abused. In the course of a single day—perhaps an unusually dark day—I encountered the term as it was used to refer to the death of a friend's pet, an individual's long struggle with cancer, the failure of a classroom test and what that portends for the course grade, Shakespeare's *Macbeth,* the development of still another block of condominiums in what was once lovely rolling Tennessee Valley farmland, the extinction of a particular species of bird, and the consequences of certain aspects of US foreign policy. Each is in its way a serious matter. But how can a term so widely used to describe this range of situations and events, drawn from so many distinct contexts, also serve usefully in the analysis of narrative material contained in the Hebrew Bible? This question is all the more critical in that the Hebraic literary corpus on the whole does not appear to provide fertile ground for the development of the theological implications inherent in tragedy or the tragic vision (Humphreys). Can a term used to denote the unfortunate, the untoward, a disaster, the results of stupidity, wrongheadedness, blindness, greed, and several other very human characteristics still retain a more restricted and specific field of meaning, one that will allow us to be sensitive to what are often neglected dimensions of the Hebraic tradition?

Clearly I believe the answer to be affirmative, and in *The Tragic Vision and the Hebrew Tradition* I explored some of these neglected dimensions. This essay by J. Cheryl Exum, as well as contributions by her and others in *Semeia* 32 (1984), also explores these possibilities with, I believe, important fruits resulting from the labor. The material dealing with King Saul in 1 Samuel and the Book of Job provide the most obvious units on which to cast the

perspective provided by tragic vision, and I and others have examined them in this light. I did not take up the "Case of Jephthah"
in my work, for I was not then impressed with its tragic potential,
and I therefore welcome Exum's present effort both as an attempt
to expand the range and complexity of material sensitive to study
from this perspective as well as to make clearer some of the limitations on its usefulness. Is it possible to slip into uses of the terms
"tragic" and "tragedy" that, while reflective of everyday usage,
also become too vague or vacuous to support careful literary analysis? In recent years the darker sides of human experience and
even of Israel's God have been underscored in several studies that
bring new perspectives to the Hebrew Bible (see, e.g., Crenshaw;
Trible; Exum and Whedbee; Fretheim; Humphreys). While not all
overtly work with the category of the tragic, these studies lay bare
dimensions of the Hebraic traditions generally neglected by most
earlier literary and theological studies, shaped as they were by a
vision of a covenanting God.

Exum distinguishes with others between "tragedy" as a literary form often defined within Aristotelian categories and the
"tragic vision" as a perspective that sensitizes us to what she calls
"a particular dimension of biblical narrative." Perhaps wisely she
does not delve into complexities of a definition that would entail
sustained engagement with a vast and complex body of literature,
some of which has been taken up in my work (Humphreys: 1-9)
and that of David Gunn (23-31). This makes it, however, all the
more important that some clear sense of limits be maintained as
the term slides between a rigid set of formal categories that define
a literary genre and usage of the term to make reference to almost
anything that seems unfortunate or untoward. In this respect it
appears especially important that a sense of balance or tension be
maintained within the tragic vision between what is generally
termed "fate" ("the hero over against an arbitrary and capricious
world") and "flaw" as often discussed in terms of classical *hubris*
and *hamartia*. There appears to be a necessary tension between
fate and flaw that must be held if the tragic vision is to be sustained. However much a particular work may tilt toward one or
the other, failure to hold them in some balance results in a sapping
of the essential force of the term "tragic," and in literature the
result can be either melodrama or a form of morality play (Humphreys: ch. 1).

I find Exum's analysis of the Jephthah story on the whole
most engaging and sensitive. She brings impressive literary skills

to the rhetorical dimensions of the text, and we will all read Judges 11-12 with deeper appreciation because of her efforts with this material. Rather than rehearse the strengths of her study, which are clear enough to appreciative readers, I will focus on her use of the perspective provided by the tragic vision. To what extent and in what ways can the story of Jephthah (and his daughter?) be usefully termed tragic? She poses this question herself as she notes that she seeks to examine not only how the story might fit her notions of the tragic but also how it "resists interpretation along tragic lines" (par. 1.5). It is certainly important to bear in mind that the vision of tragedy denotes less something a unit is or is not, than something approached, flirted with, avoided, skirted, or even (as in the Book of Job) transcended (note the title of K. Jasper's useful study: *Tragedy Is Not Enough*). Is Exum able to maintain a distinct and definite force in her use of the term tragic? To what degree does the material finally lend itself to her notion of the tragic?

As I indicated, at first blush I did not find the story of Jephthah and his daughter to display the stuff of tragedy, to be the sort of material that would make useful an approach to it through the perspective defined by the tragic vision. Jephthah's vow seemed simply unnecessary and possibly even stupid. As Exum develops the point so tellingly (3.9), we have already been told that Yhwh's spirit was upon Jephthah. Surely the result of this is to be more than an excursion through Israelite territory to that of the Ammonites (11:20), and the larger context of the whole collection of savior stories in Judges further encourages the expectation that this is all the assurance needed of success in any engagement with the enemy (3:10; 7:34; 13:25; cf. 1 Sam 11:6). If the vow is unnecessary, it is also stupid, again as Exum nicely suggests (4.7). It is made without apparent thought concerning the clear possibility of just who most likely will come from his house to meet him as he returns the victor. It is unlike more typical vows of this sort in that it has no clear link with the actual conflict, for example, through dedication of the spoils of victory or something of that sort.

Additional perspective is gained if we compare Jephthah's vow with the oath laid on the army of Israel by Saul in 1 Sam 14:24. The latter is at once spontaneous and yet understandable, enveloped in an ambiguity that Jephthah's lacks. In Saul's case, while the rout of the Philistines triggered by Jonathan seems well underway, the oath could be construed as intended to insure complete success in the destruction of the enemy forces, an issue that in context is still in doubt. While Jonathan's absence has been noted by both Saul and the reader, his chance coming upon some honey in the field seems to be the sort of thing that one might well not anticipate, especially as in Saul's case, when one is very much caught up in the tug and pull of a battle that seems to have taken on a life of its own. In hindsight Saul's oath may be perceived as both rash and as counterproductive: pursuit of the routed enemy is halted while the unwitting violator of the oath is identified, condemned by his father the king, and only then saved by the army. Yet, acting in the heat of battle, Saul could not anticipate all possible contingencies. By contrast the actual concrete occasion of Jephthah's vow is not clear. It appears set amid summary statements (11:29 and 32-33), and he seems remarkably blind to the one contingency that should be apparent: that his only child would be the one to appear in celebration when he returned in victory to his home.

Set side by side, Saul's experience appears much more the stuff of tragedy. Caught in the sweep of events that are initiated by another and seem to have taken on a life of their own, he attempts to assume a control that, as the scene transpires, it becomes clear he no longer has. His oath is based on the premise of control and knowledge that he no longer possesses. Events have moved beyond his grasp (1 Sam 14:16-19). In this assumption of a knowledge and control that is not his, he appears flawed, and his flaw seems designed to conspire with the course of events now moved by forces beyond his control to thwart his desire and trigger a downward course that will finally take the desperate king to Endor and then to the heights of Gilboa. The events of 1 Samuel 14 came to epitomize that which would later befall him.

There is no qualification to the description of Jephthah's total defeat of the Ammonites; they do not return to "their own place" (1 Sam 14:46b). Yet, with another ironic twist, Jephthah must lose his only child while the army prevents the execution of Jonathan (who will live on to die with his father), and we are just at this point in the narrative informed that Saul has, in fact, other children. 1 Sam 14:49-51 makes it clear that his was a rather extensive family, a stark contrast to the solitary pair of Jephthah and his daughter.

Exum brings to our reading of Jephthah's vow still other dimensions, however, and these merit attention. The logic and tempo of Judg 11:29-32 is broken by vv 30-31. The larger context simply reinforces our expectation that we can pass quickly with Jephthah, governed by the spirit of Yhwh, across Israelite territory to meet the Ammonites and on to a successful engagement with them that ends in total victory, recounted in a summary statement replete with still more items of geography. Verses 29 and 32-33 are in summary just what we might expect. Verses 30-31 intrude, but whether as a jarring and dark counterpoint within the field of action provided by Yhwh's spirit (cf. the evil spirit of Yhwh that afflicts Saul in 1 Sam 16:14, 23; 18:10), or as a human counterpoint to the saving action of the spirit, is not clear. In fact, it is only as Exum brings to the story the perspective shaped by the tragic vision that we have opened before us the former possibility and thus a potential for ambiguity in what on earlier readings appeared an example of simple, if very human, folly.

We might well ask whether our new openness to this dark potential for ambiguity in this text is more revealing of the reader and the times than of the text, especially as the latter is considered in its larger context in the Book of Judges. I am reminded of the opening sentences in the Book of Job, and of the natural assumption they draw from the reader about the relationship of the two elements in the description of Job, especially a reader steeped in the Hebraic tradition. That is, being informed of Job's position as a paragon of virtue ("blameless and upright, one who feared God, and turned away from evil") and then of his standing as a man of substance, most readers seem naturally to assume a causal link between the first and second—the good get goods. But unless the simple juxtaposition of statements can be said to suggest causation, it is the reader who provides this interpretative link, a link between virtue and prosperity that the Satan will indeed immediately call into question and the book as a whole leaves very much in doubt. The fact that Exum is able to read Judg 11:29-32 as she proposes, and that we are willing to an extent at least to follow her down this course and consider vv 30-31 as a possibly dark dimension of the activity of Yhwh's spirit, is certainly revealing of the context within which biblical texts are being read by some in this day (note her own caveat in par 1.5). Whether through the lenses provided by the tragic vision per se or through other perspectives sensitive to the terror in some texts, to the torment that draws some lives into a whirlpool, or to the suffering even of God, more traditional lenses are being challenged and conventions of reading are being questioned by new readers.

Presumably readers cannot, however, simply adopt whatever lenses seem to suit their fancy. The text must to some degree cooperate with the reader. Our interpretation above of Saul's oath is enhanced by the fact that it is part of a larger pattern in his downward spiral from his only full success as king (his defense of the citizens of Jabesh-gilead in the face of the threat posed by the Ammonites!) to his death at his own hands on Mount Gilboa. Saul is clearly under the control of the spirit of God in his success (1 Sam 11:6). There is no hint that his ill-taken oath and later his failure rigidly to observe the ban in his defeat of the Amalakites are so directed, and the latter is left remarkably without clear motive of any sort in spite of his excuses. His initial attacks on David are sparked by the evil spirit from Yhwh and then by his own obsessive jealousy as well. Driven as he is by forces beyond his ken or control, he also manifests qualities of character that permit his own flaws to work hand in glove with fate to bring him to the cave at Endor and then to Gilboa. By contrast, Jephthah's vow is an isolated instance, isolated both in the flow and logic of its immediate textual setting and as an event in the pattern of his life. It is the one point in his bargaining with another that he gets what he seeks; the negotiations do not here break down. There is bitter irony in all this, but behind all such irony need not lie the vision of the tragic. The text seems reluctant to cooperate wholly with the reader who would discover in Jephthah's vow the work of Yhwh's spirit, who would find here more than the disastrous results of short-sighted human folly. In fact, to shift the initiatives from Jephthah to the spirit is to move the balance from flaw to fate, but not clearly to maintain the tension essential to the tragic vision.

Exum notes other points in her analysis where the text seems reluctant (4.4). One symptom of a struggle with a reluctant text may be seen in what I suspect to be a breakdown in the use of the term "tragic" that is related to my opening observations. There are points at which use of the term seems at best loose, more in line with popular parlance than with the more circumscribed use of the term in literary discussion. Thus we are told in 4.7 that poignancy is lent to Jephthah's *tragedy* through his vowing the ultimate, his only child, and not the more obvious or logical. We are told in 5.2 that his daughter does not share in his *tragedy* so much as she shares her own personal *tragedy* with her female companions. Twice more in 5.2, Exum will speak of her *tragedy*, even in the same paragraph in which it is pointed out that she does not really attain tragic stature in the story. Indeed she is not even named and is generally viewed from a perspective defined by her father's interests. She does not protest, she does not "fight her fate"; while not quite as passive as Isaac, like Abraham in Genesis 22 she seems too willing to allow the terrible deed to be executed. Earlier in 4.4 we have been told that Jephthah also "departs from our expectations of a tragic figure." At best there seems something about him "which disposes him to tragedy." The term "tragedy" in all of this seems played on in two keys, the one of everyday speech and the other more rarefied.

My desire here is not to quibble about words, or to adopt some purist stance with respect to the use of language. Yet attention to the usage of the term "tragic" is important and revealing. The perspective of the tragic vision does provide a quite distinct vantage point on both human beings, as reflected in the figure of the hero, and on the fundamental nature of the cosmos within which they must live and act and speak, which can become for them a chaos. Jephthah is a failed man in important ways, disaster strikes him and his daughter, even as in one aspect of the basic framework that shapes his story, he is a success: Israel is delivered from the Ammonite threat and he attains leadership. Exum nicely demonstates that this success is essentially blunted, however, and not only in the loss of his only child and therefore the termination of his family line. He is a flawed negotiator both when dealing with the enemy and with his own people. The terse note that he judged Israel six years, died, and was buried in his city in Gilead (reading 12:7 with the LXX) is the best that can be said in summary of his moment in the cycle of leaders during those "days when the judges ruled."

Even in his origins he comes up short as he spans social extremes and is clearly not the classical man of substance (cf. Saul in 1 Sam 9:1-2 and Job in Job 1:1-3) who appears as the tragic hero. He is given to extremes and is foolishly unthinking. Nevertheless, he is not a wicked or a bad man. Nor is he, however, heroic. He does not struggle against his fate, as his words reveal when his daughter comes forth from the house to celebrate his return from war. There is pathos in this figure of Jephthah, and in that of his child, and sadness in the end of each. There is a muted terror at his isolation and her "incompleteness," but there is not awe and dread. In the figure of Jephthah we are not taken to the boundaries of human potential. We do not experience the dimensions of human being as stretched and thereby defined in both its potential and its limits. In the figures of Saul and Job, each in his own way, we experience what humans might fully be as well as what they are not, as they struggle to be what they are and beyond to what they cannot be. Just this testing of the boundary situations is a vital component in the tragic vision (Sewall). Finally, there is nothing to effect a literary distancing of us from Jephthah, no Creon and Chorus to speak the final lines and provide perspective, no Horatio to take the stage, no men of Jabeshgilead to cremate, bury, and honor a fallen leader who at the end fought again his people's wars as their king. David can sing of Saul and Jonathan together and of their exploits for Israel (2 Sam 1:19-27). The daughters of Israel lament each year for Jephthah's daughter, but even this reflection of him in her memorial is not our last view of Jephthah. Jephthah is last perceived in an action in which forty-two thousand Ephraimites die.

I am not therefore convinced that we can in a serious way speak of the tragedy of Jephthah or of his daughter. To do so betrays a looseness in our speaking that may be a symptom of the struggle Exum must engage in as she seeks to bring to the story the perspective of the tragic vision. Nor am I convinced that in the end we salvage a tragic thrust by suggesting that it lies finally not in divine enmity against Jephthah (as in the case of Saul) but in divine silence (5.5). In fact it seems to be a case of both enmity and silence in the story of King Saul: divine hostility is expressed at critical points through a ringing silence (1 Sam 28:3-7). What sets Saul apart from Jephthah is his desperate seeking of links and words with his God, not only in 1 Samuel 14 in the aborted use of the ephod (the ark of the MT) and then the oath, but above all in his approach to the dead Samuel through the medium at Endor (1 Sam 28). Jephthah speaks readily enough of Yhwh to others (11:9, 21-24, 27, 35; 12:3), as does his daughter (11:36), but except in the moment of the vow there is no attempt to seek the deity out by whatever means are at hand. Jephthah is just not in the same league as the God-haunted Saul.

Indeed Jephthah may be more akin to his more immediate successor in the biblical material in certain respects. Samson, like Jephthah, at only one point really seeks out his God. This is in his final prayer for vengeance (16:28) in which he also seems blind to the full potential consequences of its fulfillment in retribution for his lost eyes. Both Samson and Jephthah find their prayer and vow answered in that they receive what they request. That they get more is ironic, but it is an irony that undergirds the pathetic and is not that of genuine tragedy. The fact that Samson's one attempt to make contact with his God comes at the end of his life provides him little time for reflection, but then he was not of a reflective disposition anyway (compare the figure as finely crafted by John Milton in his *Samson Agonistes*). Jephthah's vow is placed earlier in his life; yet he seems, as Exum notes, distraught but accepting of his misfortune from his first and virtually only words (11:35) to his daughter (his one word assent [11:38] to her request for two months—"Go"—seems almost like a dismissal of her from his life) throughout the remainder of her life. "Silent transcendence" may raise questions about divine benevolence for a reader encouraged by a tragic perspective to ask them. But Jephthah is apparently no more attuned to pursue them or his God than is Samson, and just this blunts the potential for tragedy in his story. The unreflecting Samson seems bound on one side by the tragic figure of Saul and by the pathetic figure of Jephthah on the other. Each provides a distinct, if not wholly unrelated, perspective by which to view the "dark side of existence," and a thorough analysis of the stories of the three as juxtaposed in their present context, as well as in isolation, would be rewarding.

I raise one additional point, and do so with some hesitation in response to this fine study to be published in a series devoted to new modes of literary study of biblical material with their recurring celebrations of the synchronic. If indeed the Hebraic tradition provides generally rather thin soil for the tragic vision and material that reflects it to take root, then those points where there seem at least to be flirtations with the tragic—and Exum's study suggests we have at least this in the story of Jephthah and his daughter—may provide just the occasion for some diachronic perspective on the developmental history of a unit. What was by all accounts material that seemed difficult for the larger tradition to digest was nevertheless incorporated into it. Broad traces of the digestive process may be apparent especially as we are sensitive to the tradition's struggles to swallow the theological implications of the tragic vision, with what it implies about the deity. I attempted such an admittedly hypothetical diachronic analysis of the book of 1 Samuel that builds on analysis of the story of King Saul as perceived from the tragic perspective (Humphreys: chs. 2-3). The potential for the tragic in the Jephthah story—limited as it now may be—invites us to consider just how this might have been blunted as the material was incorporated into the twin cycles that shape the book of Judges.

There is, of course, first the well-recognized cycle marked by Israel's rebellion, delivery into alien hands, cry of distress, and deliverance by Yhwh through the efforts of a savior. Exum notes (3.3) the unexpected manner in which this pattern is nuanced in the Jephthah story, with Yhwh's refusal to intervene and Israel's open declaration of repentance (the only instance of this in Judges) and then the wonderful lack of clarity in the response of the deity. It could be suggested that those traits of the material that are highlighted by the tragic vision may have made this one unit more difficult than others to digest within the larger theological framework of Judges. Of course the deity does deliver Israel, but possible traces of a vision of Yhwh that emphasized traits other than justness and benevolence peep through.

The second cycle is a type of counterpoint to the first and finds behind the success of each savior a pattern of increasing disintegration that finally reaches its climax in the so-called appendix of Judges 17-21, the crassness of Eli's sons, and the loss of the ark. Simply put, after the first two accounts of Othniel and Ehud—both briefly related—each successor has her or his triumph progressively more tarnished. Jephthah fits nicely between the near civil war in the time of Gideon and the troubles his ephod caused, along with the abortive reign of Abimelech, on the one side, and the debacle that sums up the life of Samson and is most manifest in his greatest victory that is also his death (Judg 16:30b) on the other. Whatever destruction he wrought on the Philistines and their gods and temple is forgotten by 1 Samuel 4 when all seems in good repair again. Viewed in this progression the accent falls on Jephthah's vow as one more example of human perversity, as part of a line that leads from Barak's reluctance (4:9), Gideon's occasion for apostasy (8:27), Abimelech's violence and grab for power, and on to Samson's impulsive drives for sex and aggression, and to the complete distintegration pictured in chs. 17-21 and beyond. In this context even heroes with the potential for tragedy can easily be made to appear the villain.

What tragic potential there is in the story of Jephthah is most apparent when the material is read apart from its larger contexts. In fact, the potential is greatest when the reading is focussed on Jephthah and his daughter, that is, on Judges 11 rather than Judges 11-12, let alone Judges 11-12 joined to the Samson material in chs. 13-16. Of course, as readers we can select to read shorter or longer segments of a text, and can read them in or out of ever larger contexts. But the Jephthah material is there, as a whole as well as in at least two possible distinct segments in chs. 11 and 12. And it is also set in contexts, both in relation to the material dealing with Samson, in the book of Judges as a whole with its own editorial structures, and even in the larger deuteronomistic history. Attention to this does suggest possibilities concerning the development of the material as it grew and came to be placed in its several settings and about its shape and tone at each potential stage. Possibilities of this sort could provide an avenue for a fruitful rapproachment between the synchronic and the diachronic, between perspectives whose advocates seem at times to want to force into opposition, as if they can only bear fruit if one supplants the other from the field of biblical studies.

WORKS CONSULTED

Crenshaw, James L.
    1984   *A Whirlpool of Torment*. Overtures to Biblical Theology, 12. Philadelphia: Fortress Press.

Exum, J. Cheryl and J. William Whedbee
    1984   "Isaac, Samson, and Saul: Reflections on the Comic and Tragic Visions." Pp. 5-40 in *Tragedy and Comedy in the Bible*. Ed. J. Cheryl Exum. *Semeia* 32. Decatur, GA: Scholars Press.

Fretheim, Terence E.
    1984   *The Suffering of God*. Overtures to Biblical Theology, 14. Philadelphia: Fortress Press.

Gunn, David M.
    1980   *The Fate of King Saul: An Interpretation of a Biblical Story. JSOTSup* 14. Sheffield: JSOT Press.

Humphreys, W. Lee
    1985   *The Tragic Vision and the Hebrew Tradition*. Overtures to Biblical Theology, 18. Philadelphia: Fortress Press.

Jaspers, Karl
    1952   *Tragedy is Not Enough*. Boston: Beacon Press.

Sewall, Richard B.
    1952   *The Vision of Tragedy*. New Haven: Yale University Press.

Trible, Phyllis
    1984   *Texts of Terror.* Overtures to Biblical Theology, 13.
                  Philadelphia: Fortress Press.

THE STORY OF EHUD (JUDGES 3:12-30)
THE FORM AND THE MESSAGE

Yairah Amit
Tel Aviv University

ABSTRACT

The following analysis of the Ehud story (Judg 3:12-30) seeks to demonstrate how the text directs the reader to see the connection between human tactics and divine salvation. In this story the narrator has composed a plot out of a series of stratagems, and the reader advances from one to the next having encountered no realistic delays or complications. In spite of the detailed description relating mainly to Ehud's earlier tactics, however, the reader, at the end of the story, is convinced that the opening words about God's raising up a deliverer (3:15) should be taken literally. The text leads the reader to the conclusion that Ehud's ability to execute the tactics without any disruptions, but, rather, being helped by things that occurred along his way, can only be the result of God's involvement. Thus, the construction of the story in its details, from the exposition to the ending, serves to express its message: the success of human planning is brought about by the divine will.

1. Preface: Success of the Human Scheme Due to Divine Will

1.1   One's first impression when reading the story of Ehud is of a victory won by a succession of human tactics. The special dagger Ehud used and the way it was carried; the ceremony of offering tribute to the king and dismissing the tribute bearers in order to win the king's confidence; the secret word Ehud had for the king and the murder in the summer chamber, which Eglon had to himself alone; locking the chamber doors, so the king's men would think that he was in private; and finally, taking the fords of the Jordan—all form a succession of tactics that emphasize human planning and the human ability to carry it out, leaving only a small place for the intervention of God. Thus, the reader, like many commentators, may think that Ehud's victory was the result of his skill; i.e., his plans and improvisations.

1.2   On the other hand, at the opening of the story (Judg 3:15) and at the end (3:28), there is a clear indication that the victory was won by the will of God. This argument is supported by the introduction to the book of Judges (2:16-18) and by the victory of Othniel, the son of Kenaz, over the king of Aram Naharaim (3:9-10), both of which show that the judges were sent by God and that their victories were God's response to the crying out of the oppressed Israelites.

1.3   Thus the question: how can the author clarify to his readers that Ehud's success was the result of God's intention? I suggest that in this story, the narrator emphasizes God's salvation by constructing a detailed plot that describes the succession of tactics Ehud used, while avoiding information about the actual difficulties he might have had in carrying out his plan. This systematic refusal to describe even expected difficulties makes Ehud's tactics appear as a series of successful coincidences, and causes the reader to doubt that human planning alone could be responsible for it. Thus the narrator proves to the reader that the success of any human plan must be connected with and guided by divine intention.[1]

---

[1] The considerable amount of "reasonable data" which appears in the story has led interpreters to reconstruct the details of performance and to follow up Ehud's strategic plan. Josephus (*Antiquitates*, V, 4, 188-196) already described Ehud as familiar with Eglon's royal palace. According to his reconstruction, in order to stay alone with the king, Ehud relied on the hot weather and the guards' neglect of duty after finishing their lunch. Ehud, in Josephus's story, had good connections with the inhabitants of Jericho, and they helped him to gather together the army. Recent commentaries tend to reconstruct the event on the basis of data given and on the process of gap-filling. So E. G. Kraeling (205-210), who claims that the author neglected his duty only in the description of the passage to the summer chamber, while the rest of the story flows smoothly. E. Täubler (21-42) thinks that the understanding of the story is due to the reconstruction of the geographical data. M. Garsiel is aware of the considerations of reasonability and describes the main action as taking place east of the Jordan. H. N. Rösel supports

1.3.1 In other words, the presentation of Ehud in the exposition (3:15) as a savior sent by God arouses the reader's expectations for "great work" (cf. Judg 2:7), for a miracle, or for the revelation of God's spirit. At the same time, the reader's familiarity with Ehud's plan and tactics reduces God's part in the deliverance. Therefore we find that the narrator makes a special effort to convince the reader of an existing "double causality" (Seeligmann), which explains that the success of human planning is preconditioned by God's will and power and that only the fact that Ehud was sent by God guarantees the effectiveness of his tactics. This point is made by leaving out important information while moving from one scene to the next, or from one tactic to another. The disregard of necessary information in the intermediate stages prevents the reader from reconstructing the events. The reader who follows Ehud's plan and its implementation realizes that it is impossible to organize the given facts into a successive and causal chain of events. He or she therefore has to admit the existence of "weak" links in the chain that could have complicated events, but somehow did not prevent Ehud from acting. For example, the special dagger and the way it was hidden indicate that Ehud expected to be searched when entering the king's palace. Nevertheless, there is no mention of such a search, and the reader simply views Ehud offering the tribute. There is also no explanation of when and why the king moved to the summer chamber, which undoubtedly was the convenient place for acting out the "perfect murder." This technique of leaving out relevant information and putting the reader into the center of the event is supported by a string of propitious coincidences: Ehud locked the door of the summer chamber and left just before the king's servants arrived. Somehow the king's servants tarried awhile, thereby allowing Ehud to escape in the direction of Seir, from where he would blow the trumpets in the hill country of Ephraim and proceed to take the fords of the Jordan. The narrator does not give us any hint that Ehud was concerned with the timing of the events, and thus the reader might think that Ehud succeeded by coincidence alone.

1.3.2 When the reader discovers that s/he is being asked to make connections between the events by assuming coincidence rather

---

too the possibility of Ehud's double visit to the palace. Alter concludes that "... it is perhaps less historicized fiction than fictionalized history." For a different view, see J. Elizur, who stresses the element of improvisation.

than careful planning on Ehud's part, s/he realizes the limitations of human planning and accepts the need for divine guidance. As Ps 127:1 puts it, "Unless the Lord builds the house, those who build it labor in vain; unless the Lord watches over the city, the watchman stays awake in vain." This rhetorical technique, where coincidences and tactics appear side by side, convinces the reader that Ehud's ability to carry out his tricky plan is predetermined by God's desire to deliver the people. The repeating of fortunate coincidences points to someone behind the incidents, who knows their outcome and responds to human requests (cf. Isa 41:22; Prov 19:21; Gen 24:12, 42; cf. also Gen 27:20).

1.4   The following analysis of the Ehud story will demonstrate how the text directs us to see the connection between human tactics and God's salvation, so that at the end of the story the reader will be convinced that "when the Lord raised them up judges, then the Lord was with the judge, and delivered them out of the hands of their enemies" (Judg 2:18).

2. *The Structure of the Story*

2.1   Careful analysis of the structure of the story reveals both the systematic use of tactics by Ehud and the lack of detailed information between one unit and the next. The division of the story into the following structural units is based on the scenic principle.[2]

1st	Unit	The exposition	vv 12-15
2nd	Unit	The description of making the dagger	v 16
3rd	Unit	The description of offering the tribute	vv 17-18
4th	Unit	The murder scene	vv 19-23
5th	Unit	The description of the servants' delay	vv 24-25
6th	Unit	The description of the war and the victory	vv 26-29
7th	Unit	Summary report	v 30

2.2   According to this division, there are five stages between the exposition and the ending. Each stage describes Ehud's tactics as

---

[2] The division according to scenic principle is based on changes in time, place, characters, and manner of narration. As the biblical story is generally short, the transitions from situations of telling, in which the narrator functions openly, to situations of showing, in which the narrator is concealed behind the characters, are conspicuous. Moreover, the sudden sharp transition from scenic descriptions to summarizing reports, that at times cover events of many years, highlights the place and function of the scenic situation.

they are planned or carried out. Each occurs at a different time and a different place and has different characters. When making the dagger, Ehud is alone in the territory of Israel. When offering the tribute, Ehud is accompanied by the tribute bearers, and the event takes place in Eglon's territory. In the murder scene we find Ehud and Eglon in the summer chamber; the servants are described as waiting near the king's door. In the war, Ehud, as leader of the Israelite army, moves from the hill country of Ephraim to the fords of the Jordan.

2.3   Each unit forms a necessary step toward the desired victory, although each stage does not necessarily follow as a result of the previous stage. Moving from one stage to the next, however, we find that relevant details are missing—details that could disrupt and complicate events. Lacking that information, and finding her/himself in the midst of the next stage, the reader concludes that everything turned out well.

2.4   The Gaps in the Intermediate Stages and Examples of the Lack of Relevant Data.[3]

The exposition

What information did Ehud have about the palace of Eglon, king of Moab; how did he get the information; how did the information affect his planning; what details were missing in the information; did he have any alternatives; did he share his secret with others; etc.

Preparing the dagger

How did Ehud get to the hall where the tribute was offered; were there any guards present at the entrance; was he searched; were there guards in the palace;

---

[3] It is possible to argue that not all the gaps mentioned in this list are relevant to the biblical story; however, I mention them here since they are frequently adduced in scholarly reconstructions. See above, n. 1.

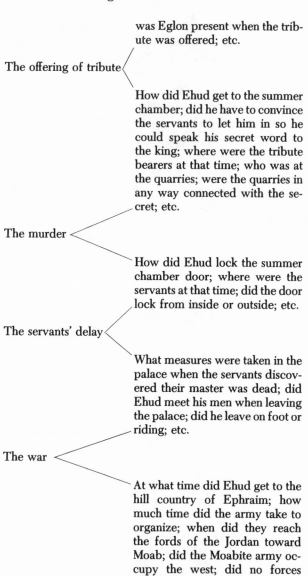

The offering of tribute — was Eglon present when the tribute was offered; etc.

The murder —
How did Ehud get to the summer chamber; did he have to convince the servants to let him in so he could speak his secret word to the king; where were the tribute bearers at that time; who was at the quarries; were the quarries in any way connected with the secret; etc.

The servants' delay —
How did Ehud lock the summer chamber door; where were the servants at that time; did the door lock from inside or outside; etc.

The war —
What measures were taken in the palace when the servants discovered their master was dead; did Ehud meet his men when leaving the palace; did he leave on foot or riding; etc.

The ending —
At what time did Ehud get to the hill country of Ephraim; how much time did the army take to organize; when did they reach the fords of the Jordan toward Moab; did the Moabite army occupy the west; did no forces come from the east; why did no part of the army flee in other directions; etc.

2.5 The units are organized symmetrically. At the end of the story a new static reality is described, different from the reality of oppression described at the beginning—eighty peaceful years. The dynamic event that brought about the change was the murder of Eglon. Ehud used two tactics in carrying out the murder. The peace was also won through two tactics.

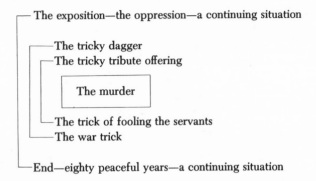

The exposition—the oppression—a continuing situation

The tricky dagger
The tricky tribute offering

The murder

The trick of fooling the servants
The war trick

End—eighty peaceful years—a continuing situation

The symmetrical structure also emphasizes the extent to which Ehud's story is constructed of tactics that turn the reader's mind from the reality of oppression to the totally different new reality of long-lasting peace. On the other hand, the gaps between one stage and the next contribute to the curious awareness that none of the tactics encountered any obstacle. This ambivalent description, emphasized by the structure of the story, helps us comprehend its meaning.

3. Analysis of the Units
3.1   The complicated role of the exposition (vv 12-15)

3.1.1   The exposition in the story of Ehud ends at v 15. At that point the first scene occurs, or, to put it differently, the more dynamic elements in the plot appear. The details in vv 12-15 are proportionally static in comparison with the dynamic description of preparing the dagger. The choice of Ehud as a deliverer is a decision that does not relate to a definite time of action, and his selection as tribute bearer does not determine the time of deliverance. Hence, in the exposition, we do not learn when Ehud will deliver the Israelites, or how many times he will lead the tribute bearers. Only the making of the dagger, in unit 1, offers a dynamic event that points to a plan that might change the situation of oppression.

3.1.2   God's part in the events is clearly expressed in the exposition by the repetitive formulas that appear throughout Judges:
"And the people of Israel again did what was evil in the sight of
the Lord" (v 12); "and the people of Israel served" (v 14); "when
they cried out to the Lord" (v 15); "the Lord raised up for them
a deliverer" (v 15). These repetitive patterns represent the four
periodic stages that tie the story of Ehud to the cyclical pattern of
Judges and, again, emphasize the controlling role of God.

3.1.3   It is important to note that only in the exposition of our
story does the author emphasize God's dominant role by adding
phrases that do not appear in the parallel patterns (cf. 2:11–19;
3:7–11; 4:1–3; 6:1–6; 10:6–10; 13:1).

> —The expression "and the Lord strengthened Eglon the
> king of Moab" (v 12b) occurs instead of the familiar "to
> give into the hand" or "to sell into the hand."

> —The causal clause "because they had done what was evil
> in the sight of the Lord" (v 12c) explains and highlights the
> idea expressed at the beginning of v 12a.[4] This kind of
> argumentation does not appear in the analogous patterns of
> sin.

3.1.4   These expressions force the reader to think that the
strength of Eglon king of Moab and his ability to defeat Israel is
in God's power. On the other hand, reading closely every detail,
we find that the king of Moab did not trust his power or any divine
power, and therefore he summoned the people of Ammon and
Amalek before going to war with Israel. Relying on this cooper-
ative human force, he possessed the city of palms, which probably was in Israelite territory. Ammon and Amalek do not appear
in the story apart from the exposition, where they lend support to
the idea of double causality. Even though the king of Moab may
attribute his victory to his use of massive forces, the reader realizes that the plan worked because it corresponded to God's plan
to punish Israel. In other words, the main theme of the story is
presented by the author already in the exposition, where he alerts

---

[4] The causal clause is also prominent in its place due to the unusual preposition
that opens it: עַל כִּי, which occurs only four times in the Bible: Deut 31:17; Jer 4:28;
Mal 2:4; Ps 139:14.

us to the existence of double causality by placing two different pieces of information side by side:

> v 12b: and the Lord strengthened Eglon the king of Moab against Israel, because they had done evil in the sight of the Lord
>
> v 13: and he gathered to himself the Ammonites and the Amalekites, and went and defeated Israel, and possessed the city of palms

3.1.5   Comparison of these verses shows us for the first time the parallel existence of two systems that work according to different norms, the human system and the divine system. The human world works according to causal laws that characterize it, as in this case the use of a large force for conquering enemy territory; whereas the successes and failures of this world are determined by God, without any connection to tactics used in the human world. The reader knows that the Moabite oppression is the result of God's wanting to punish his people, whereas Eglon, king of Moab, does not realize that he is being used as the "rod of God's anger." Therefore he acts according to human considerations and raises a large army.

3.1.6   A similar situation occurs in the appointing of Ehud as a deliverer.

> v 15b the Lord raised up for them a deliverer, Ehud, the son of Gera
>
> v 15c and by him the Israelites sent tribute to Eglon, the king of Moab

The reader, following the sequence, knows that Ehud was raised up by God as a deliverer after the Israelites cried to him for help. At the same time, the Israelites, who do not know that Ehud will be their deliverer, send tribute to Eglon king of Moab by the hand of Ehud, son of a Jemenite, a lefthanded man. The narrator here avoids using the phrase, "the Lord was with him" (2:18) or "the spirit of the Lord came upon him" (3:10), in order to emphasize the separate existence of the two systems and the gap between human and divine considerations. Already in the exposition stage, when faced with the question of Ehud's appointment, the reader is exposed to two perspectives: according to one, God elected

Ehud as deliverer; according to the other, the Israelites chose Ehud to carry the tribute. Thus the reader is left to ponder how at the same time Ehud could be the people's messenger (a tribute bearer) and God's messenger (a deliverer).

3.1.7   The biblical writer, usually succinct, characterizes Ehud by different terms, some of which seem at first redundant. The reader's attention is drawn to the second detail, בן הימיני (son of Jemini). The mention of גרא already connects Ehud with the tribe of Benjamin, therefore the distinct mention of the tribe is not strictly necessary.[5] All the same, the writer prefers to use the combined phrase בן הימיני (son of Jemini) and not מבנימין (from Benjamin). This separation (בן—ימין) creates the foundation for the repetition of ימין in a new combination, יד ימינו (his right hand). Identifying Ehud as a left-handed man, describing him as איש אטר יד ימינו, and repeating the word יד in the phrase, "the Israelites sent tribute by his hand," focus attention on Ehud's skill and direct the reader to form an assumption that Ehud of Benjamin will act upon the strength of his left hand. It seems that mentioning left-handedness and the tribe of Benjamin are to be understood in a context of war, and the use of איש אטר together with מבנימין was an idiomatic combination that referred to fearless warriors from the tribe of Benjamin (cf. Judg 20:16; 1 Chr 12:6). Characterizing Ehud by this combination of phrases not only teaches us that he is a great warrior with special skills, it also provides the key for forming a hypothesis of what is bound to happen: the one, who in the future will bear the tribute to Eglon king of Moab will be Ehud, son of Gera, a great warrior, who has excellent command of his left hand, and who might in the future use his special physical advantage when bearing the tribute, and thus deliver his people.

---

[5] Gen 46:21; cf. also 2 Sam 16:5; 19:17, 19; 1 Kgs 2:8; and see 1 Chr 7:10; 8:3,5,6,7. It is important to point out that the mentioning of the tribal origin of the judge in the exposition stage occurs only in the Samson story (Judg 13:2). In the other cases, this kind of information is obtained from the larger context; so in the cases of Othniel, Gideon, Jephthah, and Abimelech, but it is not clear if Deborah's tribe is Ephraim or Issachar or another tribe. The origin of Shamgar ben Anath is not known either. In the case of the minor judges, their residence or their burial place does not necessarily indicate their origin, and see Judg 10:1. It seems that Jair the Gileadite is a member of the tribe of Manasseh (Machir); cf. Num 32:41; Deut 3:14; on other assumptions, see B. Mazar.

3.1.8   In conclusion, we can say that the exposition serves a number of purposes. First and foremost, it functions to provide the reader with the basic data that is connected with the world described in the story and important for the understanding of what transpires. Thus the reader learns about the Moabite oppression that lasted eighteen years and about Moab's rule over the city of palms. S/he is introduced to the main figures: Eglon, king of Moab, and Ehud, a fighter from the tribe of Benjamin. Second, the exposition connects Ehud's act of deliverance with the cyclical pattern that characterizes the era and clarifies for the reader the order of the world described. Already in the exposition the reader learns of the double causality principle and of the success of human action when coupled with the divine plan: the victory of Moab and the appointment of Ehud. Finally, the exposition directs the reader's eye forward and encourages the formation of a hypothesis of what is bound to happen. It seems to me that understanding the various roles of the exposition enables us to appreciate its details and to see it as an inseparable part of the story.

3.2   Analysis of the stages that build the plot and its transitions

3.2.1   The five stages that comprise the main part of the plot are characterized by a selection of material emphasizing Ehud's tactics and by its organization as a chain of successive stages that lead him to victory. These stages give the story a realistic character. The narrative presentation helps the reader appreciate the effectiveness of Ehud's tactics. Even in those places where premeditation on Ehud's part is in doubt, the reader has to acknowledge Ehud's skill in improvising. But as more data is given and as timing serves Ehud's purpose, the reader may ask who is behind all this timing. The conclusion will be that the success of the human plan is preconditioned by the will of God.

3.2.2   The description of preparing the dagger (v 16)

3.2.2.1   The tactic in this stage concerns the description of making the dagger and the way it is hidden. The transition from Ehud's appointment to lead the tribute bearers to the description of making the dagger is sudden. The reader has no information about Ehud's previous knowledge of the palace, about the way the palace was guarded, or about the king's customs. No hint is given whether Ehud had visited the palace before, whether it was

his first visit, or whether he tried to get information from the other
tribute bearers or from other sources. The reader who was trans-
ported into the middle of the description of making the dagger
and the way it was worn concludes that Ehud planned his moves
carefully, giving thought to every detail. But the options are un-
limited, and the reader has to close the gaps.

3.2.2.2   The description of making the dagger is characterized
by the careful selection of descriptive details. Preparing the dagger could be part of the preparations for offering tribute, but the
writer provides no details about the tribute bearers and focuses
solely on Ehud's dagger. The result of this careful selection is that
apart from Ehud's dagger, the mission of the tribute bearers is no
different from any previous mission. The writer provides four
types of information about the dagger that can be classified in
different ways:

a	b	c	d
two edges	of a cubit length[6]	under his clothing	upon his right thigh

(1) material that describes the dagger itself, a + b
(2) material that describes the way it was worn, c + d
(3) material that suggests the hiding of the dagger and
     Ehud's ability to carry it secretly into the palace, b + c
     + d
(4) material that suggests the special way this dagger was
     used, a + b + d.

3.2.2.3   Examination of the details describing the dagger reveals
qualities that are not clearly mentioned. The reader senses the
calculated tactics: the two-edged dagger is effective for a quick
act (see Yadin), and perhaps this is the reason for its small dimensions. Likewise, wearing the dagger in an unusual way, on the
right thigh, together with its small size, contributes to its effective
concealment under his garments and enables Ehud to draw it
without arousing any immediate suspicion. The reader's attempt
to supply connections among the details turns the description into
a preparatory stage that helps the reader develop and enlarge the

---

[6] The length of *gomed* is unknown. Many interpreters follow the Jonathan
Translation: אמה. In any case, their tendency is to minimize its measure, see Rashi;
Ehrlich (48 [Hebrew]).

hypothesis of what is bound to happen. Now the reader is able to guess how Ehud will deliver his people: Ehud, the left-handed man, probably planned to murder Eglon king of Moab when the tribute was offered, using his special secret dagger.

3.2.2.4   According to the description, Ehud acts independently. This fact is clear not only from the absence of mention of any partners but also from the addition of the pronoun לו, "Ehud made himself a dagger" (v 16). The impression we get is that Ehud planned this stage of the event by himself. At this stage the reader lacks details to help reconstruct the murder hypothesis and is able only to wonder and to ask questions such as: How many guards did Ehud pass before arriving before the king? Will Ehud lead his people or be simply one among them? Will the tribute be offered in the king's presence or the presence of his delegates? Will the act of delivery be accomplished by the king's murder only? Could Ehud be a casualty of the delivery? Is Ehud going to murder the king while offering the tribute or afterward?

3.2.3   The description of offering the tribute (vv 17-18)

3.2.3.1   The ceremony of offering the tribute takes place inside the palace. The direct transition to the ceremony and the description of the ceremony without any delay reveal that the first stage was successful. With the absence of information to ensure or dismiss the different questions raised by the reader at the end of the dagger-making stage, the reader tends to close the gaps and assume that Ehud succeeded in fooling the palace guards as a result of the preparation and hiding of the dagger. In this stage the reader sees Ehud as he stands (in front of the king?) with his dagger hidden on his thigh, and the tribute bearers around him. The reader realizes that again s/he is in the midst of the event, disregarding possible difficulties. Now it is clear to the reader that s/he does not have enough data for a systematic reconstruction of the event. The reader does not know Ehud's future plan. Meanwhile the description brings to light another obstacle that might complicate the murder: "Eglon was a very fat man," while Ehud's dagger is small, "of a cubit length." Obviously, Ehud knew of the king's obesity, so the question arises whether he took it into consideration. Only at the end of the description of the tribute does the reader learn that this stage, in which many people were in attendance, was not chosen by Ehud for the murder. This scene

serves as a preparatory stage and as a way to demonstrate full
surrender, thereby winning the trust of the king and his men. The
writer sets the atmosphere of a prolonged ritual ceremony, where
a large tribute is offered. The lingering ceremonial atmosphere is
achieved by the following rhetorical tactics.

3.2.3.2 *The transposition of a well-known idiom in a certain
range to a different range.* The use of the verb קרב in the *hiph'il*
next to the noun "tribute" מנחה lends an atmosphere of ritual ceremony to the description. The common biblical use of קרב in this
form (about 158 times) is connected to the temple service, or to
religious ceremonies; it appears in a non-ritual context only a few
times. The same is true of the word מנחה, and the combination of
the two forms appears in the Bible only in the context of ritual
ceremonies. The verbs that accompany מנחה in the sense of "tax"
are many and different, but קרב is not among them. Thus language
from the realm of ritual has been transferred to the secular realm
of tax offering to the king. Though the time was not one of religious persecution, and Ehud was not forced to offer the tribute,
this linguistic trick gives the secular ceremony a ritual atmosphere.

3.2.3.3 *Choice of vocabulary.* The word מנחה is repeated three
times; the root קרב in the *hiph'il* is repeated twice. Besides these
words, we find others that are connected with the ritual world,
and all this occurs within a stage that comprises only two verses.
The name of the king (עגל(ון) hints of a ritual, whether as the subject of adoration (a calf ritual) or as an offering. The adjective
"fat" also fits the association of a fatted animal. Moreover, the
description of people bearing tribute strengthens the impression
of a large tribute, rich and honorable.

3.2.3.4 *Delaying devices.* It is hard to imagine a splendid ritual
ceremony that is acted out quickly, and therefore the writer uses
some delaying devices; e.g., 1) slowing the story's pace by adding the title "king of Moab" to Eglon's name and adding the
phrase, "a very fat man"; 2) the use of temporal emphasis, "and
when he had made an end," that points out the duration of what
was described earlier and creates the impression of a drawn-out
ceremony; and 3) creation of a situation in which the reader tends
to find connections between clauses. The reader wonders why the

detail describing Eglon as fat is added, and the time s/he spends speculating about it slows the pace of the story by delaying the reading process.

3.2.3.5   As a matter of fact, the reader does not get clear information about Ehud's tribute to the king. S/he does not know, for example, whether or not Eglon was present at the ceremony, and only by virtue of the techniques mentioned above does s/he enter the ritual atmosphere at the center of which was the large tribute. The reader identifies the writer's rhetorical techniques with Ehud's tactics and concludes that Ehud planned for the usual tribute offering to become a full-blown ceremony, as that would serve him in creating a favorable atmosphere and thus facilitate the murder plan.

3.2.3.6   At the end of this stage, the reader again considers the murder hypothesis. Eglon, who served as the central object in the tribute ceremony, is seen as the target of the murder, and the reader has no doubt that access to this target will be accompanied by many difficulties. The reader is anxious to discover how Ehud will murder Eglon, how he will solve the problem of the attendants at the ceremony, and how he will maneuver between the dagger that is "of a cubit length" and Eglon who was "a very fat man." Raising these questions points to the importance of this stage: it stresses the difficulties Ehud will have in carrying out the murder, and it creates interest and suspense concerning the future deeds of Ehud, who, so far, has appeared to carry out a well-planned mission. The description ends with the fact that Ehud sent away "the people that carried the tribute."[7] It seems that Ehud the loner does not have any thought of a brutal attack upon the king and his men.

3.2.4   The murder scene (vv 19-23)

3.2.4.1   In v 19, after the tribute bearers are sent away, we witness a new scene in which Ehud, Eglon, and the king's servants

---

[7] Although Ehud is not mentioned as the subject, there is no reason to assume a change of subject; see Tur-Sinai (41). It is also reasonable to assume that Ehud was interested in dismissing the people who carried the tribute because this situation enabled him to act alone and quickly. See Rashi, modern scholars, and recently Soggin (50).

appear. One of the difficulties in this scene is its location. Does it take place in the room where the tribute was offered or in the summer chamber? The difficulty lies in the fact that the report of the king's sitting in the summer chamber is given only in v 20, and the reader wonders if earlier, when Ehud said, "I have a secret message for you, O king"—and the king reacted by sending away his servants—his words were said in the summer chamber. Without the information concerning the king's movement from one place to the other, the reader concludes that the whole scene took place in the summer chamber and that the writer omitted the intermediate stage between the tribute ceremony and the scene in the summer chamber just as he did in the transition from the description of making the dagger to the stage of the tribute offering. The murder scene opens with a description in which the gaps become increasingly meaningful, and the reader realizes that again s/he is brought into the midst of the action. In the opening of the scene we read, "But he himself turned back at the quarries that were by Gilgal." As a matter of fact, it is impossible to tell who was at the quarries and when. From what is told later on, however, we may assume that the visit to the sculptured stones made the king willing to listen to Ehud's secret. The other possibility is that the king visited the quarries, and as a result of his visit was interested in Ehud's secret. In any event, it seems that the quarries play a central role. Ehud, when fleeing the murder scene, returned and passed the place of the quarries (v 26), and this hints at the relevance of mentioning the place.

3.2.4.2   Connecting this scene with the preceding one raises the possibility that Ehud relied on his former achievements. If, at the tribute ceremony, Ehud had won the king's and his servants' trust, when he was left alone, he did not raise suspicion or fear. Thus he was allowed to remain with the king in complete privacy. The results of the tribute-offering stage explain the surprising situation of the private interview.

3.2.4.3   In this stage the reader witnesses another sequence of techniques used by Ehud: 1) proclaiming the existence of a secret, after which the king sends away his attendants (v 19)[8];

---

[8] Alter (40) finds double meaning in the word דבר: the secret and the sword. Many commentators think that the meaning of the secret was an oracle (Kraeling: 206; Täubler: 38; Garsiel: 291-292). Rösel (270) assumes that the reference is

2) causing the king to rise by mentioning God's name: "And Ehud said, 'I have *a message from God for you, and he arose* from his seat" (v 20). That the king rises is very important, given the lack of proportion between the tiny dagger and the fat king. With the king's belly stretched, Ehud could use his double-edged dagger to its full advantage. 3) It is possible that Ehud planned to leave the small dagger in the king's belly, where it would be concealed by the fat closing over it, thus assuring Ehud of a "clean murder." Moreover, Ehud did not dirty himself with blood, while the king, who probably suffered internal hemorrhaging, would appear to have died suddenly rather than to have been murdered. 4) Ehud closed the doors of the summer chamber and locked them. This stratagem enabled him to escape while the king's servants sat outside and waited for the king to open the doors from the inside. Ehud's tricky action is accompanied, in this scene, by the writer's tricky rhetoric, expressed by the following elements.

3.2.4.3.1 Repetition of Ehud's words with slight variation emphasizes the trick of making the king rise. The narrator puts into Ehud's mouth two speeches that repeat the same idea in slightly different terms: "I have a secret message for you, O king"; "I have a message from God for you." Comparing the two statements reveals the different role each plays. After the first speech, the king sent his people out of the room. Returning from the quarries encouraged the king to believe that Ehud actually had a secret word. In the second stage, Ehud approached the king and repeated his words, substituting the word "God" for the word "secret" and omitting the address, "O king." Omitting the address highlights the importance of God, who is the real king, and the importance of what might be said later in his name. Eglon's rising in response shows us that he too realized this. Since Ehud could have made the king rise with a different excuse, the repetition serves to emphasize Ehud's trick. From the fact of the two stages—gaining a private audience and the king's rising—we may assume that Ehud left himself an emergency exit. If in the first stage, the king had not sent his servants away, or, if in the second stage, he had not risen from his chair, then Ehud could have used any oracle or some fictitious secret. Thus he would have "frozen" the secret murder plan, that was known to him only, and would have gotten away.

---

to state secrets; see also Kaufmann: 108. E. M. Good (33-34) shows two sides of irony in connection with this word.

3.2.4.3.2 The details given in vv 21-22 enable us to follow the punctual and systematic realization of the murder hypothesis. The writer enables the reader to follow the situation with the help of superfluous information, while making sure there is a tight verbal and interest connection between the hand, the dagger, the right thigh, and their appearance in former stages. The description of the murder could have been summarized briefly; e.g., "He thrust the dagger into his belly and he could not draw the dagger out." Such a summary would have represented the haste of the murder stage in proportion to the rest of the story. But the writer prefers to enlarge the scene by repeating phrases and explanatory descriptions, thus presenting the trick in progress and showing the tight connection between the plan and its execution.

15-17	*21-22*
וישלחו בני ישראל בידו	וישלח אהוד את יד
אטר יד ימינו	יד שמאלו
ויעש לו אהוד חרב	ויקח את החרב
על ירך ימינו	מעל ירך ימינו
איש בריא מאד	בבטנו ... החלב
גמד ארכה	גם הנצב אחר הלהב

An impression of excess is created by the use of repeated expressions in places where there is redundant information as well as by the use of descriptions of an explanatory nature. It seems that in order to murder Eglon, the left-handed Ehud used his left hand and took the dagger from his right thigh. The writer is interested in giving us details, explaining that a left-handed man (אטר יד ימינו) used his left hand, and that the "fat" (בריא) Eglon had a lot of fat (חלב), so that the cubit-length dagger, shaft and blade, disappeared in the king's belly. This technique of story telling helps the reader reconstruct some of Ehud's earlier plan.

3.2.4.3.3 The occurrence in this scene of three consecutive cases of the breaking of an imperfect (*wayyiphᶜal*) sequence by the perfect (*paᶜal*) draws the reader's attention to the repeated use of similar syntactic patterns. If we read the scene without the perfect tenses, we find fewer difficulties in the strategic level of the story: ". . . and said, 'O king, I have a secret message for you.' Then the king said, 'Silence,' and dismissed from his presence all the members of his following . . . and Ehud said to him, 'O king, I have an oracle from God for you.' Then Eglon arose from his throne . . . having closed behind him the doors of the upper room. . . ." The syntactic pattern of the perfect prevents the posing of questions, such as who was at the quarries and when, and blunts sharp questions, such as: when did the king move to the summer chamber and when did Ehud arrive there? When did Ehud lock the parlor doors, or could Ehud have locked the doors after he left the summer chamber and stood on the porch exposed to the king's guards?

3.2.4.4 Obviously we are faced with phrases that share something on the formal level that points to difficulties on the strategic level as well as gaps that prevent exact reconstruction of Ehud's tactics. Every effort the reader makes to explain the exchanges in the syntactic structure and the subsequent difficulties emphasizes the relevance of the gap to the understanding of the event. The appearance of a verb in the perfect in a sequence of imperfects points to a different scene of action, to simultaneity, or to the past perfect. In our case, the phrasing, "and he returned from the quarries," probably hints at a former visit (Garsiel: 291 n. 19). Ehud's immediate proclamation about a secret word creates a possible connection between the secret word and the king's interest in the quarries. The success of Ehud's tactic depends on the king's expected interest in the quarries. Thus Ehud comes to be alone with the king. The dismissal of the tribute bearers earlier also creates the impression of someone who might have quit and perhaps even betrayed his men. In the second stage, Ehud uses the secret word to gain access to the king. At the same time the king orders his men to leave, Ehud approaches, a simultaneity emphasized by the phrase "and Ehud came unto him." Alternatively this clause might be understood as a past perfect, indicating that Ehud had come to the chamber room before the other people had left. The reader lacks the background information to decide between the different options and may feel that the writer systematically hides important details that could help reconstruct Ehud's plan and act. The description of locking the door alludes to the tactic used by Ehud to delay the discovery of the murder. Here also the use of the perfect is problematic. When did Ehud lock the doors? Were the doors locked at the same time they were closed or had Ehud locked the doors earlier (past perfect) so that closing them could simultaneously lock them? The use of the perfect, however, eliminates the unlikely possibility that Ehud stood outside the chamber and locked the doors since one would expect the imperfect if the emphasis was on successive actions. Further questions (for example, where did Ehud get the key to the chamber?) lead the reader to consider that locking the doors and using a key were not planned by Ehud ahead of time but rather somehow occurred to enable him to carry out the perfect murder.

3.2.5   The description of the waiting servants (vv 24–25)

3.2.5.1   Though the writer does not introduce any more tactics in this stage, the description in its entirety shows the results of the closing and locking of the doors and the results of the "clean" murder. The report opens with the effect produced by the locked doors. The servants do not open the doors. Rather, they wait, and the longer they wait, the better are Ehud's chances to get farther away from the scene of the murder and to flee to a place of safety.

3.2.5.2   The description opens with two verbs in the perfect followed by a sequence of imperfects (יצא/באו . . . ויראו/ויאמרו/ויחילו/ ויקחו/ויפתחו). The imperfect sequence describes the consecutive actions of the servants while the two perfects emphasize the timing by which the meeting between Ehud and the servants next to the chamber was avoided. This coincidence, like getting the key to close the doors, presents a situation beyond every possible plan Ehud had, and the reader is thus led to ponder the system in the coincidence.

3.2.5.3   There is no doubt that from this stage until the stage when Ehud conquered the fords of the Jordan, he needed time. In order to convince the reader that Ehud had enough time, the writer conveys the sense of passage of time by creating the illusion of a discussion followed by a conclusion. This impression is given by quoting the words of the servants. The servants' "conversation" consists of one short sentence, presented as a collective response, that can be explained as a conclusion accepted by all present. The servants said, "He is only relieving himself in his summer chamber." Since these words appear as an acceptable conclusion, obviously there was some previous discussion that is not mentioned in the text. More than this, the concluding words "and they waited until they were utterly at a loss," convince us that a long time passed before the servants dared open the chamber door.

3.2.5.4   A sense of time passing slowly is achieved by the writer's penetration into the perspective of the servants. Three times he uses a syntactic structure that expresses amazement, opening with the word (והנה) after a dynamic description, ". . . and they saw that (והנה) the doors of the chamber were locked . . . and they waited until they were utterly at a loss and (והנה) he still did not open the doors . . . and they opened them and (והנה) their lord lay dead on the floor." The use of והנה is one way a biblical writer presents the point of view of a specific character (see Bar-Efrat; Sternberg). The triple repetition of והנה describes the unexpected events the servants experienced and expresses their wonder. It enables the reader to share the servants' experience of the situation from an initial stage of wonder and naive assumptions, through fear and worry which find expression in the opening of the doors, to the shock created by the sight of the dead king.

3.2.5.5   These devices, which create a sense of elapsed time, lay the foundation for the reader's trust in what is said at the beginning of the next stage, "and Ehud escaped while they delayed." The reader was given flexible data, so that descriptive time could be stretched. The illusion of the conversation, the sense of a growing process of wonder, the delay, and the fact that the servants thought their master had died—and had not been murdered—all these accumulated reactions are not defined within a particular time frame. The fact that the reader has the opportunity to prolong the time strengthens the impression of elapsed time during which Ehud flees and arrives at Seir.

3.2.5.6   The writer reports the flight and the war at a critical juncture, after the servants discovered their master dead. The writer's choice of the word "dead," without any other description, indicates that the servants did not connect their king's death with murder. Thus, this stage can be seen as a clue to filling the gaps around the questions: when was it discovered that the king was murdered? was Ehud immediately suspected? were the war preparations undertaken immediately? or were messengers sent to catch Ehud? The *discovery* of the death, and not *how* it happened, allows us to construct various hypothetical situations pertaining to the Moabite response; for example, they did not know about the murder but announced a public mourning. The exploitation (even partly) of the various possibilities, of which I mention only one, enlarges the time span Ehud had to flee and muster his army.

3.2.5.7   The description of the servants disrupts the connection between the reader and Ehud. The reader is interested in knowing what happened to Ehud after he left the king's palace, whereas the writer forces the reader to stay with the waiting servants. This technique is at odds with the reader's curiosity—s/he for the first time in this story parts from Ehud—and emphasizes the delay rhetoric, the use of synchronism that delays the dynamics of the plot. The reader is dealing with secondary information that can be avoided, and only in the next stage, when s/he realizes that while s/he "stayed" in the king's palace with the perplexed servants, Ehud had time to flee and even pass the quarries, s/he understands the connection between the period of delay s/he experienced and the delay in time Ehud gained.

3.2.6   The description of the war (vv 26-29)

3.2.6.1   This unit, like the one before it, opens by pointing to the exact timing, using the perfect tense: "And Ehud escaped while they delayed." The time "while they delayed" enabled Ehud to flee, cross the quarries, and come to Seir. Whereas synchronism is gained by the use of the perfect, there is also an element of simultaneity. Mentioning the quarries as a destination in Ehud's flight course strengthens the reader's assumption that there was a reason for the mention of the quarries in the murder scene, that they are connected with Ehud's secret and the king's interest. Also the use of התמהמהם in which the word מה is repeated helps to confirm the reader's assumption about the servants' conversation (cf. Boling: 87).

3.2.6.2   The second stage in Ehud's flight is described using the imperfect form successively: ויאמר . . . . ויתקע . . . . וימלט השעירתה . . . . The questions raised in this stage are many and meaningful: where actually did Eglon sit? where was he murdered? was it west or east of the Jordan? did the Israelite army know of Ehud's plan to murder the king and therefore wait for him? This time, too, the reader has insufficient data to fill the gaps and realizes that it makes no difference where Eglon sat, and that there was someone who arranged that Ehud would have enough time to flee. It makes no difference, then, if the army was aware of Ehud's plan; someone saw to it that the army got organized immediately. The reader in this stage has no doubt that God is behind Ehud's success, and s/he tends to take Ehud's words literally, "for the Lord has given your enemies the Moabites into your hand" (v 28). Another sign of God's intervention can be found in the results of the battle: "not a man escaped."

3.2.6.3   By and large, Ehud's war and his victory are also based on a trick—to get the bewildered Moabite army in a bottleneck area, "the fords of the Jordan toward Moab." This trick was to the advantage of Ehud's small and untrained army. The combination of the human trick and God's intervention suits the double causality principle and clarifies the hierarchical status of the duality: the success of the human plan is due to divine protection.

4. Summary of the Five Stages

4.1   The dynamic of the story is the result of the complex of strategies that appear in it, whether at the time they are planned, or at the time they are carried out, or while exploiting their full results. In the structure of the story, we find chiastic symmetry that emphasizes the importance of the murder scene and the functional parallelism of the units that "cover" it. The murder is the climax of Ehud's plans and tactics, and it is carried out taking into consideration that the death of the leader is an important factor that can cause bewilderment, chaos, and lack of motivation in the enemy army—results that bring tactical advantages to Ehud and his men. Two diversionary tactics, the offering of tribute and the locking of the chamber doors, contribute to the success of the plan. The delay and distraction gained in the tribute stage are the conditions for the murder; the distraction and delay in the stage of the servants' waiting make it possible for Ehud to flee the murder scene and arrive at Seir. Two tactics on the military operational level gave Ehud the ability to carry out the murder: the dagger, on the one hand, and the domination of the fords of the Jordan, on the other.

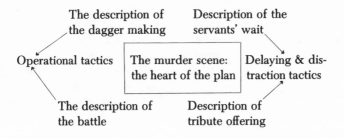

4.2   Examining the structural organization of the stages shows us
that Ehud knew how to use the advantages and disadvantages of
each stage, and they led to his overall victory. The writer's focus
on the various tactics helps emphasize the human plan and strat-
egy. Nevertheless the transitions—that were full of gaps—from
one stage to the next strengthen the reader's sense that tactics
alone were not enough and that Ehud's success was assured with
"coincidences" controlled by God.

5. *The Conclusion of the Story*

5.1   Ehud's story is sealed by concluding formulas that report the
defeat of Moab and the peace that lasted eighty years, thus providing a solution to the problem presented in the exposition. The
ending also hints at the main problem in the story. The passive
phrasing, "so Moab was subdued . . . under the hand of Israel,"
arouses the reader's curiosity regarding who defeated Moab—the
hand of Israel, the hand of Ehud, or the hand of God? Every effort
to answer this question brings the reader back to the problematic
relationship between human hands and the divine hand. Although
the style is stereotypical, the opening and the ending exhibit a
thematic and linguistic connection to the message of this specific
story, and these repetitive formulas characteristic of the book of
Judges were shaped to fit the story's needs and serve the story's
main idea, as does each of the other parts.

6. *Summary*

6.1   In order to achieve his purpose, the narrator transports the
reader from one stage to the next, while skipping over possible
obstacles. As a result, the reader has no tools to reconstruct the
details. Various scholarly interpretations that attempt to fill the
gaps by proposing different reconstructions, sometimes contrary
to each other, clearly miss the story's structure and its message.
These interpretations are no more than speculations, while the
reader has no textual basis for preferring one over another. The
narrator left out some stages and gathered coincidental data so
that the reader would sense God's part in the events. Reading the
story without paying attention to these points misses the main
purpose of the story. Through the dynamic of the reading process, the reader is led to affirm that the deliverer is God's messenger and that in delivering his people Ehud is simply
implementing God's will.

6.2   The story of Ehud shows us the biblical narrator's ability to walk a thin line between the reasonable, convincing tactics in the realistic world he describes and the outstanding, exceptional deliverance. Thus the everyday event, which can be explained reasonably, will now be understood not as a result of human achievement but rather as a result of God's plan, in which human beings have only an acting hand.

WORKS CONSULTED

Aharoni, Y.
    1971   "Palms City." *Encyclopedia Biblica* 6:218 [Hebrew].

Alonso-Schökel, Luis
    1961   "Erzählkunst im Buche der Richter." *Biblica* 42:143-172.

Alter, Robert
    1981   *The Art of Biblical Narrative*. New York: Basic Books.

Bar-Efrat, S.
    1979   *The Art of the Biblical Story*. Tel Aviv: Sifriat Poalim [Hebrew].

Boling, Robert G.
    1975   *Judges*. Anchor Bible, 6A. Garden City, NY: Doubleday.

Budde, Karl
    1890   *Die Bücher Richter und Samuel*. Giessen: J. Ricker.

Burney, C. F.
    1918,   *The Book of Judges*. New York: Ktav.
    repr. 1970

Dexinger, F.
    1977   "Ein Plädoyer für die Linkshänder im Richterbuch." *ZAW* 89:268-269.

Ehrlich, A. B.
    1969   *Mikra Ki-Pheschutô* 2. New York: Ktav [Hebrew].

Elizur, J.
    1966   "The Story of Ehud ben-Gera." Pp. 403-413 in *Studies in the Book of Judges*. Israel Society for Biblical Research, 10. Jerusalem: Kiryat Sepher [Hebrew].

Garsiel, M.
    1971   "The Story of Ehud ben-Gera in the Book of Judges." *Beit Mikra* 16:285-292 [Hebrew].

Good, Edwin M.
    1965   *Irony in the Old Testament.* London: S.P.C.K.

Kaufmann, Y.
    1962   *The Book of Judges.* Jerusalem: Kiryat Sepher [He-
                brew].

Kraeling, E. G.
    1935   "Difficulties in the Story of Ehud." *JBL* 54:205-210.

Mazar, B.
    1958   "Yair." *Encyclopedia Biblica* 3:415-416 [Hebrew].

McCarthy, D. Y.
    1980   "The Uses of W*ehinneh* in Biblical Hebrew." *Biblica*
                61:330-342.

Moore, G. F.
    1895   *Judges.* ICC. Edinburgh: T. & T. Clark.

Richter, Wolfgang
    1964   *Die Bearbeitungen des "Retterbuches" in der deuter-
                onomistischen Epoche.* Bonn: Peter Hanstein.

Rösel, H. N.
    1977   "Zur Ehud Erzählung." *ZAW* 89:270-272.

Seeligmann, I. L.
    1963   "Menschliches Heldentum und Göttliche Hilfe: die
                doppelte Kausalität im alttestamentlichen Ges-
                chichtsdenken." *TZ* 19:385-411.

Soggin, J. Alberto
    1981   *Judges.* The Old Testament Library. Trans. J. S. Bow-
                den. London: SCM Press.

Sternberg, M.
    1978   *Expositional Modes and Temporal Ordering in Fic-
                tion.* Baltimore: Johns Hopkins.
    1979   "The Truth vs. All the Truth: the Rendering of Inner
                Life in Biblical Narrative." *Hasifrut* 29:110-146 [He-
                brew].
    1983   "World and Perspective in Biblical Narrative Art:
                Free Indirect Discourse and Modes of Covert Pene-
                tration." *Hasifrut* 32:88-131 [Hebrew].
    1985   *The Poetics of Biblical Narrative: Ideological Liter-
                ature and the Drama of Reading.* Bloomington: In-
                diana University Press.

Täubler, E.
    1958   *Biblische Studien: die Epoche der Richter.* Tübingen:
                J. C. B. Mohr.

Tur-Sinai, N. H.
    1965   *Peshuto shel Mikra* 2. Jerusalem: Kiryat Sepher [He-
                brew].

Wiese, Kurt
    1926   Zur Literarkritik des Buches der Richter. BWANT III,
                4. Stuttgart: W. Kohlhammer.

Yadin, Y.
    1966   "The Story of Ehud ben-Gera." Pp. 413-415, 429-430
                in *Studies in the Book of Judges.* Jerusalem: Kiryat
                Sepher [Hebrew].

Zakovitch, Y.
    1977   "The Synonymous Word and Synonymous Name in
                Name-Midrashim." Pp. 100-115 in *Shnaton: An An-
                nual for Biblical and Ancient Near Eastern Studies,* II.
                Ed. M. Weinfeld. Jerusalem-Tel Aviv: M. Newman
                Publishing House [Hebrew].

RIGHT-BRAINED STORY OF LEFT-HANDED MAN:
An Antiphon to Yairah Amit

David Jobling
St. Andrew's College, Saskatoon

For Mary Edwardsen

0.   The context for these remarks is my ongoing work on the debate between "liberation" (feminism, Marxism, etc.) and deconstruction, a debate to which biblical scholarship is only beginning to pay attention (see my essay "Writing the Wrongs of the World" in a shortly forthcoming issue of *Semeia*, edited by Gary Phillips). Yairah Amit's reading of the Ehud story resonates with what I have been thinking, and I shall try to organize the resonances; or, taking her reading as a symbol, I shall express the thought to which it has given rise. I shall develop a discourse which, in deconstructive fashion, takes unseriously distinctions between text, commentary, and "meta-commentary," passing fluidly from the biblical text, to Amit's text, to the current state of biblical studies. So I offer this piece not as an assessment of Amit's work, not as a tally of agreements and disagreements with it, but as a *response*, an antiphon.

1. *"Multiple causality" in the Ehud story*

1.1   The reader of the story of Ehud, according to Amit, is led to a point of (what others have called) "undecidability." The reader cannot make a choice between human planning and divine guidance in the achievement of the narrative events. The story appears to be in a "realistic" mode, and makes the reader frame responses appropriate to that mode, but then it undermines these responses by failing to make the minimum narrative connections which the realistic mode requires.

1.2   One of the terms Amit proposes (following Seeligmann) is "double causality." The term is perhaps too general, since the co-presence of divine and human causality is surely a universal characteristic of the Bible. As a single, striking example, take the narrative of Rehoboam and the northern Israelites in 1 Kgs 12:1-20. This is a story which enlightens us about human decision-making and its motivation to an extent which is unusual in the Bible; yet the decision-making looks like a pointless charade in the light of the fact that the outcome has already been divinely decided (11:26-40). What Amit is pointing to is something more particular, something more embedded in the detailed verbal formulations of the narrative. How atypical Judg 3:12-20 is in this regard would be a matter for comparative work on many biblical stories; but I agree intuitively that something unusual in going on. To sense it, one need read no further than v 15: "But when the people of Israel cried to Yhwh, Yhwh raised up for them a deliverer, Ehud. . . . The people of Israel sent tribute by him to Eglon the king of Moab." How on earth is one to read this? Yhwh chose a deliverer and maneuvered to have him made tribute-bearer? The people chose a tribute-bearer and Yhwh opportunistically made a deliverer of him? Ehud experienced Yhwh's call and maneuvered to have himself made tribute-bearer? At least, initiative from the side of Ehud, of Israel, and of Yhwh might be in play, so that "multiple causality" is more to the point than "double causality." Though I am not altogether happy with it, "multiple causality" is the term which I shall use as a clue for developing my discourse.

2. *Multiple causality* of *the Ehud story*

2.1   While Amit's analysis succeeds in convincing me of multiple causality as a special feature of Judg 3:12-30, I find deeply unsatisfying her accounting for this textual effect entirely in terms of the intentional skill of a "narrator." What she does is to propose a story of the text's coming into being, a story which assumes single causality! Why is the text the way it is; why does it evidence in a special way the phenomenon of multiple causality? I do not think the question is answerable, if what we are seeking is a compelling explanation. But a framework for understanding can be built by asking a different question—given the phenomenon of multiple causality, to what can we relate it, to what are we invited to relate it? This procedure may help us glimpse what *kind* of story might be an adequate (or better, perhaps, a usable) story of the text's coming into being.

2.2 To begin with, we can relate multiple causality to narrative, to literature, as such. Many have argued that literature provides the most compelling instance of the infinite "dissemination" of meaning in discourse. Thus narrative may be perceived as "on the side of" multiple causality, as characteristically obscuring and problematizing cause and effect relationships. A range of questions comes into view around the Bible's preference for narrative theologizing.

2.3 A link which seems inviting is between multiple causality and the theme of left-handedness in the Ehud story. For the notion has become current that left-handedness is correlated with right-brainedness, or with cerebral bilaterality. Thinking dominated by the left hemisphere is supposed to be logical and linear, while thinking dominated by the right hemisphere is more holistic, instinctive, and so on. One way of expressing this difference is precisely as an opposition between single and multiple causality—the more influence of the right hemisphere, the more tolerance of "explanation" in terms of multiple causality. Perhaps multiple causality as a narrative structure and left-handedness as a narrative theme have an affinity for each other. In invoking this link between bilaterality and left-handedness, I am well aware that its "scientific" status is a matter of controversy. But it has entered our current (quasi-scientific) folklore, and to pit "hard" science against the folkloric is precisely to take a left-brained approach to right-brainedness! No doubt the causality of the folklore is multiple, in belief, prejudice, etc., as well as in observation. But such a piece of folklore is not only an effect, of whatever causes, but also a cause of cultural effects, impinging on our real attitudes to left-handedness—is it a minor handicap (cf. the literal Hebrew meaning, "handicapped in the right hand") entailing specific disadvantages (can-openers, etc.), or is it a sort of privilege? Ehud's left-handedness provides unexpected opportunity. (Another attractive line of approach, which I am not following here, would be via the theme of left-handedness in comparative folklore.)

2.4 A more far-reaching link, between bilaterality and femaleness, has likewise become part of our quasi-scientific folklore.

Women are suspected to be more bilateral in brain function than men. There are no women in the Ehud story, but the essay before us is by a woman. She chooses to write about the story of a left-handed man, and traces in it, more than any previous commentator, multiple causality. I enter here on dangerous ground, that of sexual stereotyping—but one will not get very far in reading our culture if one steers clear of dangerous ground. Why, for example, are women scholars so disproportionately well represented among those who approach the Bible as literature? Is the feature of multiple causality in the Ehud story magnified by the eye of a woman reader?

2.5   Our pursuit of possible correlates of multiple causality has now led us into the arena of political struggle for liberation in our own day. But such struggle, in another day, is, of course, the main theme of Judg 3:12-30. It is one of a series of six stories (Judg 3:7-16:31, with omission of the "minor judges") telling of Israel's liberation from foreign oppression. The question arises of why there needs to be such a long *series* of stories; the problem is not merely the sense of repetition, but also that each liberative event issues only in new bondage. Various proposals have been made, but I would suggest that one thing achieved by having a series is the establishment in the text of a second level of political liberation, a liberation within a liberation, in that the individual judges represent groups subordinate within Israel. Ehud, Deborah, Gideon, and Jephthah are respectively, and pointedly, left-handed, female, youngest son, and illegitimate. (In this connection, Othniel is no doubt a "neutral" case, but what are we to make of Samson?) Along with liberation *of* Israel must go liberation *within* Israel. (It is interesting, in relation to the preceding paragraph, that *women* are the class of people to be liberated from obscurity and subordination in the very next story after Ehud.)

2.6   If the significance of the Ehud story is tied up with its being part of a series, we may ask how its multiple causality functions in relation to the series. I would suggest that it functions to liberate the text of Judges, at the first possible moment, and in a violent way, from a certain bondage; namely, from conformity to the "standard" shape of a judge-cycle. The standard shape (which is to be discerned in the Othniel cycle of 3:7-11 even more clearly than in the programmatic statement of 2:11-19) has as one of its obvious aspects the sharp definition of divine and human roles, and their proper sequence, in the work of political liberation; but the great virtue of Amit's essay is to show how utterly these definitions are shattered—through the multiplication of causality—in the very first cycle after Othniel's. This story of the liberation of Israel, of the liberation of the left-handed, also achieves textually a liberation from the prescriptive divine pattern for history, as divine and human initiatives are compounded and problematized.

2.7   Why is Judg 3:12-30 the way it is? Around the unanswerable question I have raised some possibilities—that the multiple causality which is a special feature of this text may be related to its theme, to its larger literary context, to the nature of narrative as such, to the location of the reader. (Nor do I want to deny narratorial intentionality; while it is implausible to think of such a variety of textual effects as being under conscious control, we will want to consider the extent to which a number of narrators—of Ehud, of Judges, of the Primary Narrative—were consciously in tune with what is going on in the text.) How shall we tell of the text's coming into being? Not by a single story of a single cause, nor yet (the pluralist paradigm) by alternative stories of different causes. Our aim (for which no paradigm yet exists) should be a single story, but one which tolerates, and even focusses attention on, the multiple causality of the text.

3.   The revolution in biblical studies/biblical studies in the revolution

3.1   A profound change, everyone agrees, is coming over biblical studies, a change having much to do with literature—narrative especially—and its particular way of being. A bid is being made for liberation, from historicist domination of the field, from the need for singleness of explanation. What needs to be added, and explored, is that this bid for liberation occurs within a context deeply influenced by other bids for liberation—the political liberations to which liberation theologies, and in particular feminist theology, refer. Political liberation is a biblical theme, and the Bible functions within liberation theologies. What is the connection between the liberation of biblical method and the way the Bible may function in relation to political liberation movements?

3.2   On the one hand, the change in biblical studies (and in other fields which have been dominated by historicism) is part of a real power-shift which cannot fail to have institutional implications. To subvert entrenched ways of thinking is to subvert the structures which embody them, including structures of oppression. Methodological change becomes effete if it ignores its political location and implications.

3.3   On the other hand, how are we to excercise our responsibility, as biblical scholars, vis-à-vis movements for political liberation? There is no easy answer, for the question entails a hard look at our own social location. But if methodological and structural change do indeed at some level go together, then the methodological revolution implies a need for liberation to come to terms with its "handedness," that it is of the Left. The problem with the Left is that it desperately needs to be right, assumes that it is right; understandable as this may often be, the result is that "successful" revolution notoriously reestablishes the structures of oppression against which it strove. Ehud's story (though it is a touch bloody) is not about reversing the structures of domination, but about having the freedom of one's own territory, having no more tribute to pay. Resistance to the dominant, whether methods or structures, needs a certain left-handedness, a certain bilaterality. It needs to be attuned to the multiple causality of change, to refuse the dominance of linear historical models of change, to note that change is often happening where it is not conscious of itself (and often is not happening where it *is* conscious of itself!). How, after all, do we perceive this revolution of which we are a part? We perceive it, as Amit perceives the revolution of Ehud, at one level as something planned for and achieved, but at another level as something stumbled upon, something simply to hand, something which all of a sudden surrounds us—as grace, if you will. Multiple causality!

3.4   In her apparent need for singleness of explanation, Amit is still paying tribute to the dominant paradigm in biblical studies; but, in forcing to prominence the feature of multiple causality, her reading nevertheless contains a "secret message," even one "from God"! If she fails to follow her own clue, her reading is not therefore any less a part of the change occurring in biblical studies; for, as the deconstructionists remind us, we never avoid repeating, somehow, the gestures of power which we have internalized. The point is to make and to let happen, to go on, and a woman exploring multiple causality in the story of a left-handed man is refreshment on the way.

IN SECURITY:
THE DAVID OF BIBLICAL NARRATIVE

David M. Gunn
Columbia Theological Seminary

ABSTRACT

To tame the story I write a paper; and to tame the
paper I write an abstract. But one taming is more than
sufficient. Suffice, then, to say that this essay asks the
question, who is David? It seeks to hear some voices in
the text. And, lest it silence them, it attempts to come to
no certain conclusion.

I

1.1 Who is David? The "sweet psalmist of Israel," reply sundry
titles on my bookshelf.[1] It is a much-honored label and drawn,
appropriately for my purpose, from the closing chapters of the
story of David in 1 & 2 Samuel and 1 Kings 1–2 (2 Sam 23:1, to be
precise). Yet, aptly, it is not a prose label but a catch of poetry,
embedded in prose. It links beginnings with ends: the day of
deliverance from Saul (at the Rock of Escape?—"Yahweh my
rock and my stronghold and my deliverer," 2 Sam 22:1-2; cf.
1 Sam 23:28) with the day of "last words" (2 Sam 23:1). Perhaps
here, then, with these "last words" of the sweet psalmist, we may

---

[1] I dedicate this essay to the members of my exegesis class on Saul and David,
Columbia Seminary, Spring 1985. An inimitable class, I thank them for their stim-
ulation and many insights. Essentially completed at the end of 1985, the essay does
not take account of some fine work that has since appeared and which is listed in
the bibliography [Jan 1987].

seek the final word on David. Here are words of one raised on high, the anointed of the God of Jacob, one who rules justly in the fear of Yhwh, oracular words (*rex et propheta*, David was called in the Middle Ages), confident words: "For a lasting covenant has he made with me, ordered in all and secure." Confident words, strong words, yet hedged about with questions. "For is it not thus, my house, with Yhwh? . . . Will he not cause [all my deliverance and desire] to spring forth? "[2] Rhetorical questions, yes, but susceptible to the merest shift of tone. Is the sweet psalmist's security open to question?

1.2   The poem secures itself by shifting focus back to the field (cf. v 4), not to the flourishing grass but rather to the threatening thorns and the "weapons" of those who root out the forces of chaos (vv 6-7). Here, surely, is a sure world, David's world, where good arms itself for battle with evil, David against Goliath (but which of them armed himself with iron and the shaft of a spear?). Thus the poem dissolves into a listing and recounting of weaponry: of the anointed's mighty men, their deeds, their ordering (vv 8-39). We are back in a world only briefly left behind—to make room for the psalmist—where Philistines are foes and mighty men battle for their lord (2 Samuel 21).

1.3   Yet some curiosities inhabit this world, raising questions of the psalmist and disturbing our certainties. Where is David? In an unguarded moment he buys water at the price of other men's blood, though a price unpaid (2 Sam 23:13-17). A careless David perhaps? A David commanding intense loyalty certainly. A David who can forbear mightily, mightily alert to Providence as he refuses to drink that water and pours it out to Yhwh, blood upon the ground. We are reminded of the David who would not reach out against Saul, Yhwh's anointed (1 Samuel 24 and 26). Or, as Absalom seized power (2 Samuel 15-20), the David who turned Abishai's sword back to its sheath when Shimei of the house of Saul threw stones and cursed him on the path from Jerusalem into exile while all the mighty men stood round about. "Out, out, man of blood, man of chaos! May Yhwh bring upon you all the blood of the house of Saul," cried Shimei to David. "You are ruined. For you are a man of blood!" (2 Sam 16:6-8).

[2] Reading MT. For an ingenious emendation, see McCarter's fine commentary (1984:478).

1.4   Following Shimei's train of thought we may remember an earlier time when David's needs were purchased with blood—and the price paid (1 Samuel 21-22). Fearful for his life, David had fled from Saul's court, obtaining provisions and a weapon from Ahimelech, the priest at Nob, thus enraging Saul. Goliath's sword and a few loaves of holy bread cost the blood of eighty-five priests and more, as Doeg's sword, at Saul's command, devours Nob, the city of priests, "men and women, children and sucklings, oxen, asses and sheep" (22:19). It is the slaughter of the Amalekites all over again (cf. 15:3) but in a ghastly parody! And is Saul alone responsible? For a moment, David and Saul, so different, look so alike: "And David said to Abiathar [Ahimelech's son, escaped (like Agag!) from the slaughter—a dangerous remnant]: "I knew that day that Doeg the Edomite was there, that he would indeed tell Saul. I have turned upon every living being in your father's house" (22:22). Yet not so alike—that extraordinary confession has its own disarming power; it is vintage David.

1.5   We have travelled some distance. To return to our passage: "'Far be it from me, Yhwh, that I should do this. . . . ' And he refused to drink it! These things did *the three mighty men*" (2 Sam 23:17, resuming vv 9, 11, 13, 16). Even as we come back to the enlivening gesture, the rhetoric—with a laugh?—plucks us away from the gesturer! That parallels our journey, just travelled. Just when we have David, he is plucked away. As we grasp the essence, the paradigm, the ideal king, the just king, the covenant king, we grasp instead a man of blood, man of chaos, man of the sword, man of mighty men.

1.6   Who did these deeds? Who built the house of David? His song on the day of deliverance (2 Samuel 22) is a song of "I" and "Thou," with no hint of "we." A touch disingenuous, perhaps, suggests ch. 23, for no "I" is an island. Whereupon, as if to reinforce the point, the narrator speaks of other mighty men, first Abishai who, we recall, saved a weary David from a giant (21:15-17)! Within a verse or two another name—Elhanan, from David's home town—has disturbed our memory of the young David, splendid against Goliath (1 Samuel 17), by resurrecting that unsettling anecdote of Elhanan (another Elhanan?) and Goliath (2 Sam 21:19). Who *did* kill Goliath? And that prompts a fundamental question. Have we too readily accepted our narrator as infallible ("reliable")? Is the author trying to shake us free, unwilling to become (via the narrator) the object of our idolatry? We may recall that even at the beginning we were warned, with competing tales of David's introduction to court as musician and as slayer of the Philistine.

1.7   So, too, with the rest of this chapter of mighty men: names and incidents send us throughout David's story, further unsettling the sweet psalmist's assurance, the anointed king's confident righteousness, and our own certainties.

1.8   Asahel, brother of Joab, recalls those moments when the kingship hovered (2 Samuel 2-4), when young Asahel, too swift of foot, fell to Abner's back-hander, when Joab avenged his brother's blood and removed rival power, all in one deceptive blow.

1.9   Abishai, Zeruiah's son and brother of Joab, and Benaiah, killer of Joab (1 Kings 2), are a potent combination. Their mention not only evokes the remarkable David who twice restrained Abishai from striking down Shimei ("What is there between us, you sons of Zeruiah, that you become my opponent today?"; see 2 Sam 16:5-13; 19:16-23) but also foreshadows the sequel of Shimei's story (1 Kgs 2:8-9, 36-46). "You shall not die," the king had said to Shimei, "and the king swore him an oath" (2 Sam 19:23). When it is David's time to die (1 Kings 2), however, he will charge Solomon to "hold [Shimei] not guiltless" and to "bring his gray head down with blood to Sheol." Solomon obliges, but, like David with Uriah, at arms length. Benaiah acts the hatchet man (vv 25, 34, and 46). So Abishai prevails in the end and David dies, convicted by his own rhetoric, enfolded in a tale of posturing and conniving (1 Kings 1-2, Solomon's succession to the throne) matched only by his own special contribution to the genre, the tale of David, Bathsheba, and Uriah (2 Samuel 10-12).

1.10   That tale, also, is conjured up by the list of mighty men. Names jump out: Eliam (Bathsheba's father? cf. 11:3), Nathan, Zobah and the Ammonites, Joab. Finally (v 39) the list comes to rest upon none other than Uriah the Hittite! One hears oracular words: "Why have you despised the word of Yhwh, doing what is evil in his sight? Uriah the Hittite . . . you have slain with the sword of the Ammonites: so now a lasting sword will not turn aside from your house . . ." (2 Sam 12:9-10). One also hears, with a strong sense of irony, snatches of poetry: "Yhwh rewarded me

according to my righteousness . . . I was blameless before him
. . . Therefore Yhwh has recompensed me according to my righteousness" (22:21-25). "The Rock of Israel has said to me: 'When
one rules justly over people . . .' For is it not thus, my house, with
Yahweh?" (23:3, 5).

1.11   What has happened to the sweet singer? David's story has
a way of shifting out from under us. The story refuses to be
tamed, secured, or neatly ordered.

II

2.1   Who is David? "The man after God's own heart," say sundry
other titles on that bookshelf: the model man, the ideal king. This
is the David of Jewish and Christian piety—the David who is so
different from Saul. David is obedience, Saul disobedience; David
is the future, Saul the past.

2.2   "Saul is a foil to David," writes many a commentator. Alternatively David is a foil to Saul. When we begin at 1 Samuel 8, with
the people's request for a king, the story is Saul's and even beyond
1 Samuel 15 (Saul's rejection after the Amalekite raid) it continues
to take up dangling threads. Who will be chosen as Saul's successor? When and how will his replacement occur?

2.3   On the other hand, a new starting point (1 Samuel 16) or a
simple exercise of choice by the reader, and Saul's story becomes
a fragment of David's story. In the last analysis the stories are
inseparable. To be David is not to be Saul. To be Saul is not to be
David. (That is neatly encapsulated in the symbolism of clothes:
see 1 Sam 17:38-39 and 18:3-4.) The motive power driving the
plot, what binds the two characters together in this sometimes
cruel harmony of seeming opposites, is Yhwh's will.

2.4   The people ask Samuel for a king. Samuel consults Yhwh,
who says, "Listen to their voice (obey them!), and make them a
king" (1 Sam 8:22), whereupon the prophet anoints Saul, declar-
ing Yhwh's commission (10:1). Then, however, comes the sacrifice
at Gilgal (ch. 13) and another declaration to Saul: "But now your
kingdom shall not continue: Yhwh has sought out a man after his
own heart" (v 14).

2.5   Here is a story of insecurity (the people's), sovereignty
(Yhwh's), and choice (the people's and Yhwh's). What makes David a "better" person than Saul to reign over Israel (15:28)? It is
not that he is made from a better pattern, more finely honed to
produce that special image of God, a "man after God's own
heart." The issue of Saul's rejection is at heart the issue of choice.
At heart Saul is the people's king, Yhwh's king only on sufferance.
Yhwh *chooses* to establish David's sovereignty, not in response to
the people's demand for security—as though Yhwh was not sovereign enough—but because Yhwh chooses to do so, in freedom,
according to his own wishes, his own devices, after his own heart
(cf. 2 Sam 7:21). Yhwh's sovereignty cannot be traduced. Yhwh
cannot be coerced. Saul and David, therefore, enact for us this
theology—Saul ever constrained, coerced by the spirit of God
and denied the future; David blessedly free, granted the future.
Saul struggles against a constricting word and seeks in vain a
silenced oracle; David moves intuitively with an establishing
word and acts upon a most talkative oracle.

2.6   So, too, the people's cry to Samuel to make them a king (an
understandable cry, as Lyle Eslinger helps us to see) turns out to
be of crucial importance to the plot, the necessary condition of
Yhwh's reluctant acquiescence in this experiment in human sovereignty; and in turn the seeds of this cry lie further back in the
story, with Samuel and the house of Eli. The David of the books
of Samuel starts life in Hannah's royal hymn (1 Sam 2:1-10), as
Hannah gives thanks for the gift of a child.

2.7   As the child is a special gift to the barren woman, so the
kingdom is a special gift to David. Both gifts are freely given by
God. David, moreover, has a gift for knowing how to allow others
to make their gifts freely. Giving and grasping constitute a major
dynamic of the David story.[3] When David allows choice to lie in
the hands of others, especially Yhwh, he most flourishes and provokes us to recreate for ourselves a model of forbearance that
recognizes Providence as reality (e.g., 1 Samuel 24 and 26; 2 Samuel 15-16). When he cannot rest content with the risk entailed or
with the injured esteem issuing from rejection, he falters. Then we

---

[3] See Gunn, 1975, 1978: ch. 5. That analysis owed much to Walter Brueggemann's insights; among a succession of stimulating works, see esp. Brueggemann,
1972, 1974.

are forced to recognize that our model is a vision of a transcendent reality to be lived out in the midst of the reality we know only too well, the reality that makes us judge the David story as "realistic," as "plausible" (Wharton).

2.8   The pivotal story of David grasping is, I believe, that of David, Bathsheba, and Uriah (2 Samuel 11-12), framed by the war against the Ammonites (ch. 10) and the taking of Rabbah (12:26-31). The rape of Tamar that follows (ch. 13), together with the murder of Amnon and the seizing of the kingdom by Absalom (chs. 13-20), all replay, ironically and perversely, key elements of this central episode, a turning point in the larger story (Carlson, 1964). Yet it would be a mistake to think that here is something essentially new. The ingredients are incipient, for example, in the much earlier episode of David, Abigail, and Nabal (1 Samuel 25; see Gunn, 1980:91-106; cf. Gordon, 1980; Levenson). Framed by episodes of David's restraint against Saul, when the kingdom might have seemed to another to be in his grasp (1 Samuel 24 and 26), is an account of violence breathed against Nabal (whose folly is his proud dedication to the notion of his own sovereignty) for refusing to "give" what David thinks his due. Only the intervention of Abigail—combining roles later to be transformed and played out separately by Bathsheba and Nathan—averts this eruption of the other reality in David. The taking of Abigail, when it comes, is by her invitation (1 Sam 25:30, 40-42); the taking of Nabal, when it comes, is by Yhwh's choice.

2.9   To act "after his own heart" is Yhwh's prerogative. Yhwh alone is sovereign. In Yhwh alone is security, found in a gift and found in giving, found as Yhwh's freedom is risked and accepted. Perhaps, then, it is in that risk, that insecurity, that we glimpse a David "after God's own heart."

III

3.1   Who is David? My bookshelf now fails me, knowing no other such popular titles. But, as we saw, Shimei can help. "A man of blood," he replies. That reply is jaundiced, we retort, the label simplistic. "Let him alone, and let him curse," says David, "for Yhwh has bidden him" (2 Sam 16:11). We are back to that downward path from Jerusalem (2 Samuel 15-16), which was also a way to a peak of trust, when David offered freedom: to Ittai, his mercenary captain, to Shimei, who cursed him, to God, who had given him the kingdom. There, where the king set the crown again in Yhwh's hands, God responded to prayer and met David at "the summit where God was worshipped" (15:31-37; 17:14).

3.2   In a perverse sort of way, however, Shimei was right. In seeking the sweet psalmist did we not instead find a man of blood? And Shimei's death underscored the point. Here was an old man, never more than a growler, a thrower of impotent stones, a parody of young David before Goliath, a figure resurrected by the text (1 Kgs 2:8-9, 39-46) solely to act out the part of crippled Mephibosheth, who also "dwelt in Jerusalem" at a king's behest. And in a single-minded, blinkered act of folly—Shimei so reminds us of that other independent intemperate, Nabal—he seeks some slaves and finds . . . Benaiah, the grim reaper, instead. "You shall bring down his gray head with blood to Sheol" (1 Kgs 2:9), says the king who offered freedom, who swore to give life, who set the crown in God's hands.

3.3   Do ends justify means? At least ends require beginnings, and the beginning of that little story of Shimei, champion of the house of Saul, itself requires an earlier beginning, forcing us to review the new king's rise to power and his relationship to the house of Saul. We know Shimei to be wrong when he believes Yhwh to be avenging upon David the blood of the house of Saul by giving the kingdom to Absalom (2 Sam 16:8); for it was precisely Yhwh who gave the kingdom into the hand of David, to reign in Saul's place (and, we are soon to learn, who will ordain that evil befall rebellious Absalom). That the blood of Saul's house is upon David is contradicted by compelling accounts of forbearance, especially at the cave in the wilderness of En-Gedi and in Saul's camp on the hill of Hachilah (1 Samuel 24 and 26). Yet the story will in turn attempt to subvert that contradiction as it draws us into those fragments of David's life in 2 Samuel 21-24 and tells of the Gibeonites' revenge, of David's acquiescence in the hanging of the seven sons of Saul for the sake of "bloodguilt."

3.4   Shimei's outburst also takes us to David's own house. "Yhwh has given the kingdom into the hand of your son, Absalom" (2 Sam 16:8)—Absalom, who had had Amnon struck down (as David had had Uriah struck down); Amnon, who had seized and raped Tamar (as David had taken and lain with Bathsheba). "So now," says Nathan the prophet, "a sword will not turn aside from your house, a lasting sword. . . . Thus says Yhwh: 'Behold, I am raising up evil against you from your house'" (2 Sam 12:10-11).

3.5   "I gave you," says Yhwh, "your master's house . . . I gave you the house of Israel and of Judah" (v 8). The house of Israel and the house of Judah. The house of Saul and the house of David. "House" is nation, kingdom; "house" is dynasty; "house" is extended family.[4] Nathan probes another kernel of meaning in our story. David's political and private lives are correlates, mirroring each other and curiously intertwined (especially in 2 Samuel 10-20; see Gunn, 1975, 1978:87-111; Gros Louis). The ethos of private life has a way of impinging on the ethos of political life. The point is expressed in the ambiguity of Nathan's phrase, "your master's house." Does that mean house of Israel or house of Saul (i.e., Saul's family—Michal and Jonathan, Ishbosheth and Mephibosheth), or dynasty, or God's (Adonai's) own house, or all of these? The houses give expression to each other. They are integral parts of the organism that is "all Israel," the people of Yhwh.

3.6   Why does the pivotal Bathsheba/Uriah episode come where it does? Because, I believe, only here is the king on the point of securing his house. All enemies "round about" have been defeated. War against the Ammonites is the final phase, the seizure of Rabbah spells completion. It offers David the crown of empire. Victory is imminent. David need not even go out to battle. Internally, the house of Saul is subdued, Michal (Saul's daughter) and Mephibosheth (Jonathan's son) have been assimilated into the new king's house.

3.7   Dynasty, the "house" which eluded Saul, is promised by the oracle of Yhwh through Nathan (2 Samuel 7). Validation has also come through the cult in another way, for now the ark, too, like Mephibosheth, dwells in Jerusalem (2 Samuel 6). Chapters 5-10 spell consolidation of power, legitimacy, security (Flanagan, 1983; see further 1988). They also bring to completion a story which began even before David, before Saul and the feuding years,

---

[4] Paula Bowes, especially, helped me to focus on this key term and to ponder its multivalence: "A Literary Interpretation of the Court Narrative" (unpub. Ph.D. diss.: Hebrew Union College, Cincinnati, 1979), esp. pp. 69-73. (She, in turn, expresses a debt to James W. Flanagan.).

back in the opening chapters of 1 Samuel, with issues of external
threat, a lamented and peripheral ark, failed leadership, and a cry
for a king. With David these issues are resolved. Here, indeed, is
security.

3.8   Yet here, precisely as those mighty men of David's are seizing Rabbah and its crown of crowns, David seizes Bathsheba. As
one house (the house of Israel) is secured, another (the house of
David) begins to crumble with David's attack on the house of
Uriah. Wittingly or unwittingly, Uriah refuses to go down to his
house (see 11:8-9 and the reiteration of "house"), refuses to com-
promise his own house in an act that could only further embed the
corruption in the king's house, though that forbearance will cost
him his life. As David's pinnacle of power is reached, it is Uriah
("Yhwh is [my] light") the Hittite who rules in Jerusalem.

3.9   In those mighty men who fought before Rabbah lay both
strength and lethal weakness for David. The trappings of kingship
germinate the seeds of failure (that's old wisdom). Kingship is no
talisman, God-given or not (cf. 1 Samuel 8 and Deuteronomy 17).
Our story retells a story told and retold in the great history from
Genesis through 2 Kings: Yhwh alone is sovereign, Yhwh alone
offers security, and even then the people of Yhwh cannot secure
that security, fashion it their own way (and Saul, pathetically pious, Yhwh's loyalist to the end, epitomizes that last truth).

3.10   Thus David here embodies the nation that is given the land
but falters in the very realization of the gift (cf. Judges).[5] Solomon, too, plays his part in this iconoclastic story. Established on
David's throne, secure in the gracious promise of a house (2 Samuel 7; cf. 1 Kings 8), he builds further security, a house for Yhwh.
We are dazzled by the description, swayed by the rhetoric of
prayer and proclamation, pushed by both subject matter and
style back to that formative, prescriptive period at Sinai and in

___

[5] The Book of Judges is a downwards spiral until the judge, unrecognized, is
turned over to the Philistines. "Do you not know that the Philistines are rulers over
us?" say the men of Judah to Samson, with sweet reasonableness (15:11). If Samson demonstrates that it is not the Philistines, not Dagon, but Yhwh who rules in
the land, this is a message that has to look outside the text for an audience. The final
chapters (21–24) parody a national life where God is mostly excluded, to be invoked and yoked to a chaotic society only as an expression of idolatry or, in the
interests of self-interest, as a god of last resort.

the wilderness. The glory of Yhwh's house, however, soon gives way (1 Kings 9-11) to the expanding glory of Solomon's house (via, ironically, his God-given gift of wisdom), as it also gives way to an account of extraordinary devotional failure incubated within his own house (the thematic parallel with David's failure, 2 Samuel 11-12, is striking). Solomon, secure in the glory of the house of Yhwh, serves other gods! Thus the house of Israel is torn from his house (leaving Judah, for Yhwh's bond to David, his chosen, remains strong). This division of David's kingdom was intimated, we now recognize, in the account of Sheba ben Bichri and the house of Israel subsequent to Absalom's rebellion, which itself represented the near division of David's own house (2 Samuel 20, esp. v 1; cf. 1 Kings 12, esp. v 16).

3.11 The house of Yhwh is no talisman. The story ends with its ruin, the people dispersed. Nor does the house of David guarantee security. To be sure, the relationship intimated in Nathan's prophecy (2 Samuel 7) surfaces from time to time in the subsequent tale. At these moments the narrator speaks as prophet, locating at least part of Yhwh's forbearance in this particular bond with David and the promise emanating from it (cf. 1 Kgs 2:4; 8:22-26; 9:4-5; 11:30-39; 15:4; 2 Kgs 8:19). Yet after the fall of the northern kingdom (2 Kings 17), and despite the tale of Josiah's urgent reforms,[6] the remaining story of southern survival turns out to be a coda. By the end, like the house of Yhwh and the house of Israel, the house of Judah has disappeared. The erstwhile king of Judah, of the house of David, eats, like Mephibosheth of the house of Saul, at the usurper's table!

3.12 The ambivalence of the promise to David, conditional or unconditional, is not a historical but a theological question.[7] God offers grace that is lasting—grace to Abraham, to Moses, to David. But God cannot be taken for granted. A banal comment, a truism, yet one that catches the story of the nation, from entry into the land to exit. The promise of a "house" is grace ordered, institu-

---

[6] Some critics see Josiah as a *David redivivus;* e.g., Cross, 1973: 274-89, esp. pp. 283-85. Alternatively, David is *Josiah redivivus* (Nelson, 1981: 125-26). Much more is Josiah a Moses, promulgating the law, and grinding into dust the golden calves.

[7] See also the sensible comments by Burke O. Long (1984: 16-17) in a perceptive critique of the "dual redaction" hypothesis of the "deuteronomistic history."

tionalized. Yet that is a paradox, for grace confounds order and institution—as Jonah knew and resented. No institution secures, no institution *is* secure. The promise, suggests our story, cannot be presumed upon; it is not a crutch but an invitation to share in God's grace for the future.

3.13   David, therefore, is not an ideal character, a paradigm for emulation. Rather the story to which he belongs encodes in a variety of ways, negative as well as positive, key parameters of a relationship between Yhwh and humankind that is still "plausible" for the reader who "today" (which is where, as Deuteronomy makes clear, stands the reader of Genesis-Kings) seeks to build or rebuild a "house." Despite the ambiguities of the narrative and its unwillingness to let us "type" David, despite what we may feel as David's mighty men (2 Samuel 23) unsettle us, or as the passing moments of his kingship in 1 Kings 1-2 both uphold and mock the past, the larger story does not allow him to crumble, to disappear in shades of gray. If we cannot grasp him, yet we can allow him the freedom to provoke us, enliven us, and challenge our securities.

IV

4.1   Who is David? "A man of blood," says Shimei. Yes and no, we answer. Yes, says God (according to David) in the other great narrative account of David in 1 Chronicles. Addressing Solomon, David explains why he will not himself build a house to Yhwh's name: "There came upon me the word of Yhwh, saying, 'Much blood have you shed and great battles have you waged; you shall not build a house to my name; for much blood have you shed upon the earth before me'" (1 Chr 22:7-8; cf. 28:3). Despite that affirmation of the label and its allusion to Samuel and Kings, if we seek David the man of blood in 1 Chronicles we will not readily find him. In Samuel the sweet psalmist led us to the man of blood (and perhaps directed us to the Psalms). Here the man of blood will give place not only to a psalmist (2 Chr 29:30) but above all to a great patron of liturgy and the music of worship, and a planner of institutions, indeed of *the* institution, the house of Yhwh. It is not that the warrior is gone: in 1 Chr 11:4-9 the taking of Jerusalem is recounted and later come summary accounts of wars against foreign foes to recall the glory of empire (1 Chr 18:1-13). Yet these have, by and large, a rather aseptic character, at least as far as David is concerned. The Ammonite war is there (19:1-20:3), but no longer framing a story of adultery and murder. Bathsheba and Uriah have vanished. Completing this cluster of battle reports is the story of Elhanan slaying Lahmi, Goliath's *brother,* and of David's brother and the great man of Gath. No David and Goliath, *nor* even a disturbing Elhanan and Goliath. The threatening fragments at the end of 2 Samuel are tamed.

4.2   Tamed also is the story of census (cf. 1 Chronicles 21 with 2 Samuel 24), inasmuch as the Satan now stands between David and total culpability, though Joab's remonstration with the king (more vehement than in Samuel) prevents a total idealization of David. The Chronicler, too, knows that there is no perfection in humankind. Yet even this strange story is deftly woven back into line, for Ornan's threshing floor (where the story ends) becomes the site of the temple. The census story thus issues in praise to God's name. For the house of God in Chronicles is above all the building of praise and thanksgiving.

4.3   When, therefore, we review David's story from its narrative inception in 1 Chronicles 10, the death of Saul, we see that the concerns of peace have enveloped and permeated the accounts of war. The divisions of north and south, house of Israel and house of Judah, are bridged as all Israel gathers. The mighty men gather, a muster transformed into a congregation, to hear Amasai (a fortuitous reconciliation of 2 Samuel's rebel Amasa and aggressive Abishai!) shout "Peace!" (12:18). Battles against the Philistines are encompassed by a greater purpose for the congregation, namely the bringing of the ark to Jerusalem. In ordering and activating the great praise due to God, David finds life in the Chronicler's narrative.

4.4   As the ark story in 1 Chronicles 13 and 15-16 envelops the Philistine battle accounts in ch. 14, so the celebrations of chs. 15 and 16 at the installation of the ark and the intimations of house building in ch. 17 eventually envelop the campaigns of chs. 18-20. Though death touches Israel itself in the pestilence of ch. 21, there is a rapid shift from repentance to mercy and back into the dominant frame, the promulgation of worship in the building of Yhwh's house, by the end of the chapter (and from there to the end of the book and David's reign). The issue of succession is digested in a verse (23:1), swallowed up by more important issues. Charges have to be made (Be strong and build!), leaders have to be assembled, divisions established (divisions for harmony!). The organizing of divisions for temple and community in chs. 23-27 lies within a frame of ordering speech (the pattern is typical). David's charge to Solomon (and to the leaders) in ch. 22 leads to an assembly in ch. 23, while after the details of the divisions a newly constituted assembly follows in ch. 28 with a resumed charge to Solomon (and to the whole assembly). The focus of all the organization is the sustenance of the house of Yhwh: priests and levites, musicians and gatekeepers, commanders of this, chief officers of that, all are ordered to such an end.

4.5   The very style orders our understanding. It processes; lists and careful descriptions, prayers and exhortations are its subject matter. It is above all monologue rather than dialogue; it harks back to Leviticus and Deuteronomy, to Samuel's sermon (1 Samuel 12) and Nathan's prophecy (2 Samuel 7). Rather than creating "gaps," ambiguities, openness, in the text—as in so much of David's story in Samuel-Kings—it closes around us and marches us toward "plain" understanding. We become less attuned to those ironies and paradoxes that inhabit Samuel-Kings. There is a deliberate, measured quality about this material. The reader has to march with it, mark time, develop stamina. This is the style of commitment.

4.6   It also has the effect of turning us *away* from David, to the *task*, the *many* actors, and the *community.* Indeed, before we enter the narrative proper (ch. 10) we become enmeshed in the web of community through the extensive genealogical lists. Again, it is striking that the hymn of ch. 16 is no longer David's (compare the "I" of 2 Samuel 22-23) but *appointed* by David to be sung by the appropriate leaders for the worshipping community.

4.7   David's life as a character in the text comes predominantly (there are exceptions, such as 1 Chr 15:29) through "ordering" or through being the focus of other people's activity (such as the warriors who "came to David" in ch. 12). Another source of life is allusion: those charges to Solomon in chs. 22 and 28, punctuated by the call to "Be strong and of good courage. Fear not; be not dismayed!" (23:13; cf. 28:20), are redolent of Moses to Joshua as well as Moses to the people (Deuteronomy 31) and Yhwh to

Joshua as well as Joshua to the people (Joshua 1). The task at hand is like the possession of the land (hence 1 Chr 28:8, "Seek out all the commandments of Yhwh your God, that you may possess this good land," comes as no surprise). Like Moses, David mediates God's word directly and in this and other respects he inherits, and wears discreetly, a prophet's mantle (Newsome: 210-212). These are tones that lend authority to the ordering speech. They do not really constitute personality. The figure remains flat and curiously self-effacing.

4.8   At the center of the community is the house of Yhwh, not David's house, nor even Jerusalem. Thanksgiving is fundamental. *Giving* is fundamental. David's purchase of the site of the house is paradigmatic. The whole community can contribute, beyond those who directly serve in the house. The narrative moves toward an exhortation to give (ch. 29); and in the context of this inexorable knitting together of myriad persons, all with their allotted role, who can turn away from the call to commitment?

4.9   The end of Kings is a gaping hole which, when we peer into it, loops us back to Deuteronomy, to where we stand "today" before Moses, "outside," pondering the invitation to enter and participate in a new gift. The end of Chronicles bridges that gulf surely, converts desolation into a sabbath (2 Chr 36:21), and marches us resolutely toward an unambiguous goal—to build Yhwh a house. Cyrus' decree (36:23; Ezra 1:3) strikingly resumes David's charge to Solomon (1 Chr 22:6, 18-19).

4.10   Invited into the Books of Ezra and Nehemiah by the resumption of Chronicles in Ezra 1 (Clines: 2-12), we stand once more before David (fashioned now in the form of Cyrus), as we are ordered to be up and building a new building. The vision of David stays in the text, too, as the people offer gifts and praise Yhwh at the foundation of the new house, and as Ezra and Nehemiah themselves charge, exhort, and celebrate. As in Chronicles, the great moments are those of giving and thanksgiving in the service of Yhwh by a community which finds its identity in its ordering in and around his house.[8] Ultimately this is the only house that matters. At the dedication of the wall—the bulwark

---

[8] On giving, see, e.g.: Ezra 1:6-7; 2:68-69; 6:16-17; 7:11-25; 8:24-36; Nehemiah 3; 7:70-72; 10:32-39; 12:43-47.

around the house and its servants (cf. Neh 12:44-47)—Ezra's company of praise processes with the musical instruments of David, the "man of God," *above* David's house (12:31-37).

4.11 Yet the *actuality* of house-building competes with David's vision: there is no end to the business of establishment (Neh 13:30); rather the story is one of struggle and contention and ever renewed invitation, by exhortation or paradigm (see, e.g., Neh 12:47), to *give*. Again and again we see commitment lapse. The ending, set against the celebration in ch. 12, with Nehemiah once more attempting to untangle the potential damage done by ever resurgent self-interest and ordinariness, is realistic, if a touch pathetic: the zealot berates, curses, contends, chases, and pulls out hair. Remember the forces of evil, he urges God; and "remember me, O God, for good" (13:23-31). The sentiments are not unlike those of David's last words, which is where we began! Vision and actuality compete. Righteousness risks mocking itself.

4.12 David's vision in Chronicles–Ezra–Nehemiah is a splendid one, a call to build a house in order to seek Yhwh in the service of praise and thanksgiving—a call which reverberates particularly readily with today's reader in church or synagogue. The vision reasserts, alongside the liberating ironies of Samuel and Kings, the constructive power of order and institution.

4.13 Yet for me to end thus in security may be to betray both stories. For insecurity is also their burden. Better perhaps to break off with a question.

4.14 Must it always end thus, David's story—not with praise and thanksgiving but judgment and claims to righteousness?

WORKS CONSULTED

Ackroyd, Peter R.
  1981   "The Succession Narrative (So-called)." *Int* 35:383-96.
Alter, Robert
  1981   *The Art of Biblical Narrative.* New York: Basic Books.
Berlin, Adele
  1983   *Poetics and Interpretation of Biblical Narrative.* Bible & Literature Series, 9. Sheffield: Almond Press.

Brueggemann, Walter
1972   "On Trust and Freedom: A Study of Faith in the Suc-
        cession Narrative." *Int* 26:3-19.
1974   "On Coping With Curse: A Study of 2 Sam 16:5-14."
        CBQ 36:175-92.
1985   *David's Truth in Israel's Imagination & Memory.* Phila-
        delphia: Fortress Press.

Carlson, R. A.
1964   *David, the Chosen King.* Stockholm: Almqvist &
        Wiksell.

Clines, D. J. A.
1984   *Ezra, Nehemiah, Esther.* New Century Bible. Grand
        Rapids: Eerdmans/London: Marshall, Morgan &
        Scott.

Conroy, Charles
1978   *Absalom Absalom: Narrative and Language in 2 Sam
        13-20.* Analecta Biblica. Rome: Biblical Institute
        Press.

Cross, Frank Moore
1973   "The Themes of the Book of Kings and the Structure
        of the Deuteronomistic History." Pp. 274-89 in *Canaan-
        ite Myth and Hebrew Epic.* Cambridge: Harvard Uni-
        versity Press.

Eslinger, Lyle M.
1985   *Kingship of God in Crisis: A Close Reading of 1 Sam-
        uel 1-12.* Bible and Literature Series, 10. Sheffield:
        Almond Press.

Flanagan, James W.
1983   "Social Transformation and Ritual in 2 Samuel 6." Pp.
        361-72 in *The Word of the Lord Shall Go Forth.* Ed.
        Carol L. Meyers & M. O'Connor. Winona Lake, IN:
        Eisenbrauns.
1988   *David's Social Drama: A Hologram of Israel's Early
        Iron Age.* The Social World of Biblical Antiquity Se-
        ries, 7. Sheffield: Almond Press.

Fokkelman, J. P.
1981   *Narrative Art and Poetry in the Books of Samuel.*
        Vol. I, *King David.* Assen: Van Gorcum.

Gordon, Robert P.
1980   "David's Rise and Saul's Demise: Narrative Analogy
        in 1 Samuel 24-26." *Tyndale Bulletin* 31:37-64.

1984   *1 & 2 Samuel*. Sheffield: JSOT Press.

1986   *1 & 2 Samuel*. Exeter: Paternoster.

Gros Louis, K. R. R.

1977   "King David of Israel." Pp. 15-33 in *Literary Critical Studies of Biblical Texts*. Ed. Robert W. Funk. *Semeia* 8. (Also in Gros Louis, ed., with James S. Ackerman, *Literary Interpretations of Biblical Narratives*, Vol. II. [Nashville: Abingdon, 1982], 204-19.)

Gunn, David M.

1975   "David and the Gift of the Kingdom." Pp. 14-45 in *Classical Hebrew Narrative*. Ed. Robert Culley. *Semeia* 3.

1978   *The Story of King David: Genre and Interpretation*. JSOT Supplements, 6. Sheffield: JSOT Press.

1980   *The Fate of King Saul: An Interpretation of a Biblical Story*. JSOT Supplements, 14. Sheffield: JSOT Press.

Jobling, David

1978   "Jonathan: A Structural Study of 1 Samuel." Chapter1 in *The Sense of Biblical Narrative*. JSOT Supplements, 7. Sheffield: JSOT Press.

Levenson, Jon D.

1982   "I Samuel 25 as Literature and History." Pp. 220-42 in *Literary Interpretations of Biblical Narratives*, Vol. II. Ed. K. R. R. Gros Louis, with James S. Ackerman. Nashville: Abingdon.

Long, Burke O.

1984   *1 Kings*. The Forms of OT Literature. Grand Rapids: Eerdmans.

McCarter, P. Kyle

1980   *I Samuel*. Anchor Bible, 8. Garden City, NY: Doubleday.

1984   *II Samuel*. Anchor Bible, 9. Garden City, NY: Doubleday.

Miscall, Peter D.

1983   *The Workings of Old Testament Narrative*. Semeia Studies. Philadelphia: Fortress Press/Chico: Scholars Press.

1986   *1 Samuel: A Literary Reading*. Indiana Studies in Biblical Literature. Bloomington: Indiana University Press.

Nelson, Richard D.
    1981   *The Double Redaction of the Deuteronomistic History.* JSOT Supplements, 18. Sheffield: JSOT Press.

Newsome, James D.
    1975   "Towards a New Understanding of the Chronicler and his Purposes." *JBL* 94:201-17.

Perdue, Leo G.
    1984   " 'Is There Anyone Left of the House of Saul . . . ?' Ambiguity and the Characterization of David in the Succession Narrative." *JSOT* 30:67-84.

Polzin, Robert
    1980   *Moses and the Deuteronomist. A Literary Study of the Deuteronomic History,* Part 1. New York: Seabury.

Rosenberg, Joel
    1986   *King and Kin: Political Allegory in the Hebrew Bible.* Indiana Studies in Biblical Literature. Bloomington: Indiana University Press.

Sternberg, Meir
    1985   *The Poetics of Biblical Narrative.* Indiana Literary Biblical Series. Bloomington: Indiana University Press.

Wharton, James A.
    1981   "A Plausible Tale: Story and Theology in II Samuel 9-20, I Kings 1-2." *Int* 35:341-54.

FOR DAVID'S SAKE:
A Response to David M. Gunn

Peter D. Miscall
St. Thomas Seminary

ABSTRACT

1 Samuel 16–1 Kings 2 presents a shifting David who
can't be secured or fixed; divine freedom dominates.
The Chronicler presents a consistent image of David, he
who establishes the temple. The temple is not perfect
and requires renewal. The Chronicler can be equal to or
in conflict with Samuel–Kings; new readings arise that
mirror the conflicts of Samuel–Kings. In 1 Kings the
Lord shows his freedom to shift; David is his righteous
servant for whose sake he stays the destruction of Judah.
God rewrites the past and refashions the future.

In "In Security: The David of Biblical Narrative," David
Gunn has given us a thought-provoking presentation of the material on David in 1 Samuel 16–1 Kings 2, 1 Chronicles 10–29, and
Ezra–Nehemiah. The article is organized around the question
"Who is David?" Gunn's first response is the "sweet psalmist of
Israel" (2 Sam 23:1). The context of the statement, however, leads
to weapons, warriors, and war and to David, Shimei's "man of
blood" (2 Sam 16:6-8). This is a David skilled in intrigue; we are
far from the sweet singer. "David's story has a way of shifting out
from under us. The story refuses to be tamed, secured, or neatly
ordered" (1.11). Shifting, disorder, and wildness are hallmarks of
Gunn's reading of David in Samuel and Kings; whenever we think
that we have David cornered and identified, we find ourselves
elsewhere and with someone else.

The second response is "the man after God's own heart," i.e., the model man and ideal king. This dissolves with the realization that David and Saul are foils for each other and are not so different morally. The force that both unites and distinguishes them is Yhwh's will. David is not a better man, one more after God's own heart, than Saul. "Yhwh *chooses* to establish David's sovereignty, not in response to the people's demand for security . . . but because Yhwh chooses to do so, in freedom, according to his own wishes, his own devices, after his own heart" (2.5; his italics). Yhwh's freedom, grace, and sovereignty are central terms for Gunn. God *gives* the kingdom to David but the gift is frequently complicated and fouled by David's inveterate grasping, particularly in the Abigail and Bathsheba stories.

In his third answer, Gunn returns to "the man of blood," the David of violence and death from the conflict with Goliath to his deathbed "hit list" for Solomon. The title leads Gunn into an interesting meditation on "houses": those of Saul, David (the dynasty and the kingdom), Israel and God (the temple). The ambiguity of the word "house" is expressive of the complicated and complicating relationships between the private and public spheres. Just as David is on the verge of establishing his house, he grasps Bathsheba and almost loses "his house": family, dynasty, and kingdom. Yhwh's freedom and sovereignty intervene and David is saved.

But Yhwh's freedom gives no eternal and unconditional promises. What he gives, he can take away, as another learned. Neither "house," that of God or that of the dynasty, can save the kingdom or David's family; both end in ruin and dispersal. Order and institution cannot provide certain guarantees. God's promises can invite into the future but they are not a crutch or a talisman.

In the second part of his paper, Gunn locates the search for such guarantees in order and institution in Chronicles. Chronicles depicts a musician, a liturgist, and above all "a planner of institutions, indeed of the institution, the house of Yhwh" (4.1). The house of the Lord is preeminently a place for praise and thanksgiving. David's last words in Kings and in Chronicles support Gunn's contrast. "You shall bring his gray head down with blood to Sheol" (1 Kgs 2:9) and "Bless the Lord your God" (1 Chr 29:20).

Chronicles is a story of "lists and careful descriptions, prayers and exhortations. . . . Rather than creating 'gaps,' ambiguities, openness, in the text—as in so much of David's story in Samuel-Kings—it closes around us and marches us toward 'plain' understanding" (4.5). This clarity and understanding, however, take us away from David who disappears behind the community, the work, and the orders. David is reminiscent of the great "orderers" of the past: the Lord, Moses, and Joshua.

I would add that Chronicles shows more interest in the Mosaic tabernacle. "The tabernacle of the Lord, which Moses had made in the wilderness, and the altar of burnt offering were at that time in the high place at Gibeon" (1 Chr 21:29; cf. 16:39-40). In Kings, only a high place and altar are at Gibeon (1 Kgs 3:4). David substitutes for Moses and Joshua, and the house of the Lord for the wilderness tabernacle.

Unlike the earlier "orderers," the focus for David is not the nation, the land, or even his own dynasty; it is the house of the Lord. All of Chronicles revolves about this institution and its established orders. Gunn could have strengthened his argument by noting the intensity of the theme of choice in Chronicles. 1 Chr 28:1-10 summarizes the progression: the Lord has chosen Judah from among all the tribes, David's family from that tribe, David from among his father's sons, and Solomon from among David's sons (vv 4-5). Solomon is to build the temple in Jerusalem, the city that the Lord has chosen.

2 Chronicles ends looking ahead to Cyrus's rebuilding of the house, and this leads into Ezra and Nehemiah which detail the rebuilding of temple, city, and community, all figures for each other. Gunn regards Cyrus, Ezra, and Nehemiah as "David figures" who are perpetually involved in the business of reestablishing and rebuilding the community and the house. Order and institution may be constructive for them but, Gunn argues, the continual need to renew them is evidence of a falling away and of a lapsing commitment.

I might quibble with some of Gunn's statements and conclusions, but it would be only quibbling. On the other hand, I can elaborate and further complicate his depictions of David; much of this I have done in *Workings* and *1 Samuel* and hope to continue at a future time. For now I confine myself to two general categories of comments. First are some added ways of reading Chronicles, Ezra, and Nehemiah (referred to as the Chronicler for short) in comparison and contrast with Samuel and Kings; these would recast Gunn's presentation in different literary models of reading. The focus would be on issues of textuality and on the relations of texts more than on the characterizations in the separate texts. Second is a closer look at the references to David in the rest of 1 and 2 Kings; Gunn stops with 1 Kings 2.

The Chronicler

The Chronicler emphasizes *place*, the temple as the site of the community. The emphasis is balanced by one on *time* and time in the sense of duration, not just of proper succession. This is mythic and metaphorical time, not metonymical time, not a series of individual historical events and characters. The combination of the house of the Lord (tabernacle and temple), the community of Israel, and everlasting praise should last forever. Tabernacle and temple and Moses, Joshua, David, Cyrus, Ezra, and Nehemiah are all substitutions for one another; they are not just members of a legitimate line of succession. They are all figures for the Lord's one creative act of choice and charge. (I adapt the insight from Bloom: 57.)

In Samuel and Kings, place may be important but we must always ask which place, e.g., Judah or Israel; Jerusalem or Babylon? And time goes on. There is no one pattern or originating act in Genesis–Kings; there may be similarities but there are not identities. David may be like Moses but he is not Moses. The word of the Lord must always be interpreted and reinterpreted as people, place, and setting change (cf. Polzin and Miscall, 1986). The command to build the house of the Lord, whether tabernacle or temple, does not bind the narrative together.

As Gunn so ably demonstrates, the David of Samuel–Kings is not a fixed and stable character to be described in secure and identical terms. His character and characteristics shift and change. The sweet psalmist is a man of blood; the pious shepherd is a great warrior; the anointed of the Lord is a conniver who doesn't miss a chance to advance his own fortunes. The Chronicler attempts to tame this chaotic flux by fixing David in one, secure image. The Chronicler's "vision reasserts, alongside the liberating ironies of Samuel and Kings, the constructive power of order and institution" (4.12). Gunn, however, closes with the comment that the burden of both Samuel–Kings and the Chronicler is security and insecurity. The Chronicler can't fix and secure David, and Samuel–Kings "does not allow him to crumble, to disappear in shades of gray" (3.13).

The pictures of the Chronicler and of Samuel–Kings are more poles on a spectrum than mutually exclusive views that cancel each other. The two texts can be read as intertexts, as texts that are present at the same time and that are of the same status. The Chronicler may tame and settle Samuel–Kings but the latter is always there to unsettle and release the former. The Chronicler hasn't replaced Samuel–Kings or deceived any reader with his more consistent presentation of David. Samuel–Kings is always there as a reminder of the flux and inconsistency that accompanies any attempt to depict David. On the other hand, the Chronicler is always present in a reading of Samuel–Kings. The gaps, ambiguities, and undecidabilities of the latter are limited and checked by the securities of the former.

The two works unsettle one another but they do not cancel each other out; it is not a matter of choosing one or the other as "the true picture of David." This is attempted in historical treatments of the two works. The Chronicler is later and has "cleaned up" David and presented a historically false picture of him. (This allows for the acceptance of particular details and events in 1 Chronicles as historically accurate; it is the big picture that is false.) This is too neat and easy since, historically, Samuel–Kings was known by the reader of Chronicles; true or false historicity is not the issue. To adapt Gunn, the tensions between the two works are "not a historical but a theological question" (3.12). For "theological" we can also read "literary" and maintain a historical order of authorship in which Chronicles is later than Samuel–Kings.

This does not negate the intertextual model and reading since intertexts do not have to have been actually written at the same time. *Hamlet* can illuminate and even complicate *Oedipus Rex* and *Oedipus Rex* can do the same for *Hamlet*. This would allow, as another approach that would swerve from the above, the application of a version of Bloom's theory of the anxiety of influence, of the burdensome feeling of belatedness, and of the conflict with the precursor. (Bloom's *The Breaking of the Vessels* is a fine, short statement of his theory.) At this time I can only hint at what this reading would look like.

The Chronicler does not refashion Genesis–Kings simply because he wants to but because he has to. He has been "chosen" by this work and becomes an author in wrestling with it, in attempting to write his own book. His work, his existence as an author in his own right, can only be by displacing this precursor, Genesis–Kings. The above intertextual reading would be modified and replaced by one replete with themes of conflict, catastrophe, striving for priority, replacement, and costly victory. Bloom frequently makes the conflict and striving for priority a version of Freud's family romance.

This would be a fascinating and rewarding exercise since Bloom's themes are already those of the story of David and of a considerable portion of the Hebrew Bible. Genesis 1-11, "repeated" in 1 Chronicles 1-9, sets the scene in which the Bible is a "family romance" of conflict, of striving for priority, and of attempts of one person to supplant another. Our theory and practice would already be contained in the text that we would be reading. Congruence between text and reading, in which each mirrors the other, is a characteristic of much contemporary criticism; Felman's study contains excellent and lengthy discussions of it.

Congruence applies to my comments on David's article. I have shifted out from under his essay and have wandered far but that is what he says happens with David's story. "The story refuses to be tamed, secured, or neatly ordered" (1.11). Indeed I, like the Chronicler, seek to tame and replace David. Read me, not him!

1 and 2 Kings

David's dying words reflect the picture of him developed in Gunn's article. He opens as the man after God's own heart. He speaks as a Moses or Joshua in charging Solomon to be strong and to "keep the charge of the Lord your God, walking in his ways and keeping his statutes . . . as it is written in the law of Moses" (1 Kgs 2:2-3). He refers to the dynastic promise from the Lord in 2 Sam 7:5-16 and shifts it away from the unconditional proclamation: "I will establish the throne of his kingdom forever . . . I will not take my steadfast love from him" (2 Sam 7:13-15). David speaks of the Lord's word: "*If* your sons take heed to their way, to walk before me in faithfulness with all their heart and with all their soul, there will not fail you a man on the throne of Israel" (1 Kgs 2:4).

This is the David of 2 Samuel 22, particularly vv 21-25, who speaks of faithfulness, righteousness, and the Lord's statutes and ordinances; keeping them has earned him the Lord's reward. This is not the sweet psalmist who talks of "an everlasting covenant, ordered in all things and secure" (2 Sam 23:5). This is a David like unto Moses and Joshua, who orders and who speaks of keeping statutes and ordinances.

The second part of David's dying statement is twice as long as the first and is spoken by Shimei's man of blood who charges

Solomon to be wise and to kill Joab and Shimei. David is the interpreter, the man skilled in speech.[1] "I swore to him [Shimei] by the Lord, 'I will not put you to death with the sword'" (1 Kgs 2:8). David keeps his oath to the Lord by interpreting it in terms of "I"; Benaiah, not David, will put Shimei to death. Who is David? "A man of blood." "A man skilled in words." "A consummate casuist."

The Chronicler is not the first to attempt to tame David in one secure image and to use this image as a guarantee of order and stability. Solomon attempts it. Death and blood are upon Joab and his descendants, "but to David and to his descendants, and to his house, and to his throne, there will be peace from the Lord for evermore" (1 Kgs 2:33). Shimei will die but "King Solomon will be blessed, and the throne of David will be established before the Lord forever" (1 Kgs 2:45). Solomon may not be intoning the unconditional dynastic promise of 2 Samuel 7, but he is not as explicitly conditional as David.

The Lord is explicit, "If you [Solomon] will walk in my ways, keeping my statutes and my commandments, *as your father David walked*, then I will lengthen your days" (1 Kgs 3:14). Who is David? "The man who walked in the Lord's ways and kept his commandments." Like David in his closing words, the Lord speaks of conditions: "if . . . then." David earned his reward, his lengthened days, because of his righteousness (2 Sam 22:21-25 and 1 Kgs 3:14). This is not the divine grace and freedom that Gunn found in his material. Who is David? "The man rewarded by the Lord for his righteousness."

After the dedication of the temple, the people "blessed the king and [were] . . . joyful and glad of heart for all the goodness that the Lord had shown to David his servant and to Israel his people" (1 Kgs 8:66). Who is David? "The servant of the Lord."

The Lord responds to Solomon's prayer. *If* Solomon keeps the Lord's statutes as David his father did, *then* the Lord will establish his throne as he promised David his father, and "there will not fail you a man upon the throne of Israel" (1 Kgs 9:4-5).

---

[1] David's skill or prudence in speech is first introduced in 1 Sam 16:18 in the description of David by one of Saul's retainers. It can be taken in the positive sense that David's speeches are wise, accurate, and beneficial (Rose: 63-65). "It can also be taken in an ironic sense; David knows well the public and political effect of speech and therefore chooses his words carefully, wisely, for maximum public and political benefit" (Miscall, 1986: 119).

The latter is a quote from David's final words (1 Kgs 2:4) and not from the dynastic promise in 2 Samuel 7. The Lord closes with a threat. *"But if* you turn aside from following me . . . *then* I will cut off Israel" (1 Kgs 9:6-7). "If . . . then" dominates. David earned his reward. Now it is up to Solomon and his descendants to earn theirs.

Gunn spoke of "the ambivalence of the promise to David, conditional or unconditional, [which] is not a historical but a theological question. God offers grace that is lasting. . . . But God cannot be taken for granted" (3.12). The passages we have discussed resolve the ambivalence—the promise is conditional for both David and the Lord—but reemphasize that God cannot be taken for granted, that his actions and words are paradoxical and confounding. God's freedom may beckon us into the future, but it does this by extending into the past and reinterpreting and rewriting it. The Lord makes no mention of an unconditional dynastic promise, speaks of David as righteous and deserving of reward, and quotes David as a legitimate source for his (the Lord's) own words.

This picture of David from 1 Kings 2 on is a decided change from the preceding portrayal. Gone is the man of blood, the victorious king who is God's free gift to his people Israel. "Yhwh *chooses* to establish David's sovereignty . . . because Yhwh chooses to do so, in freedom, according to his own wishes, his own devices, after his own heart (cf. 2 Sam 7:21)" (Gunn: 2.5; his italics). Apparently the Lord gives up his freedom in binding himself to the conditional "if . . . then" framework that he intones from 1 Kings 3 and that he projects back onto the David beginning with 1 Samuel 16: his servant who walked in his ways and kept his commands. Yet the projection itself is a mark of the Lord's freedom; he can rewrite the past.

Because of his wives, Solomon's "heart was not wholly true to the Lord his God, as was the heart of David his father . . . Solomon did what was evil in the sight of the Lord, and did not wholly follow the Lord, as David his father had done" (1 Kgs 11:4-6). Solomon has broken the "if" and the "then" follows: the loss of the kingdom as punishment. But the Lord is not bound. "Yet for the sake of David your father I will not do it in your days, but I will tear it out of the hand of your son. However, I will not tear away all the kingdom; but I will give one tribe to your son, for the sake of David my servant and for the sake of Jerusalem which I have chosen" (1 Kgs 11:12-13; cf. 11:32-39). David has merited this position by walking in the Lord's ways, doing what is right in his eyes and by keeping his statutes and ordinances (11:33, 38).

This David continues into 1 and 2 Kings. "My servant David, who kept my commandments, and followed me with all his heart, doing only that which was right in my eyes" (1 Kgs 14:8). To depart from this pattern, to act other than David did, is evil and should merit punishment and total destruction. Solomon, Jeroboam, Abijam, Jehoram, and Ahaz all do evil by not walking in the ways of the Lord "as David their father had done" (cf. 1 Kgs 11:4-6, 33; 14:8; 15:3-5; 2 Kgs 8:19; 16:2). (The other evil kings of Judah are not contrasted with David.) But the Lord is not bound. "For David's sake the Lord his God gave him a lamp in Jerusalem, setting up his son after him, and establishing Jerusalem; because David did what was right in the eyes of the Lord, and did not turn aside from anything that he commanded him all the days of his life, except in the matter of Uriah the Hittite" (1 Kgs 15:4-5). In his statements, the Lord omits the matter of Bathsheba and Uriah the Hittite which was evil in his eyes (2 Sam 11:27).

The Lord is not bound.[2] He can refashion the past—David is all good and wholly true to the Lord—and then use it to shape the future in ways different from a strict "if . . . then" pattern. The kings of Judah do evil and do not follow the Lord but punishment does not follow "for the sake of David my servant."[3]

Yet this has a dark side. Josiah "did what was right in the eyes of the Lord, and walked in all the way of David his father, and he did not turn aside to the right hand or to the left" (2 Kgs 22:2). Indeed, "before him there was no king like him, who turned to the Lord with all his heart and with all his soul and with all his might, according to all the law of Moses; nor did any like him arise after him" (23:25). Josiah stands above David—therefore there is no mention of the latter—and is even more like Moses (cf. Deut 4:29; 6:5; 10:12; 11:13; 13:3-4; 30:2-10 which speak of heart, soul, and might). But this does not issue in reward and good for Josiah.

---

[2] Neither is the narrator bound, but this is for another work. I am gliding over many significant literary issues, particularly those involved in the refashioning of previous parts of Samuel-Kings. A Bloomian model could be employed with the Lord and the narrator as strong readers and writers but with the added twist that the precursor texts are their own!

[3] This is a simplified account. I am leaving out the role of Jerusalem and the story of the northern kingdom and its evil kings. I am also omitting treatment of the details of the separate references to David in 1 and 2 Kings; they are not word-for-word the same and the differences would be instructive in a fuller reading.

Evil has been decided upon for Judah (cf. 2 Kgs 21:1-16 and 22:16-17), but it is delayed and Josiah is to be spared the evil. Unlike Solomon, the sparing is due to Josiah's penitence. "You humbled yourself before the Lord . . . you will be gathered to your grave in peace, and your eyes will not see all the evil which I will bring upon this place" (22:16-20). This places Josiah in mixed company: Hezekiah and Ahab (cf. 2 Kgs 20:1-11 and 1 Kgs 21:27-29). Hezekiah lives fifteen more years and is apparently gathered to his grave in peace. Not so Ahab and Josiah. Both die in battle (cf. 1 Kgs 22:29-38 and 2 Kgs 23:29).

The Lord is not bound. This grand king, who turned to the Lord more than all before him including David, does not become the Lord's servant for whose sake the Lord will stay the destruction of Judah. His turning to the Lord delays only his own demise. He won't see the evil; he will die in peace. The latter does not occur. The Lord is not bound.

Destruction comes for "houses": those of Judah, of the Lord, and of David. "The erstwhile king of Judah, of the house of David, eats, like Mephibosheth of the house of Saul, at the usurper's table!" (Gunn: 3.11). David's house and Saul's end in similar manner. However there can be a future, for another can rewrite the past and fashion a new future. The house of Judah and of the Lord can be rebuilt and reestablished and the house of David can carry on through its replacements and figures: Moses, Joshua, Cyrus, Ezra, Nehemiah, and others.

WORKS CONSULTED

Bloom, Harold
    1982   *The Breaking of the Vessels.* The Wellek Library Lectures. Ed. Frank Lentricchia. Chicago: University of Chicago Press.

Felman, Shoshana
    1977   "Turning the Screw of Interpretation." *Literature and Psychoanalysis: The Question of Reading: Otherwise.* Ed. S. Felman. *Yale French Studies* 55/56: 94-207.
                [Issued as a separate volume in 1982: Johns Hopkins University Press.]

Miscall, Peter D.
    1983   *The Workings of Old Testament Narrative.* Semeia Studies. Ed. Dan O. Via, Jr. Philadelphia: Fortress Press/Chico: Scholars Press.
    1986   *1 Samuel: A Literary Reading.* Indiana Studies in Biblical Literature. Eds. H. Marks and R. Polzin. Bloomington: Indiana University Press.

Polzin, Robert
    1980   *Moses and the Deuteronomist. A Literary Study of the Deuteronomic History.* Part 1. New York: Seabury Press.

Rose, Ashley S.
    1974   "The 'Principles' of Divine Election. Wisdom in 1 Samuel 16." Pp. 43-67 in *Rhetorical Criticism: Essays in Honor of James Muilenburg.* Eds. J. J. Jackson and M. Kessler. Pittsburgh Theological Monograph Series, 1. Pittsburgh: Pickwick Press.

EZRA-NEHEMIAH:
FROM TEXT TO ACTUALITY

Tamara C. Eskenazi
University of Denver

Freedom. It isn't once, to walk out
under the Milky Way, feeling the rivers
of light. The fields of dark—
freedom is daily, prose-bound, routine
remembering. Putting together, inch by inch
the starry worlds. From all the lost collections.

Adrienne Rich,
"For Memory"

ABSTRACT

Ezra–Nehemiah is a book that does not merely high-light the significance of texts through descriptions such as the public reading from the Torah (Nehemiah 8). The book also exemplifies the primacy of texts by its overall structure and its innovative use of genres such as letters and memoirs. This essay shows how Ezra–Nehemiah, programmatically and pervasively, combines form and content to articulate a central theme: the actualization of the written text in the life of the community.

1.1 Hegel distinguishes between poetry and prose not merely as styles of writing but rather as ways of being. The great epic eras of antiquity reflected, for Hegel, a fundamentally poetic state of the world, or, as Erich Heller puts it, "a world in which poetry is not merely written, but, as it were, lived" (3). Hegel considered his own epoch to be an age of prose, one from which the gods had absconded, where, lamentably, the prosaic mode prevailed.

1.2   Ezra–Nehemiah is a book written in and for an age of prose. It is a book where the words of Yhwh from the mouth of the prophet have come to some kind of closure (Ezra 1:1: לכלות דבר יהוה), where poetic utterances are suspect (Neh 6:12-13), where even prayers of the heart flow in prose (Ezra 9). It is a book where God does not speak directly and where life is lived in the dailiness of placing stone upon stone. It is also a book, however, which does not long bemoan the loss of poetry and the loss of grandeur. Instead it sanctifies the prosaic, the concrete, and the common, hallowing a life that gathers together "inch by inch, the starry worlds. From all the lost collections."

1.3   Ezra–Nehemiah affirms the prosaic by its depiction of the return and restoration: what is said and what is left unsaid, how the story is structured, what of the past is recalled and what is emphasized—all of these convey Ezra–Nehemiah's interest and intention. The book's mode of narration deflects attention from the heroism of great leaders to the community living in accordance with the book. Ezra–Nehemiah replaces the veneration of ecstatic and inspired spoken word by the dogged and persistent execution of the written. It transfers authority from leaders to text.

1.4   Three dominant themes combine in Ezra–Nehemiah (Eskenazi, 1988a). First, Ezra–Nehemiah shifts the focus from leaders to participating community. Second, Ezra–Nehemiah expands the concept of the house of God from temple to city. Third, Ezra–Nehemiah emphasizes the centrality of the written text and its primacy over the oral as a source of authority. In so doing, Ezra–Nehemiah wrests power from charismatic figures and provides a more publicly accessible, and publicly negotiable, source of authority. These themes work together to depict the return and reconstruction as an era in which all the important accomplishments are not the achievement of a few illustrious and inspired men trailed by an anonymous mass of followers. Instead, these accomplishments are the product of broad-ranging communal involvement, over time, inch by inch.

1.5   This essay traces one of Ezra–Nehemiah's themes, the emphasis on text. It seeks to demonstrate that forms, structure, and thematic development in Ezra–Nehemiah combine to articulate the primacy of texts as source of authority and the actualization of texts in the community's life. The written word gains new prominence in exilic and post-exilic times. Ezekiel and Jeremiah, for example, wrestle with the issue in their different ways. Ezra–Nehemiah shares the interest in texts and replicates—as do other books—the process by which life is translated into texts. The very fact that it is a book is one example of this. Ezra–Nehemiah goes further, however, for it also reverses the direction, demonstrating how text becomes life. Indeed, one of Ezra–Nehemiah's most lasting contributions is the dialectic which not only claims that texts embody meaning but also shows how texts come to be actualized. In this sense it gives new concreteness to the notion of the fulfillment of the word (e.g., Ezra 1:1).

1.6 As the following discussion will elucidate, Ezra–Nehemiah programmatically and pervasively establishes the written documents (e.g., Cyrus' edict and the law in Ezra's hand) as decisive for the life of the community. The ultimate power behind such documents is God. But God's messages in Ezra–Nehemiah are transcribed by divinely appointed human subjects (e.g., Cyrus, Moses) into writings which become the definitive forces in the unfolding reality. In the prophets the spoken word is actualized; in Ezra–Nehemiah, the *written* text.

2.1 Ezra–Nehemiah's distinctive orientation comes to the fore when one explores the book by means of a literary analysis, utilizing the techniques refined, e.g., by R. Alter or M. Sternberg. Ironically, at a time when literary criticism flourishes, few of its insights have penetrated Ezra–Nehemiah studies. To a large extent, reconstructions of the history and of the text still predominate this particular field. As B. S. Childs observes,

> The discovery of a larger number of difficult literary and historical problems associated with the writings of Ezra and Nehemiah has caused many scholars to regard the present canonical shape of these books as confused and distorted. They have concluded that a proper understanding of these writings entails an extensive reconstruction of the present form of this collection (626-27).

2.2 Such a persistent "source oriented" (Sternberg: 15) or "excavative" (Alter: 13) approach to Ezra–Nehemiah seems to have been influenced by the categorizing of the book as historiography and the concomitant presumption that historiography is somehow exempt from literary convention. Yet, as the historian Hayden

White points out, history is not an independent reality "out there" faithfully recorded, nor is historiography the objective recording of such reality. On the contrary, putative objectivity—so often associated with historiography in contrast to literature—can be more easily granted to annals or chronicles (though, as White demonstrates, not even there). History writing, however, is distinct from those genres precisely by the fullness of its narrativity (23). Events in real life do not present themselves in the coherent manner that history presents them. The ordering of experience as history "arises out of the desire to have real events display the coherence, integrity, fullness, and closure of an image of life that is and can only be imaginary . . ." (23). Narrativity, the shaping of events and the fullness of contextual interpretation of details, thus separates historiography from annals or chronicles. Since historiography is a literary construct rather than a mirror of reality, it requires literary sensitivity on the part of the reader. Literary analysis of other historiographical books in the Bible has already produced exciting results (see, e.g., Alter, Fokkelman, and Sternberg on 1 and 2 Samuel; see also Van Seters). The literary dimensions of Ezra–Nehemiah, however, continue to be neglected.

2.3   Ezra–Nehemiah displays a remarkable reverence toward the written word that manifests itself through the many ways in which the written text is paradigmatic for the life of the community. One notes, for example, that it is from a written text that God's messages are conveyed in Ezra–Nehemiah, as the public reading of the book of the Torah clearly illustrates (Nehemiah 8). Other powers are also exercised by means of the written text, as the interplay of authorizing correspondence (Ezra 4-5) and the written oath of the people of Israel (Neh 10:1) indicate. Ezra–Nehemiah thus demonstrates a self-consciousness about the power of the written word. The concern with the literary mode—the coalescing of significance and meaning in the written text—in Ezra–Nehemiah is taken here as an invitation for an analysis of the book that attends to its literary dimensions.

2.4   A literary approach typically focuses on the text in its final form. For this study, the text is Ezra–Nehemiah in the MT, following BHS. Several preliminary observations about the scope of the book are necessary. First, it has to be noted that Ezra–Nehemiah in the MT forms a single book, in contrast to the ways it appears in most modern translations. The Masoretic notations at the end of Ezra-Nehemiah attest to the unity of this book. Unity is also reflected in the ancient manuscript of the LXX (e.g., Codex Alexandrinus). Most modern editions of the Bible ignore these earliest traditions. They complicate the reading by treating Ezra and Nehemiah as two separate books, losing the thrust of the work as a whole.

2.5 Complications accrue on account of 1 Esdras, which preserves another ancient version of the restoration era, with many parallels to Ezra-Nehemiah. The existence of two such books has often called into question the priority and integrity of Ezra-Nehemiah, as scholars attempt to discern which work preceded. Debates about priority continue. One thing can be stated with certainty: we have two sacred traditions, both going back to antiquity. The reverence for both works is evident from the inclusion of Ezra-Nehemiah in the MT and LXX and from the inclusion of 1 Esdras in the LXX, reinforced by Josephus' reliance on 1 Esdras. The fact of the two traditions demonstrates that the early writers permitted themselves a large measure of freedom in handling their material. Apparently, the persons or circles responsible for these variants did not slavishly reproduce the documents in their possession but composed their work in order to communicate a specific perception of reality. This observation heightens, rather than diminishes, the importance of a literary analysis of each book. A comparison between the two serves to underscore Ezra-Nehemiah's steady focus on texts in contrast to 1 Esdras' focus on heroes (see Eskenazi, 1986: esp. 44-49).

2.6 In what follows, Ezra-Nehemiah will be examined as an integral unit, as the MT preserves it: separate, on the one hand, from Chronicles and, on the other, forming a single book which encompasses Ezra 1-10 and Nehemiah 1-13. The analysis of the book includes a general overview of forms, followed by a sketch of the book's structure, culminating with a more detailed development of a theme within the structure. Each of these elements in Ezra-Nehemiah, it is argued, contributes to the book's overriding concern with texts and a movement from text to actuality.

3.1 To begin to explicate Ezra-Nehemiah's drive toward textualization, one needs to look at the book's forms. Much of Ezra-

Nehemiah appears, even at a glance, as a collage of unintegrated documents. The following explicitly purport to be reproduced documents:

> Cyrus' decree (Ezra 1:2-4)
> Artaxerxes' correspondence (Ezra 4:7-22)
> Darius' correspondence (Ezra 5:6-6:12)
> Nehemiah's memoirs (Neh 1:1-7:5 and at least Neh 13:4-31)
> The list of returnees (Neh 7:6-72)
> The written pledge (Neh 10:1-40)

Other portions of the book are implicitly separate, written documents, e.g., the lists of Ezra 2, Ezra 8, Ezra 10, and Nehemiah 12; most likely Ezra's memoirs (Ezra 7:27-9:15) should be reckoned as a document as well. Transitions between such documents are often abrupt (to put it mildly), differentiating this book from others. Whereas other biblical books which utilize documents typically acknowledge them only in passing (e.g., Chronicles), Ezra-Nehemiah vividly displays its reliance on numerous reproduced sources.

3.2   Scholarly concerns with these sources invariably lead to discussions of authenticity, chronology, and original readings (see, e.g., Klein: 365-70). Those who deny the authenticity of some (or most) of these documents explain their presence in Ezra–Nehemiah as the book's attempt to attribute veracity and authority to the reports. The point which must be grasped, however, is *how* Ezra-Nehemiah chooses to affirm such veracity. The book does so by reference to written documents. The implication is clear: it is the written text which carries weight. The authoritative resides in writing. Neither miracles nor prophetic declarations constitute the relevant source of authority. The "library search" replaces divine intervention.

3.3   Ironically, this "documentary" stance of Ezra-Nehemiah has proved in the past an obstacle to literary assessment of the book. Moreover, the awkward transitions have been dismissed as a clumsy splicing job. J. A. Miles' wise counsel about ancient writers' skills, their ability to conceal and their willingness to reveal their hand, should alert us to the probable deliberateness of Ezra-Nehemiah's jarring characteristics. We should recognize the presence of so many documents as a dramatic example of the book's central emphasis on texts.

3.4   Ezra–Nehemiah uses documents to tell its story. It is a book of documents. These function as an important structural device. The steps that Ezra–Nehemiah takes to preserve these documents clearly underscore their importance from the book's perspective. They demonstrate Ezra–Nehemiah's view about the power and propriety of written texts as causative principles and significant forces in human events.

3.5   Texts, rather than the spoken word, come to occupy the center of attention in Ezra–Nehemiah, reflecting thereby a significant change. As Alter observes, in most biblical narrative the dialogue is crucial. "Everything in the world of biblical narrative ultimately gravitates toward dialogue" (182). The importance of speech accounts for the frequency with which narrated information is repeated in the form of direct speech. Such valuation of speech in the Bible means, according to Alter, that "quantitatively, a remarkably large part of the narrative burden is carried by dialogue, the transactions between characters typically unfolding through the words they exchange, with only the most minimal intervention of the narrator" (182).

3.6   In Ezra–Nehemiah, however, interactions of texts replace oral dialogue. The text functions in the place of speech. Written documents, such as the correspondence of Artaxerxes (Ezra 4:7-22), or the written lists (e.g., Neh 7:5-72), dominate, influence, and propel events. Important transactions are those between texts, e.g., letters to and from Darius (Ezra 5:6–6:12). As documents become primary conveyors of meaning and wisdom, the mouth and ear are augmented and occasionally superseded by the hand and the eye as the important tools of transmission. One notes, for example, the frequent references to the "hand" (Ezra 7:7, 9, 14, 25, 28; cf. prophetic emphases on mouth and ears, e.g., 1 Sam 6:7; Ezek 2:8; Jer 1:9). Even a pivotal oral performance is depicted as the actualization of the primary written text—namely, the oral reading of the Torah in the cultic assembly (Nehemiah 8). Such oral performance becomes a memorable and influential model precisely because it is given authoritative incorporation in still another written text, i.e., Ezra–Nehemiah. It is therefore not an overstatement to describe this process as a paradigm shift. The significance and consequences of such a shift touch not only on important issues in the intellectual history of late antiquity (see Havelock) but also on current debates in literary criticism (Handelman).

4.1   Ezra–Nehemiah's basic structure further underscores the book's emphasis on the written text, since the book as a whole is fundamentally the story about the actualization of texts. The specific structure of Ezra–Nehemiah is most clearly illuminated by the elements of story which the structuralist Claude Bremond charts. Using "story" as a basic component of narrative, Bremond (cited by Rimmon-Kenan: 22) lists the three formal features of story as follows:

> Potentiality (objective defined)
> Process of actualization (steps taken)
> Success (objective reached)

4.2   Bremond's categories allow us to recognize the following structure of Ezra–Nehemiah:

> I. Potentiality (objectives defined): decree to the community to build the house of God (Ezra 1:1-4)
> II. Process of actualization: the community builds the house of God according to decree (Ezra 1:5–Neh 7:72)
> III. Success (objective reached): the community dedicates the house of God according to Torah (Neh 8:1-13:31)

4.3   The book opens with a written decree and proceeds to show how it comes to be actualized (Ezra 1:5–Neh 7:72), concluding with the celebration of the successful completion of the decree. Put in a nutshell, Ezra–Nehemiah depicts how the community builds the house of God in accordance with authoritative documents.

4.4   Ezra–Nehemiah makes the point that all that transpires from Ezra 1:1 to Neh 13:31 is unified by the command of Israel's God coupled with the command of the three kings. The initial command, stated in Cyrus' decree (Ezra 1:2-4) and restated later (Ezra 6:2-4), is the basis for all that follows. The decree is only partly fulfilled in Ezra 6:14-22. The full execution of the task entails three distinct movements, each with its own specific role within the overall project, and with its own distinctive group of participants. The first movement, Ezra 1-6, depicts the fulfillment of the edict up through Darius' time. Two other movements in Artaxerxes' time bring it to completion (Ezra 7-10 and Nehemiah 1-7). Ezra 6:14 is a linchpin, summing up what preceded and informing us of what is yet to come: the completion of the house of God in Artaxerxes' time. It declares that completion occurred: "They finished their building by command of the God of Israel and by decree of Cyrus and Darius and Artaxerxes king of Persia" [English translations of biblical quotations follow the RSV unless otherwise noted]. The dedication activities that mark the final section of the book (Nehemiah 8-13) celebrate the success in fulfilling the decree(s). The various phases of the celebration unfold in accordance with significant texts, most prominently, the Torah.

5.1 Not only is the book as a whole structured in terms of actualizing documents, but the dynamics within each of the major units express in a persistent fashion Ezra-Nehemiah's concern with texts. Tracing the thematic developments within each major structural unit, as well as the relation between these units, helps demonstrate the tenacity and sophistication with which Ezra-Nehemiah expresses its emphasis on texts.

6. Potentiality (objectives defined): decree to the community to build the house of God (Ezra 1:1-4)

6.1 The opening notes of Ezra-Nehemiah sound the themes that will be played in a variety of rhythms and keys throughout the book. The first few verses introduce the three themes: the primacy of the community as a whole, not simply the leaders, as the real subject of the book; the building of the house of God; the centrality of the written text.

6.2 Cyrus' decree urges each member of God's people to go up and to build the house of God in Jerusalem (note the jussives "let him go up" and "let him build" in Ezra 1:3). The decree defines the objective of the book or, in Bremond's terms, the decree establishes potentiality. What will follow in subsequent chapters is the process of actualizing this potentiality, i.e., the fulfillment of the decree.

6.3 The first verse identifies the real impetus not only for Cyrus' decree but for virtually all that follows: "The LORD stirred up the

spirit of Cyrus" (Ezra 1:1). This verse also establishes a fundamental *modus operandi:* God works *indirectly.* God prompts humans to action. These promptings issue in decrees, in this case in
Cyrus' decree which is both oral (בקול) and written (במכתב).

6.4   For Ezra–Nehemiah, the God of heaven is the power behind
the earthly events, stirring humans to action while remaining behind the scenes. God's presence and command continue to find
their expression in the written documents. Ezra–Nehemiah focuses on the human or, more specifically, the communal implementation on earth of this divine command found in texts. Ezra–
Nehemiah differs from other post-exilic books which stress divine
initiative, e.g. Zechariah (Petersen: 299), in that it transforms divine initiative quickly into human action and into documents
which provide the guidelines for the divinely initiated human
task.

7. *Process of actualization: the community builds the house of God according to decree (Ezra 1:5-Neh 7:72)*

7.1   Ezra–Nehemiah's major part describes the human execution
of the decree by means of three movements. This is the "process
of actualization," structured as follows:

> A. Introduction: proleptic summary (Ezra 1:5-6)
> B. First movement (Ezra 1:7-6:22)
> C. Second movement (Ezra 7:1-10:44)
> D. Third movement (Neh 1:1-7:5)
> E. Recapitulation (Neh 7:6-7:72)

7.2   A repeated list of returnees, Ezra 2:1-70 and Neh 7:6-72,
frames this section. (Ezra 1:7 is linked with Ezra 2 and thus becomes an extension of the frame. On the basis for the unity of
Ezra 1:7-11 with the list of Ezra 2, see Eskenazi, 1988b.) The
repetition re-presents the major characters, provides continuity
for the section as a whole, and unifies the events in between. The
material within this framing device divides into three different
stories, each with its own specific "potentiality" (or "objective
defined"), "process of actualization," and "success" ("objective
reached"). These individual stories are embedded in the overall
structure ("Embedding" refers to a pattern in which "one sequence is inserted into another as a specification or detailing of
one of its functions" [Rimmon-Kenan: 23]). Each story comprises

a specific detail of the "process of actualization." All of them combine to complete the task. I label these three stories "movements" because they present three journeys from diaspora to Jerusalem. They also constitute distinct movements pertaining to different streams of populations. Each movement begins with preparations "over there" in the diaspora, as well as an introduction of the main characters. Each has its unique task and tension which are satisfactorily resolved by the end of that story. The first movement builds the altar (under Cyrus) and the temple (under Darius); the second builds up the community itself (under Artaxerxes); and the third finishes the house of God by restoring the wall (under Artaxerxes). Ezra 6:14 binds the movements thematically and sums up the central event of the book, stating that the returnees built the house of God according to divine decree and the decree of the three Persian kings. The recapitulation of the list of returnees (Nehemiah 7; cf. Ezra 2) combines all of these people and their activities. It articulates structurally what Ezra 6:14 spells out, namely, that the completion of the house of God spanned the reigns of these three Persian kings. The list also reiterates the fact that the central characters in the book are all of these people together. Although a distinct group dominates each movement, this resumptive repetition combines them all and thereby forms them into a single cast of characters for the entire section.

7.31   A proleptic summary introduces this process of actualization (Ezra 1:5-6), stating in embryonic fashion what Ezra 1:7–Neh 7:72 elaborates in detail. It announces the fulfillment of Cyrus' decree (and God's). The decree has summoned a people to go up and build the house of God (Ezra 1:1-4). Ezra 1:5-6 repeats that a community rose up promptly to execute this decree, going up to build. To borrow Hillel's famous phrase, "all the rest is commentary," Ezra 1:7–Neh 7:72 being that commentary.

7.32   The structure and vocabulary of this introduction largely parallels the decree, stressing thereby the close correspondence between the decree and its fulfillment. The jussives "let him go up" (ויעל) and "let him build" (ויבן) in Cyrus' decree (Ezra 1:3) become the infinitives "to go up" (לעלות) and "to build" (לבנות) in the people's response (Ezra 1:5). The royal exhortation to neighbors to support the returnees with freewill gifts of silver, gold, goods, and livestock (Ezra 1:4) is matched by the report that the neighbors strengthened the returnees with silver, gold, goods, and livestock (Ezra 1:6). Care is taken to show that the decree was carried out fully. The three movements provide an elaboration of the details of such communal response.

7.41 The first movement (Ezra 1:7–6:22) depicts how, after some preparations in exile, the returnees build the altar, reinstitute the cult, and proceed to build the temple. The central conflict erupts due to the opposition of the adversaries to the building. Resolution comes when the king authorizes the resumption of the work. The movement ends with celebration of the completed task.

7.42 Texts play the crucial role in expressing the conflict and in its resolution. The major events in this movement are propelled by letters and adhere to writings. Documents precipitate and guide the action. Furthermore, a large portion of Ezra 1:7–6:22 consists of reproduced documents.

7.43 The decree of Cyrus had triggered the events. The restatement of the decree (Ezra 6:3-5) highlights the continuing significance of that document in shaping subsequent developments. The eventual linking of the decree with other documents, appearing alongside it or as an extension, implies that what transpires is essentially the actualization of the written word. Indeed, documents determine all important events in this section.

7.44 One such document is the Torah of Moses. The edict of Cyrus is still the necessary background. But building the altar is also governed by what is written in the Torah of Moses: "they built the altar of the God of Israel, to offer burnt offerings upon it, as it is written in the law of Moses the man of God" (Ezra 3:2b). The repetition of the phrase "as it is written" (Ezra 3:4) stresses the theme of compliance with the definitive written documents and their fulfillment in the life of the community.

7.45 Further work ensues, presumably according to the Torah of Moses, but also linked specifically to Cyrus. Monies and provisions are given to workmen "according to the grant which they had from Cyrus king of Persia" (Ezra 3:7b). This new reference to Cyrus' decree highlights the continued impact of the initial document.

7.46   The invocation of Cyrus' decree in the central conflict of
this movement undergirds the rejection of the adversaries. Having offered to participate in the building project, the adversaries
are bluntly rejected: "You have nothing to do with us in building
a house to our God; but we alone will build to the LORD, the God
of Israel, as King Cyrus the king of Persia has commanded us"
(Ezra 4:3). The claim of "merely following orders" functions both
as a justification for building the house of God and, at the same
time, a means for exclusion from the people of God. In this fashion, the decree buttresses and defines both the house of God and
the composition of the people.

7.47   A series of letters follows, signaling, like traffic lights, "stop"
and "go" for the central action of the section, the building of the
house of God. The opposition to building expresses itself in documents which, in turn, refer to other documents. Ezra 4:6, 7, and
8 all reiterate the fact that letter writing was the primary ammu-
nition used by the opposition. Ezra 4:11-16 reproduces one such
letter. The letter itself, furthermore, urges the king to look for
other documents to corroborate and verify its claims: "therefore
we send and inform the king, in order that search may be made
in the book of the records of your fathers. You will find in the book
of the records and learn that this city is a rebellious city . . ." (Ezra
4:14b-15a). This document in turn generates still another document (Ezra 4:18-22) from Kings Artaxerxes, acknowledging re-
ceipt of the letter, referring to an earlier document as the basis of
his present decree, and alluding to a future one as well: "Therefore make a decree that these men be made to cease, and that this
city be not rebuilt, until a decree (טעם) is made by me" (Ezra
4:21). The king's letter effectively stops the building: "Then, when
the copy of King Artaxerxes' letter was read before Rehum and
Shimshai the scribe and their associates, they went in haste to the
Jews at Jerusalem and by force and power made them cease.
Then the work on the house of God which is in Jerusalem
stopped" (Ezra 4:23-24a). What we observe are documents within
documents, extending their influence back and forth in time.

7.48   Documents continue to control the process in the next chapters. The divinely guided prophetic voices initiating the next
phase (Ezra 5:1) are quickly channelled into written documents
which allow the action to materialize (Ezra 5:1-6:14). The pattern
of documents invoking other documents and empowering action

recurs. Just as obstacles had been generated by documents (Ezra 4:6-24), so too resolution (Ezra 5:1-6:14) comes through documents.

7.49   In this episode (Ezra 5:1–6:14), royal representatives inform the Persian king about suspicious building activities in Jerusalem and ask for instructions. In their letter, the representatives report that the builders invoke Cyrus' decree to justify their activities and to demonstrate continuity from the time of Cyrus to the present (Ezra 5:13). They urge the king by letter (Ezra 5:6-17) to look for this document in his archives (Ezra 5:17). The search yields a memorandum about Cyrus' decree. Ezra–Nehemiah reproduces this memorandum (Ezra 6:3-5) by incorporating it into another letter (Ezra 6:6-12). Whereas the earlier "library search" ("may [a search] be made in the book of the records of your fathers. You will find in the book of the records and learn that this city is a rebellious city," Ezra 4:15) had subverted building activities, the new "library search" ("Let a search be made in the royal archives," Ezra 5:17) reverses the situation. The work resumes in the wake of this exchange of documents. Darius, the present Persian monarch, not only affirms Cyrus' decree but exceeds it in generosity (Ezra 6:13a).

7.51   We see, then, that Ezra 1-6 is practically propelled by written texts. Past and present documents work together, leading to the fulfillment of divine and royal command. A key verse is 6:14. Here the edict of God and the edict of the three kings combine both to explain the success of the Judeans and to expand the task even further into the future. Ezra 6:15 reports the completion and dedication of the temple. This, however, represents only a partial actualization of Cyrus' edict. The report is prefaced, therefore, with a statement which unifies the decree of Cyrus with those of Darius and Artaxerxes, extending it (and the work itself) into completion at some future point. Ezra 6:14b states, "They finished their building by decree of the God of Israel and by decree of Cyrus and Darius and Artaxerxes king of Persia" (my translation; the RSV obscures the analogy between royal decree and God's by translating טעם once as "command" and once as "decree"). An intriguing transmutation has taken place. Actual completion and final success must await the execution of the decree of Artaxerxes (טעם) which is combined with that of Cyrus and Darius and is simultaneously consonant with the decree (טעם) of the God of

Israel. The singular "king of Persia" applies to all three kings as a single unit, as if they spoke with one voice. Likewise the *decree* of the three kings appears in the singular as if it were a single decree. Such indeed is Ezra–Nehemiah's message: divine decree and royal decree, spanning various eras and persons, fundamentally constitute one event.

7.52   The section closes with celebration and the appointment of priests and Levites, (ככתב ספר משה) "as it is written in the book of Moses" (6:18). The significance of texts is thus again reaffirmed. Nothing of consequence transpires in this movement except by the authorizing power of a written document. As royal decree and divine written word become actualized, one is projected forward, thematically and structurally, toward the next document, the decree of Artaxerxes, and the completion of the project under Artaxerxes' guidance.

7.61   The second movement (Ezra 7:1–10:44) depicts the "going up" of Ezra and other children of exile. The book's emphasis on texts appears in two major ways in these chapters: first, in the connection between Ezra and a document, i.e., Ezra as scribe of the book of the Torah; second, in the way one document (Artaxerxes' letter) empowers another (the law in Ezra's hand). This latter point also replicates Ezra–Nehemiah's pattern in which documents precipitate action, propel the story, and propagate other documents.

7.62   The emphatic bonding of Ezra with the book of Torah in the introduction exemplifies the significance of the text. Ezra is clearly Ezra–Nehemiah's outstanding individual. The literary marking for this claim include his remarkable introduction. Ezra appears with the longest pedigree and the longest introduction in the book. The exceptional length of the introduction signifies his importance, as does the literary technique of characterization which combines pedigrees, epithets, and direct definitions by the narrator and the Persian king. Here the normally unobtrusive narrator, who rarely intrudes with privileged information in Ezra–Nehemiah, steps forth and vouches for Ezra's mission and credentials. No other person receives such an imprimatur. The narrator first defines Ezra by means of a reference to the book, quickly establishing the book's centrality. Ezra is ספר מהיר בתורת משה אשר נתן יהוה אלהי ישראל, a "scribe skilled in the Law of Moses which the LORD God of Israel had given" (Ezra 7:6). The prominence of Ezra's scribal role might surprise those who would expect a priest with such superlative credentials to be primarily associated with the cult; it highlights, however, not only Ezra's primary textual orientation but also Ezra–Nehemiah's.

7.63   Epithets designating Ezra as scribe multiply, exemplifying Ezra–Nehemiah's interest. As Sternberg, for instance, demonstrates, epithets in biblical narrative are not merely reported for the sake of realism. In the Hebrew Bible formal epithets "enter into tight relations with the patterns that surround them" (331). One of their most important functions "consists in laying the ground for plot developments. . . . Ostensibly descriptive of the statics of character, all these epithets are implicitly proleptic within the dynamics of action" (331). Epithets are "a ticking bomb, sure to explode into action in the narrator's (and God's) own good time" (339). In Ezra's case epithets recur, supplied by the narrator (Ezra 7:6, 11) and king (Ezra 7:12). All of them stress his scribal affiliation. The double emphasis in the repetition of the root ספר in Ezra 7:11 is particularly noteworthy: לעזרא הכהן הספר ספר דברי מצות יהוה. The RSV, like most translations, obscures the double emphasis, rendering, "Ezra the priest, the scribe, learned in matters of the commandments of the LORD," even though both "scribe" and "learned" are the same root. Ezra–Nehemiah, however, intensifies its emphasis by such double repetition.

7.64   The initial designation of Ezra as ספר מהיר בתורת משה (Ezra 7:6) contains certain ambiguities. The implications of מהיר are not clear, as is evident from the variety of English translations of the term. RSV translates it as "skilled." L. W. Batten speaks of "a ready scribe in the law of Moses" (304). F. C. Fensham has "a secretary well versed in the law of Moses" (97). Nor is the term ספר wholly understood (see Fensham: 72, and Ackroyd, 1973: 241). "Scribe" could reflect an official title or a profession. Scribes appear elsewhere in the Hebrew Bible, but their range of authority and expertise is not always clear (e.g. Shaphan in 2 Kgs 22:3 and Baruch in Jeremiah 36) beyond the obvious connection with writing.

7.65   Ezra is the scribe of the words of the commandments of Yhwh (Ezra 7:11), as well as a scribe skilled in the Torah of Moses which Yhwh gave (Ezra 7:6). This designation is unique in the

Hebrew Bible. Other references to "scribe" in construct forms specify the scribe of the king (2 Kgs 12:11 and the parallel in 2 Chr 24:11), the scribe of the commander of the army (Jer 52:25), and the scribe of the prophet (Baruch, Jeremiah 36). On occasion, the term occurs in the absolute, as in the case of Shaphan, the scribe who was a member of Josiah's court (2 Kings 22). That particular story makes clear, however, that Shaphan's expertise does not extend to the book of the Torah, since he is at a loss about the book's nature and the prophet Huldah has to be consulted. The scribe in the Hebrew Bible is paired, several times, with a priest, while at the same time differentiated from the priest (2 Sam 8:17; 20:25; 2 Kgs 12:11 and 2 Kings 22). All of these functions parallel the roles of scribes in the ancient Near East as royal functionaries or trained writers/readers subservient to kings or to whoever hires them (Wiseman: 30-47, esp. 35-42). Ezra's role, as defined within Ezra-Nehemiah, is clear and also unique: his master is neither king nor prophet, nor military prince, but the words of Yhwh as transcribed in the Torah of Moses. Ezra is a scribe at the service of a book; his primary affiliation and primary allegiance are to the Torah. If one glides too swiftly over the characterization of Ezra as a scribe of the Torah, it is largely because the very success of the innovation made in this era has blunted our sensitivity to Ezra-Nehemiah's peculiar synthesis. Whatever priestly Torah may have meant for the prophets or pre-exilic writers, here is a book, and its priest is first and foremost a scribe. This is the only occasion in the Hebrew Bible where the two functions are explicitly combined or, rather, fused. One of Ezra's chief contributions in Ezra-Nehemiah may in fact be this fusion. It is also Ezra-Nehemiah's contribution to subsequent Judaism.

7.66   The content and extent of Ezra's Torah remain debatable (Klein). Several different appellations occur in Ezra 7 alone: "the law (תורה) of the LORD" (Ezra 7:10), the Lord's statutes for Israel (Ezra 7:11b), "the דת of the God of heaven" (Ezra 7:12). These terms could have originally referred to diverse documents, not to what has become identified as the book of Torah (Rendtorff). Ezra-Nehemiah in its present form, however, effectively equates all these documents, largely through repetitive linking with Ezra, both in the introduction (Ezra 7:1-10) and in Artaxerxes' letter (cf. 7:12, 14b, 21, 25). Ezra-Nehemiah uses various labels for these documents as equivalencies. The inevitable inference is that for Ezra-Nehemiah the Torah of Moses is the Torah of Yhwh; it is the words of the commandments of Yhwh; and it is, finally, the חז of Ezra's God. The terms have become synonyms for the Torah whose scribe Ezra is.

7.67   This solid linking of Ezra and the book of the Torah places the text in the forefront, together with Ezra. It implies that where Ezra is, there also is the book whose scribe he is. The prominence of Ezra goes hand in hand with the prominence of the book.

7.68   Other elements in this movement also express the binding significance of texts. The function and content of Artaxerxes' letter (Ezra 7:12-26) are an example. Like other documents in Ezra–Nehemiah, the letter initiates activities, thus governing the flow of the movement. Set at the beginning of the account, before Ezra himself appears on stage, the letter reflects the recurrent pattern in which unfolding events are the fulfillment of written texts.

7.69   The report about the letter (Ezra 7:6b) precedes the report about the return (Ezra 7:7a). As in the case of Cyrus' decree—and in order to parallel it—the narrator also vouches for divine participation in this occasion. This letter, somewhat like Cyrus' decree, has God's backing in some definite, even though nebulous, fashion: "for the hand of the LORD his God was upon him" (Ezra 7:6b).

7.71   An even more pointed emphasis on texts occurs within the letter itself. In the first place, the letter authorizes Ezra to implement the law of his God. In the second place, it enforces the law of the king and the law of Ezra's God in tandem, equating them, by inference, as the authoritative documents for Judah and for the rest of Ezra–Nehemiah.

7.72   The stress on the law of Ezra's God is particularly strong in both the frame and center of the letter. Ezra is addressed by the king as "the priest, the scribe of the law of the God of heaven" (Ezra 7:12). His mission is to inquire about Judah and Jerusalem "according to the law of your God, which is in your hand" (Ezra 7:14). Artaxerxes' instructions to his officials underscore the importance of that law (Ezra 7:21-23). And finally the conclusion of the letter reiterates the importance of the law with a double emphasis:

> And you, Ezra, according to the *wisdom of your God which is in your hand,* appoint magistrates and judges who may judge all the people in the province Beyond the River, all such as know *the laws of your God;* and those who do not know them, you shall teach. *Whoever will not obey the law of your God and the law of the king,* let judgment be strictly executed upon him . . . (7:25-26).

Fensham's translation of v 26, although not literal, captures the implications: "Everyone who does not comply with the law of your God—*it is also the law of the king*—let judgment be diligently meted out to him: death, corporal punishment, confiscation, or imprisonment" (102, emphasis added). On sheer grammatical grounds, די אלהך ודתא די מלכא דתא does not necessarily have the emphasis Fensham includes. The two "laws" are simply connected by the conjunction "and." Nevertheless, Fensham is correct in drawing the implications. In Artaxerxes' letter, the bottom line (literally and metaphorically) is that the law of the God of heaven is also the law of the king. Both have been written down and are now in Ezra's hand to be implemented.

7.73   Artaxerxes' letter positions the law of Ezra's God as an authoritative document together with the law of the king. As in Ezra 6:14, Ezra–Nehemiah envisions no tension between the two (Whedbee). The Torah of Moses and the command of the king work together. The one supports the other. Adherence to the one implies adherence to the other. Heavenly ruler and earthly ruler collaborate for the sake of the house of God. Having combined these sources of authority and having established the dual affirmation of the book of the Torah, Ezra–Nehemiah can now leave behind any further references to the law of the earthly king and proceed with sole attention to the book of the Torah. Both of these writings have been already sanctioned by the king. This book of Torah, this written text, will henceforth govern communal life.

7.81   The third movement (Neh 1:1–7:5) depicts the building activities of Nehemiah and the Judeans. Although written documents seem to be less central here than in the surrounding material, the very form of the unit demonstrates the importance of texts. The heading, "The words of Nehemiah son of Hacaliah" (Neh 1:1), as an internal superscription (cf. e.g., Isa 2:1) indicates that what follows is a document. Superscriptions, after all, reflect the fact that the words "have already been committed to writing"

(Tucker: 65-66). The end of the section refers to yet another document: a list which Nehemiah uses (and the book reproduces, Neh 7:5). The perpetuation of documents thus persists.

7.82   Between these markers we find concern with documents in Nehemiah's encounter with the king and in his conflict with opponents. In the first case, Nehemiah, having been granted permission to build, boldly requests that the king's words be transcribed into letters (Neh 2:7-8). In the second case, Nehemiah's confrontations with his detractors take place through letters. Sanballat, attempting to ensnare Nehemiah (according to Nehemiah's assessment of the motive), sends letters: "Sanballat for the fifth time sent his servant to me with an open letter in his hand. In it was written, 'It is reported among the nations, and Geshem also says it, that you and the Jews intend to rebel'" (Neh 6:5-6a). The interaction with other opponents also transpires through letters (Neh 6:17-19), continuing the "dialogue" via documents. Thus Nehemiah states:

> . . . the nobles of Judah sent many letters to Tobiah, and Tobiah's letters came to them. For many in Judah were bound by oath to him, because he was the son-in law of Shecaniah. . . . Also they spoke of his good deeds in my presence, and reported my words to him. And Tobiah sent letters to make me afraid (Neh 6:17-19).

7.83   The most significant use of documents in this section occurs at the conclusion, when Nehemiah resorts to a written document in order to resolve the population problem: "Then God put it into my mind to assemble the nobles and the officials and the people to be enrolled by genealogy. And I found the book of the genealogy (היחש ספר) of those who came up at the first, and I found written in it" (Neh 7:5). The following section, Neh 7:6-72, next reproduces the document *in toto*. Here the prescription for settling the rebuilt city requires a document to which Nehemiah turns. Just as Cyrus' decree was recalled earlier to provide a model and authority (Ezra 5:13–6:5), so now the "book of genealogy" is recalled as a "voice" from the past to guide the present. It prepares the restored community for the celebration of its completed house of God.

7.9   The process of actualization concludes with "Recapitulation: The List of Returnees" (Neh 7:6-72)—a virtual repetition of the earlier list (Ezra 2). The repetition of the list constitutes one of Ezra–Nehemiah's most striking aspects and has baffled interpreters. Scholars frequently have used it as evidence against the unity of Ezra-Nehemiah (see, e.g., Talmon: 318). From a literary perspective, the repetition re-presents the major characters, i.e., the people of Israel as a whole. Since a stable set of characters helps differentiate between a genuine event and a series of unrelated episodes (Rimmon-Kenan:19), the repetition of the list, among other things, affirms the unity of the intervening material as a single event. The written list (note: "I found written in it," Neh 7:5), as a resumptive repetition of Ezra 2 in Nehemiah 7, clamps together everything and everyone in between, i.e., the earlier movements and characters from Ezra 2 to Nehemiah 7. The past is united with the present. Previous generations become partners in present events through the text. They are brought together in order to celebrate the long-awaited completion of the house of God in accordance with God's and Cyrus' decree.

8. Success (Objective Reached): the community dedicates the house of God according to Torah (Neh 8:1–13:31)

8.1   In its final section, celebrating success, Ezra–Nehemiah articulates the authority of the written text through a formal structure organized around documents, and through content describing how documents hold the community's center of attention. The structure is as follows:

> A. Four implementations of the Torah (Neh 8:1–10:40)
> B. Recapitulation: list of participants (Neh 11:1–12:26)
> C. The dedication of the house of God (Neh 12:27– 13:3)
> D. Coda (Neh 13:4-31)

People and Torah are intimately bound in this section. The book of the Torah which had already received full royal imprimatur in Ezra 7 now continues as the primary source of authority. It is from the Torah that behavior issues (Neh 8:1) and to the Torah that the community turns for further instructions (Neh 8:13). The dedication ceremonies themselves conclude with the reading and implementation of the Torah (Neh 13:1-3).

8.21   Neh 8:1-10:40 can be characterized as flowing out of and flowing into documents. The section is composed of four imple mentations of the Torah, each demonstrating not only how the reading *was* done but, more to the point, how it *should* be done and *that* it should be done. It depicts three assemblies (Neh 8:1-12; Neh 8:13-18; Neh 9:1-37; note the repetition of אסף, "gather," in Neh 8:1; 8:13; 9:1, beginning each unit) in which the reading of the Torah takes place (Neh 8:1; 8:13-14; 9:3). These readings of the text issue in a written pledge (Neh 10:1-40). One notes, above all, the public, communal character of the Torah reading. Access to the Torah, to its content and implications, is to be made available to all people: men, women, and whoever is capable of under-standing (Neh 8:3). Conversely, the Torah takes a primary place in public worship. Worship becomes "Torah-centric." At the end, Ezra vanishes. Torah remains. What is written continues to be carried out, as the repetition of "the written" in Neh 8:14 and 8:15 stresses, without Ezra's explicit presence.

8.22   The importance of the text is directly introduced when, at the very outset, the assembled people ask Ezra to bring the Torah (Neh 8:1). This opening scene (Neh 8:1-12) devotes itself to a detailed account of the public reading of the Torah, replete with repetitions of "book" and "Torah" (Neh 8:1,2,3,5,8).

8.23   There is an intense emphasis on the bonding of the people with the book of the Torah that sets the tone for the rest of the book. The people remain unequivocally in the foreground. The word עם occurs thirteen times in the first twelve verses (Neh 8:1, 3,5 [three times],6,7 [twice],9 [three times],11,12). The public reading of the Torah engages the whole community; men, wom-en, and children assemble and respond, a response that initially leads to tears but culminates in great joy (8:12).

8.31   The first reading leads to a second (Neh 8:13-18) in which community leaders come to "Ezra the scribe" (i.e., Ezra in his scribal capacity) to learn Torah (Neh 8:13). The section provides an important glimpse into the process wherein the Torah replaces the individual leader. The "heads of fathers' houses of all the people, with the priests and the Levites" (Neh 8:13) come to Ezra to become enlightened. The narrator reports that "they found it written in the law" (Neh 8:14). The text does not say, "Ezra told them," nor "Ezra showed them," but states that *they* themselves now find the commandments in the Torah. Much to one's amaze-ment, Ezra has disappeared, giving way to the book. The people themselves immediately execute the written injunction which they found and joyfully celebrate Succoth.

8.32 This second implementation of the Torah closes with the statement: "And day by day, from the first day to the last day, he read from the book of the law of God. They kept the feast seven days" (Neh 8:18). The singular verb ויקרא, without an immediately identifiable subject, has led many scholars to insert Ezra's name, even though such textual emendation is not supported, even by the LXX. The MT, however, implies that Ezra has accomplished his task and then vanished, leaving the community holding the book, as it were.

8.41 The third assembly (Neh 9:1-37) also involves a reading of the Torah (Neh 9:2b-3a). As the ceremony progresses, no single individual rises up to conduct it. The people remain the subject of the verbs. They stand up, they confess, they read the Torah. Only then do certain Levites rise up to what approximates a leadership role. One notes that they do so jointly. Again, the plural subject has a singular verb. ויקם is followed by the plural subject of several Levites in Neh 9:4, implying here, as in each of the previous units, a unison of voices. Ezra himself is not named in the MT of Nehemiah 9. The ceremony thus represents, as D. J. A. Clines says, "a popular reaction to the reading of the law, not a service conducted by Ezra" (1984: 189-90).

8.42 A lengthy prayer (Neh 9:5b-37) dominates this section and constitutes a third implementation of Torah. The shift into the prayer in the MT obscures the identity of the speakers, who could be either the Levites or, more probably (on the basis of Neh 10:1 where the community as a whole is the identified "author"), the people themselves. The breadth of knowledge of Israel's traditions that the prayer exhibits speaks well for the chanting community. As J. M. Myers observes, "The author of our prayer psalm drew upon a wide knowledge of the theology and traditions of his people, skillfully weaving into it elements of instruction, exhortation, and confession" (169-70). Such breadth of knowledge testifies loudly to the fact that the people have learned well from their teacher. Having learned Torah, having read the book of the Torah (Neh 9:3), the people demonstrate a new competence, a new understanding of what they have read, and prove able to translate these into commitment and action. This recitation of the people's history, meaningfully aware of the relationship between God and Israel, is also, thereby, another example of implementing the Torah.

8.51 The fourth unit (Neh 10:1-40) reproduces a *written* pledge (Neh 10:1) by all the people (Neh 10:1-29) to observe the Torah (Neh 10:30b), with detailed obligations for the house of God (Neh 10:31-40). There has been an incremental progression, with an ever intensifying display of commitment by the community to the Torah. As the community's response to their earlier readings (Neh 10:1) and rectification of a history of violations (previously acknowledged in Nehemiah 9), the pledge reflects yet another facet of having learned Torah well. The literary setting of the pledge, the nature of the pledge as an interpretive process of Torah, the dynamics of this event as a covenant ceremony—all demonstrate the central place of the text in the life of the community.

8.52 Scholars dispute the original setting of the pledge but usually concur that this chapter is dislocated. Clines would place the chapter after Nehemiah 13, "There can be little doubt . . . that these halakot are *ad hoc* responses to problems encountered by Nehemiah in his so-called second governorship; for all the items except the sabbatical and remission year correspond to elements of Nehemiah 13" (114). Ezra–Nehemiah, however, presents the reforms as neither Ezra's nor Nehemiah's but as the spontaneous response of a repentant community to their reading of the Torah.

8.53 The pledge which contains an oath to observe the Torah (Neh 10:30) is tightly knit—albeit awkwardly—with what preceded. The expression וּבְכָל זֹאת (10:1) establishes a definite causal relation between the preceding readings and the pledge. The awkwardness of the connection has encouraged the separation of the two chapters. But as D. J. McCarthy points out,

> The rough Hebrew may mark a join between sources, but this does not diminish the important fact: the chapters are joined. On the contrary, the struggle to put two sections together shows that the compiler—if any—found the sequence so necessary to his idea of covenant-renewal that he paid the price of clumsiness to express it (34).

What Ezra–Nehemiah expresses by means of this connection is that the people have made a written commitment to the Torah as a result of their prior readings of the Torah. The one text has led to action and generated yet another text.

8.54   This pledge (אמנה), often labelled "covenant" and understood as a covenant ceremony spanning Nehemiah 8-10, has been compared with covenant renewal ceremonies in Chronicles. Scholars from Zunz to Clines (1981: 114) allude to similarities, particularly between Nehemiah 8-10 and the famous reading of the law under Josiah (2 Chronicles 34). But a closer inspection of the two readings fails to reveal any compelling parallels. Differences in structure, content, and emphasis stand out. One searches in vain for any common denominators beyond the mere fact of a public reading followed, at some interval, by a festival (Passover for Chronicles; Succoth for Ezra–Nehemiah). Furthermore, Ezra–Nehemiah shares these few common features with 2 Kings 23 as well, discounting thereby any unique relationship between Chronicles and Ezra–Nehemiah on this subject. As a matter of fact, Chronicles' own modifications of 2 Kings at this point actually accentuates differences from Ezra–Nehemiah: 2 Chronicles minimizes the impact and import of the Torah by having the greater bulk of Josiah's reforms *precede* the discovery of the book (2 Chr 34:3-7), whereas 2 Kings shows them as a result of the implementing of the book (2 Kgs 23:4-20). In this, Chronicles goes counter to the emphases of Ezra–Nehemiah.

8.55   McCarthy sums up the important differences in covenant renewal ceremonies in these books. He notes that in Ezra–Nehemiah, in contrast to Chronicles, "there is emphasis on a written law. This is not alien to Chronicles, but the change of emphasis is notable. The Chronicler honored 'the book of the law,' but it is at the very heart of Ezra–Nehemiah" (35). Ezra–Nehemiah also differs from Deuteronomy. In Deuteronomy (e.g., Deut 26:17-19), the people pledge themselves to God; "the first step is a pledge whose object is a personal relationship, the law a guide for living out that relationship. In Nehemiah the law itself is the object of the pledge" (McCarthy: 26). For Ezra–Nehemiah, the pledge is to the Torah itself, dramatically heightening the emphasis on the book.

8.56   The link between the people and the book intensifies in Nehemiah 8-10, as does the link between the people and the house of God. The commitment to the one becomes tantamount to a commitment to each other. The community, having coalesced—

as a community, around the Torah, and in relation to the house of God—finally embodies the goals of Cyrus' decree. It has gone up and built the house of God in Jerusalem which is in Judah. It has also demonstrated who the people of God are.

8.6   The Recapitulation (Neh 11:1–12:26) is primarily made up of lists and hence, presumably, reproduced documents. Lists of settlers (Neh 11:1-36) are followed by lists of cultic personnel (Neh 12:1-26). Thus documents retrace names of cultic personnel from the beginning of the book to the present (cf. Neh 12:1 and Ezra 2:1). Only after the recapitulation of persons does the actual dedication of the house of God take place.

8.7   The Torah that opened the ceremonies in Neh 8:1 also closes the dedication ceremonies in Neh 13:1-3. As Ezra–Nehemiah reaches its conclusion, the book of Moses is read again in public (Neh 13:1-3). The written text is then implemented, interpreted to apply to the present time. Thus, the finale ("on that day," Neh 13:1) depicts a community that has purified itself from all dross on the basis of what is written. The final sentence reiterates the significance of Torah: "When the people heard the law (תורה), they separated from Israel all those of foreign descent" (Neh 13:3). The document envelopes the celebration from beginning to end.

8.81   The book closes with a coda (Neh 13:4-31). This coda, trailing like an afterthought and looping back to a time before the climax of the celebration, is anchored in the preceding event, as the beginning indicates: "Now before this" (Neh 13:4). The section functions as an appendix to the book, summarizing earlier material, but narrated this time from the perspective of Nehemiah, who is granted the last word.

8.82   The role of the text emerges from the juxtaposition of the material about Nehemiah's self-proclaimed reforms in the coda (Nehemiah 13) and the reforms in the pledge of Nehemiah 10. Nehemiah's reforms consist of purifying the cult, restoring effective tithing, enforcing observance of the Sabbath, and attacking mixed marriages. According to Nehemiah, he himself energetically imposes these measures, acknowledging no overt support from the community. These obligations, however, have been assumed by the community in the earlier pledge (Nehemiah 10).

8.83 The striking parallels between material in Nehemiah 13 and Nehemiah 10 invite an assessment of their relationship. Clines, along with others, presumes that, historically speaking, the material in Nehemiah 13 precedes Nehemiah 10 and precipitates the pledge of Nehemiah 10 (1984: 245). Accordingly, Nehemiah 13 describes Nehemiah's initial measures, namely, his direct intervention to resolve problems he encountered; Nehemiah 10 is a later, more measured, response in order to cope with these same problems on a long- term basis.

8.84 A. Jepsen, in one of the most thorough studies of Nehemiah 10, also wrestles with the similarities between the two chapters. He observes the implicit conflict between the two claims of Nehemiah 10 and 13: the pledge declares that the reforms were freely instigated by the community as a whole; Nehemiah is silent about any such previous reforms or obligations (101). Nehemiah's silence and the incongruity between the two accounts impel Jepsen to disengage Nehemiah 10 from Nehemiah himself.

8.85 What is pertinent for our present purpose is the effect of the juxtaposition of Nehemiah 10 and 13. The arrangement in Ezra–Nehemiah ascribes the reforms to the community as a whole, making Nehemiah's activities essentially the administering of communally ordained regulations. Consequently, despite Nehemiah's silence about the origin of his reforms, the book of Ezra–Nehemiah is so structured that his reforms appear to be the result of that earlier document. Nehemiah simply implements the commitments specified in the written pledge (Nehemiah 10). In this sense the book concludes with the governor's execution of the community's written religious and social commitments. Once again, life flows from writings.

8.86 By appending Nehemiah's reforms to the conclusion of the book, Ezra–Nehemiah casts shadows on the finale as a whole. This protects the reader from confusing the "ideal community" (as Clines [1984: 234] refers to it in connection with Neh 12:44–13:3) with an idyllic or idealized community. The recurrence of problems and the necessity of repeated resolutions permeate the book. They preclude an innocent illusion of a happy "ever-after." Problems have to be addressed anew in each generation. Sacred documents guide the community in the resolution of these problems. Remembrance by God and community attends those who set their heart and hand to implement these documents and thereby care for the house of God.

8.9   Ezra–Nehemiah closes with a community not so much restored to some earlier, familiar state, but rather living up to a prophetic vision in which sanctity pervades the people and city as a whole. The words of the Torah take root in the daily life of the people who recite and practice them. Unmitigated joy engulfs the celebrating community. Cyrus' decree has been finally fulfilled.

9.1   It is commonplace to credit Ezra with the establishment of the Torah as the governing document for post-exilic Israel. This study has demonstrated that Ezra–Nehemiah's drive toward textualization is far more pervasive than that. Ezra's own activities are but one component of a programmatic and persistent actualization of the text in the community's life. Ezra–Nehemiah's forms, structure, and thematic developments collaborate in articulating the significance of texts. The concern with the execution of the written text defines the shape of the book and finds expression within the smaller units. The overall structure proceeds from the decree of Cyrus to its final fulfillment, celebrated with much fanfare in Nehemiah 12–13. As the book now stands, this completion is only partly fulfilled in Ezra 6:14-21. The text sums this up: "They finished their building by the command (טעם) of the God of Israel and by the decree (טעם) of Cyrus and Darius and Artaxerxes king of Persia" (Ezra 6:14). Ezra 1:5–Neh 7:72, unified through the list of returnees, is also unified by the command of the three kings. The central command, stated in Cyrus' decree (Ezra 1:2-4) and reiterated (Ezra 6:2-4), is the basis for all that follows, supplemented by the decrees of Darius and Artaxerxes, perceived (according to Ezra 6:14) as essentially the same decree.

9.2   This drive toward textualization may be rooted in the Persian context; note, for example, the reverence toward texts in Herodotus' account (128). Whatever its origin, the emphasis on the written in Ezra–Nehemiah reaches a new height and new significance. The interplay of documents in Ezra–Nehemiah—book, letters, written edicts—acknowledges the written word as effective and active in the world. This theme is of theological and political import. It subjects human life and history to the execution of the divine mission which is given in a written document. It represents a paradigm shift from the sanctity of the oral to the sanctity of the written. Prophets still speak, but the real force behind the events manifests itself in writing. Now God's word is found in a book (e.g., Neh 8:14). The text replaces the charismatic leader. Human leaders are best when they help implement the teachings of the written document—as does Ezra. The text is (literally) an open book, a publicly accessible source of power to be shared equally with men, women, and whoever is capable of understanding (Neh 8:2), not the private channel of communication between God and an elite.

9.3   The drive toward textualization not only divests charismatic individuals from power but also places constraints on the divine impulses. J. C. Exum, who notes the ambiguous character of the deity in Judges, argues that, in Judges, the text "acknowledges God's complicity" in the chaos and dissolution. A case for the ambiguous role of God in Israel's destiny can also be made on the basis of other historical books, especially Samuel (note, in particular, the largely inexplicable rejection of Saul in 1 Sam 15:10-35). Ezra-Nehemiah curtails such powers by emphasis on the book.

9.4   The shift of the book, which Ezra-Nehemiah promulgates on multiple levels, proves decisive for subsequent Judaism and also sets the stage for the scriptural orientation of the other "peoples of the Book." The following Talmudic story provides one of many examples of the way the primacy of the text had become entrenched in rabbinic Judaism. Moreover, it illustrates something about the significance of the shift: In his dispute with the other rabbis, R. Eliezer invokes (and receives) divine intervention in support of his interpretation of Torah. The rabbis, however, dismiss even the intercession of a heavenly voice, arguing that the Torah is not in heaven. It has been given at Sinai, it is written down, and is to be interpreted communally, in accordance with majority rule. God, the rabbinic story continues, laughed approvingly over the rabbis' decision to ignore even divine intercession (b. B. Meṣ. 59b).

9.5   Ezra-Nehemiah's emphasis on the written mode combines with the other two themes to deflect the limelight from the heroic individual to a life lived in community, gathered around the book. In its own prosaic fashion, Ezra-Nehemiah has moved step by step to implement and actualize the vision of a holy people in a holy city. It does not envisage such holiness in glowing, supernatural terms but in very mundane ones. Ideals are implemented daily, inch by inch, in the process of translating Torah into life, in the tenacity of diverse and numerous people working together, in ceremonies which sanctify city, people, and book. Ezra–Nehemiah's quietistic way supersedes the dazzling splendor of the Davidic monarchy, providing an enduring model, a way of life, that the rabbinic sages assiduously seek to emulate.

WORKS CONSULTED

Ackroyd, Peter R.
   1973   *I & II Chronicles, Ezra, Nehemiah.* Torch Bible Commentaries. London: SCM Press.

Alter, Robert
   1981   *The Art of Biblical Narrative.* New York: Basic Books.

Bar-Efrat, S.
   1979   *The Art of the Biblical Story.* Jerusalem: Siffriat Hapoalim [Hebrew].

Batten, L. W.
   1913   *A Critical and Exegetical Commentary on the Books of Ezra and Nehemiah.* ICC. New York: Charles Scribner's Sons.

Berlin, Adele
   1983   *Poetics and Interpretation of Biblical Narrative.* Sheffield: Almond Press.

Childs, B. S.
   1979   *Introduction to the Old Testament as Scripture.* Philadelphia: Fortress Press.

Clines, David, J. A.
   1981   "Nehemiah 10 as an Example of Early Jewish Biblical Exegesis." *JSOT* 21:111-117.
   1984   *Ezra, Nehemiah, Esther.* The New Century Bible Commentary. Grand Rapids: Eerdmans.

Eskenazi, Tamara C.
   1986   "The Chronicler and the Composition of 1 Esdras." *CBQ* 48:39-61.
   1988a   *In an Age of Prose: A Literary Approach to Ezra-Nehemiah.* SBL Monograph Series. Atlanta: Scholars Press.

1988b   "The Structure of Ezra–Nehemiah and the Integrity of the Book." *JBL* 107.

Exum, J. Cheryl
forth-   "Narrative Strategies in Judges." Ed. Kent H. Rich-
coming   ards. *Semeia*.

Fensham, F. C.
1982   *The Books of Ezra and Nehemiah*. The New International Commentary on the Old Testament. Grand Rapids: Eerdmans.

Fokkelman, Jan P.
1975   *Narrative Art in Genesis*. Assen: Van Gorcum.

Handelman, Susan A.
1982   *The Slayers of Moses*. Albany: State University of New York Press.

Havelock, Eric A.
1963   *Preface to Plato*. Cambridge, MA: The Belknap Press of Harvard University Press.

Heller, Erich
1984   *In the Age of Prose*. Cambridge: Cambridge University Press.

Herodotus.
1972 ed.   *The Histories*. Trans. A. de Delincourt. Middlesex: Penguin Books.

Japhet, Sara
1983   "People and Land in the Restoration Period." Pp. 103-125 in *Das Land Israel im biblischer Zeit*. Ed. N. Kamp and G. Strecker. Göttingen: Vandenhoeck & Ruprecht.

Jepsen, A.
1954   "Nehemia 10." *ZAW* 66:87-106.

Kellermann, Ulrich
1967   *Nehemia: Quellen, Überlieferung und Geschichte*. BZAW 102. Berlin: Alfred Topelmann.
1968   "Erwägungen zum Esragesetz." *ZAW* 80: 373-385.

Klein, Ralph W.
1976   "Ezra and Nehemiah in Recent Studies." Pp. 361-376 in *Magnalia Dei: The Mighty Acts of God*. Ed. F. M. Cross, W. E. Lemke, and P. D. Miller. Garden City, NY: Doubleday.

McCarthy, Dennis J.
    1982   "Covenant and Law in Chronicles–Nehemiah." *CBQ* 41:25-44.

Miles, J. A., Jr.
    1981   "Radical Editing: *Redaktionsgeschichte* and the Aesthetic of Willed Confusion." Pp. 9-31 in *Tradition in Transformation*. Ed. B. Halpern and J. D. Levenson. Winona Lake, IN: Eisenbrauns.

Myers, Jacob M.
    1965   *Ezra, Nehemiah*. Anchor Bible, 14. Garden City, NY: Doubleday.

Petersen, David L.
    1984   *Haggai and Zechariah 1-8*. Philadelphia: Westminster Press.

Rendtorff, Rolf
    1984   "Esra und das 'Gesetz.'" *ZAW* 96:165-184

Rich, Adrienne
    1984   *A Wild Patience Has Taken Me This Far*. New York: W. W. Norton.

Rimmon-Kenan, Shlomith
    1983   *Narrative Fiction: Contemporary Poetics*. London: Methuen.

Rudolph, Wilhelm
    1949   *Esra und Nehemia*. HAT 20. Tübingen: J. C. B. Mohr (Paul Siebeck).

Sternberg, Meir
    1985   *The Poetics of Biblical Narrative. Ideological Literature and the Drama of Reading*. Bloomington: Indiana University Press.

Talmon, Shemaryahu
    1976   "Ezra and Nehemiah, Books and Men." Pp. 317-329 in *IDB* Supp. Nashville: Abingdon.

Tucker, Gene M.
    1977   "Prophetic Superscriptions and the Growth of a Canon." Pp. 56-70 in *Canon and Authority*. Ed. G. W. Coats and B. O. Long. Philadelphia: Fortress Press.

Van Seters, John
    1983   *In Search of History*. New Haven: Yale University Press.

Vogt, H. C. M.
1966   *Studie zur nachexilischen Gemeinde in Ezra–Nehemia*. Werl: Dietrich Coelde.

Whedbee, J. William
1984   "Ezra and Nehemiah: A Tale of Torah and City, Politics and Piety." Unpublished paper.

White, Hayden
1981   "The Value of Narrativity in the Representation of Reality." Pp. 1-23 in *On Narrative*. Ed. W. J. T. Mitchell. Chicago: University of Chicago Press.

Wiseman, Donald J.
1970   "Books in the Ancient Near East and in the Old Testament." Pp. 30-66 in *The Cambridge History of the Bible*, Vol. 1. Ed. P. R. Ackroyd and C. F. Evans. Cambridge: Cambridge University Press.

Zunz, Leopold
1832   "Dibre hajamim oder Bücher der Chronik." Pp. 12-34 in *Die gottesdienstlichen Vorträge der Juden, historisch Entwickelt*. Berlin: Louis Lamm, 1919 edition.

THE FORCE OF THE TEXT
A Response to Tamara C. Eskenazi's
"Ezra–Nehemiah: From Text to Actuality"

David J. A. Clines
University of Sheffield

1. The written as generator of the actual

1.1   There can be no doubt that Tamara Eskenazi has made her principal case cogently, with enviable lucidity and force. Which is: in Ezra–Nehemiah written documents are decisive for the flow of the narrative and for the life of the community whose life is depicted by that narrative (§1.6). Her paper is a focused literary reading of an unprepossessing text, which few would have thought a "literary" text. She professes herself surprised that Ezra–Nehemiah has not previously attracted this kind of reading (§2.1), but perhaps it is a surprise that is more justifiable after than before one has seen a demonstration of how valid such a reading can be.

1.2   Eskenazi's view of the significance of the written as the generator of the actual holds good for all the main sections of Ezra–Nehemiah.

1.21   In the opening sentences of the book, a written document—which is not only referred to but brought within the narrative as it is quoted—is the authorization for all the action down to the end of Ezra 6. Within this narrative of the building of the temple "documents precipitate and guide action" (§7.42); what transpires in the narrative "is essentially the actualization of the written word" (§7.43). In this section of Ezra–Nehemiah the documents are mainly Persian decrees, but one other foundational text is "the law of Moses" (Ezra 3:2) which determines the fashion of the building of the altar; this, be it noted, is the "written" law, and not an oral commandment.

1.211　"Past and present documents work together" (§7.51). I would like as well to see in this observation about the function of documents a hint of the *interlacing of times:* time prior to the point reached by the narrative is being interwoven with the time of the narrative. We might add that even, on occasion, time future to the narrative can be brought into relation to the narrative through a document. Thus the letter of the officials of Samaria (Ezra 4:8-16) is itself of a later date than the narrative context in which it is embedded, but at the same time manages to refer back to memoranda of Babylonian kings written long before the narrative of Ezra begins. So in its interlacing of times it can affirm that Artaxerxes *will* find, from investigating the *past* history of Jerusalem, that it *is* a rebellious city, and will, if he allows the *past* to have influence on the *present,* properly protect his *future* (Ezra 4:15-16).

1.22　In the second section (Eskenazi: "movement") of Ezra-Nehemiah (Ezra 7-10), it is again texts that are determinative. The one is the book of Torah that authorizes and empowers Ezra's functions as "a scribe skilled in the law of Moses" (Ezra 7:6). And the other is the firman of Artaxerxes (Ezra 7:12-26) authorizing the imposition of the law of Moses as the only law for Jews of the province and thus initiating the whole flow of the narrative of the section.

1.221　I would observe a second interlacing here, between the two texts. While the law of Moses recks nothing of Persians, the Persian law's principal concern is that very law of Moses! "Artaxerxes' letter positions the law of Ezra's God as an authoritative document together with the law of the king" (§7.73). But it is more than that "together with." Artaxerxes' authority is on the face of it the primary authority: it is *his* letter that gets Ezra moving from Babylonia to Judah. But we soon discover that his authority in reality does no more than make space for the authority of the law of Ezra's God: it is not Artaxerxes's law that will rule in Judah but "the law of the God of heaven" (Ezra 7:21). Artaxerxes makes a law that it is someone else's law that must be obeyed! The interlacing of the texts carries with it an irony both gentle and grave.

1.23　The third section of Ezra–Nehemiah concerns the building activities of Nehemiah (Neh 1-7). It is here not so evident that texts have an *initiative* function, and perhaps Eskenazi's global claim (§1.6, see §1.1 above) needs to be modulated somewhat. Certainly, the section begins and ends with references to texts: at 1:1 we are informed that we are to embark upon a document, "the words of Nehemiah"; at 7:5 we encounter "the book of the genealogy of those who came up at the first," reproduced *in extenso* in 7:6-73. A written text with a distinct significance in advancing the action is met with at 2:7-8 where Nehemiah receives "letters" from the king to allow him safe passage to Judah and to provide him with timber for his building operations in Jerusalem. These are a kind of low-key parallel to Ezra's royal mandate, and if they do not exactly determine the sequel of the narrative, they are certainly highly useful for it.

1.231   Here too there is an interlacing of texts. For the "words" of Nehemiah (1:1)—which means to say, his "chronicles" (דברי נחמיה like the דברי הימים)—are not just the account of his deeds but include within themselves a text from the past, from before his time (Neh 7:5), that dictates his course of action (Eskenazi: "Previous generations become partners in present events through the text," §7.9). The written text is interlaced with the current events, and action on the basis of a text becomes in its turn a text.

1.3   In the fourth section (Neh 8-13) the authority of the written text is "articulate[d] through a formal structure organized around documents" (§8.1). The book of the Torah, read aloud on three occasions (Neh 8:1-12; 8:13-14; 9:3), becomes the directive of the people's actions. The ultimate response to the reading of the text is the production of a new text, the pledge of Nehemiah 10.

1.31   There is, I would say, a new kind of interlacing of texts here. In two ways. First, the text is not only referred to (as it is in Ezra 4-5, for example) but *read aloud*, not just *read* but *read out* (British English). No doubt all reading in the ancient world was reading aloud, to some extent, but here the text speaks explicitly of a public reading. The nearest we have come to this in Ezra–Nehemiah has been when a letter from Artaxerxes is read "before Rehum and Shimshai the scribe and their associates" in Samaria (Ezra 4:23)—which letter also incidentally includes a report of a reading of the previous letter from the Samarians in the presence of the king (4:18). These have been readings of correspondence to the persons to whom the letters have been addressed; it is different here in Nehemiah where a text addressed to no one in

particular, undated, previously available, traditional, is read to an
assembly convened purposely in order to hear it read (Neh 8:1-3).
Text becomes actuality through being read aloud.

1.32   Secondly, the effect of reading a text becomes the production of another text. This is true, of course, of all the texts contained within Ezra–Nehemiah: all the texts mentioned in these
books end up in these books, by name or in full. It is something
more, though, when a text within the narrative generates another
text that will be within the narrative. The nearest we have come
to this before has been when a letter generates another letter in
response, as when the letter of Rehum and the Samarians (Ezra
4:11-16) generates the rescript of Artaxerxes (4:17-22), or when
the letter of Tattenai and the officials of the satrapy Abar-nahara
(5:7-17) explicitly calls for (5:17) and generates the rescript of
Darius (6:2-12). But these cases of response to a previously existing text fall within a conventional and predictable pattern. It is
something different when in Nehemiah 10 (the pledge document)
we find an unsolicited, unpredictable writing responding to and
generated by the reading of the law in Nehemiah 8.[1] Here then we
have a step beyond Eskenazi's "text to actuality": the fuller pattern is "text to actuality to text." And, since text, the text of Ezra–Nehemiah, is the end product of all the actuality, had we not
better use that fuller formulation not just for the particular production of the text of the pledge of Nehemiah 10 but for the work
as a whole?

1.4   The "force" of the text is generally taken to be its meaning.
Eskenazi's paper encourages us to think of it also as the effect a
text has upon reality—which is, in another idiom, its meaning,
since texts are not just words upon the page.

2. One narrative or three?

2.1   A secondary contention of Eskenazi's paper seems to me less
well-founded. It is that Ezra–Nehemiah as a whole forms a single
narrative whose parts are related to one another as the parts of a

---

[1] Perhaps we should say that it is generated at second hand by the law-reading,
for the prayer of Nehemiah 9 has intervened; the prayer is generated by the law-
reading and the pledge by the law-reading as it has led the people to a prayer of
confession.

simple story. She organizes the total content of Ezra–Nehemiah according to the structural schema for narrative proposed by Claude Bremond: *potentiality, actualization,* and *success.* Thus the first four verses of Ezra, narrating the decree to the community to rebuild the house of God, is potentiality (objective defined), the bulk of the entire work (Ezra 1:5–Neh 7:72) is actualization, and the last six chapters of Nehemiah (chs. 8–13) is success (objective reached) (§4.1–4.2). Eskenazi sees in the opening lines of Ezra the goal of the whole work Ezra–Nehemiah, namely the building of the house of God (Ezra 1:3) (§4.4), and she finds in Ezra 6:14, narrating the completion of the building of that temple, the "linchpin" of the work as a whole.

2.2   I grant that we may reasonably look for the plot of the work as a whole, this being a narrative work. But there is no reason why the plot of the work should be divulged by the first statement of intent that we encounter in the work. The fact that the book of Ezra opens with the command of Cyrus to "rebuild the house of the LORD, the God of Israel" need not mean that we are now in touch with the theme of Ezra–Nehemiah as a whole. The issue can only be settled by asking whether the theme "building of the house of the LORD" is germane to all the material of Ezra–Nehemiah. Since the completion of the temple itself is narrated as early as Ezra 6:14, Eskenazi is obliged to claim that the "house of the LORD" is extended in meaning in Ezra–Nehemiah from the temple to the city (§1.4); she can thus entitle the central section of the work as a whole (Ezra 1:5–Neh 7:72) "the community builds the house of God according to decree" (§4.2). But there is no textual warrant for supposing this transferred sense of "house."[2] Everywhere in Ezra–Nehemiah the "house" is the temple, and the city is the city, and the people are neither the house nor the city. If we were to argue that the building of the wall was *analogous* to the building of the temple, that would be a different matter. But then we would have *two* (or more) analogous stories, not one overarching story.

2.3   There is indeed one text that Eskenazi can call in aid of her view that "Ezra–Nehemiah expands the concept of the house of God from temple to city" (§1.4). Ezra 6:14 says that "they finished

---

[2] "House" sometimes of course means "family," as in Ezra 2:36, 59; Neh 1:6, or someone's private house, as in Neh 2:7; 3:10, etc.

their building by command of the God of Israel and by decree of
Cyrus and Darius and Artaxerxes king of Persia." Since the completion of the temple is here dated to the sixth year of Darius,
which is 515 B.C.E., the reference to Artaxerxes, who did not begin
to reign until more than half a century after the completion of the
temple (his dates are 464-423 B.C.E.), has seemed out of place to
previous scholars. The usual explanation given for this reference
to Artaxerxes is that a glossator has had in mind the service done
to the temple in Jerusalem by Artaxerxes in the next chapter: in
7:15-22 he sends gifts of silver and gold and of temple vessels for
the maintenance of sacrifice there and promises future funds from
the income of the satrapy. This is not, of course, assistance with
building the temple, so the gloss (if that is what it is[3]) is inappropriate. Its status as a gloss is further confirmed, in the eyes of most,
by its inclusion of the phrase "the king of Persia"; since both Cyrus
and Darius are also equally kings of Persia, it is hard to believe
that a single author would have used the title for one, and denied
it to the other two.

2.4   Eskenazi has an original explanation of the text. The singular
form, "king of Persia," she says, "applies to all three kings as a
single unit, as if they spoke with one voice," and the singular
"decree" of the three kings signifies their acting in unison. She
concludes that "actual completion" of the building of the house of
God "must await the execution of the decree of Artaxerxes"
(§7.51).

2.41   However, the more natural interpretation of the singular
word translated "decree" (Aram. טְעֵם, with the variant orthogra-
phy טַעַם when used of God's "decree") in this context is that it
means "order, command": the temple building is finished "by order of" the Persian kings. There is no explicit reference here to the
formal "decrees" of the Persians, any more than there is to any
"decree" of the God of Israel, since in the narrative of the book
God has not issued a "decree" or anything like it. So there is
nothing deeply meaningful about the singular term טְעֵם.

---

[3] Williamson (1985: 83-84) thinks it not impossible that the original author used
the phrase in "anticipation of Artaxerxes' support for the temple and its services,"
but does not explain how such an author could have understood the contribution
of Artaxerxes as part of the *building* of the temple.

2.42   And as against the inference that the presence of Artaxerxes' name in the verse signifies the extension of the building of the house of God into his reign—and thus the extension of the significance of the term "house of God"—we have to take with equal weight the statement of the following verse (6:15) that "this house was finished" on a particular day in the sixth year of Darius. The matter of fact reportorial language does not in my opinion admit of the subtlety that the "house" was both completed and incomplete.

2.43   There is perhaps a hidden assumption in Eskenazi's paper that a "literary" reading of a text must work (?exclusively) with "the final form of the text," the text we are reading being the only text we have, glosses and all. For myself, while I can see some merit in a principled attempt to make sense of everything in the text, and in asking, for example, what the effect of any presumed gloss may be on the work as a whole, I cannot see the value in allowing mere scribal errors or simple misapprehensions of a text that has already been effectively finalized to be determinative of the overall structure and meaning of the work I am considering. We have plenty of evidence for the corruption of the text of Ezra–Nehemiah, especially in lists of proper names, so the assumption of a gloss is nothing extraordinary. If one insists on identifying the Masoretic text, with its various undeniable faults, as the final form of the text, I will ask whether there is not an even *more* final form of the text that I should be concerned with, such as the RSV—which is the form in which the text has come down to *me*.

2.5   If Ezra 6:14 does not project the work on the "house of God" beyond the reign of Darius, then it becomes impossible to regard the building of the house as the theme of Ezra–Nehemiah as a whole, as Eskenazi argues. But her analysis of "three different stories," each with its own beginning, middle, and end still stands (§7.2). The question that remains is whether one can discern any other overall structure to the books.

2.6   It is not too difficult to see that the restoration of the temple, the city, and obedience to the law are the subject matter or the theme of Ezra–Nehemiah. But this does not mean that this theme is realized in one sweep of plot. Nor does it imply that the theme is ever explicitly stated. The theme-element of *restoration of the temple* is very explicit in the opening sentences of Ezra; the theme-element of *restoration of obedience to the law* is presaged in the reference to Ezra as "a scribe skilled in the law of Moses which the Lord the God of Israel had given" (7:6) and explicit in the king's authorization of Ezra's law (7:25-26); the theme-element of *restoration of the city* is hinted at in the report that "Jerusalem is broken down" in the third verse of Nehemiah 1 and becomes explicit in Nehemiah's request to be sent to Jerusalem "that I may rebuild it" (2:5). The different elements of the theme are handled differently from a narrative point of view: the first element comes to a conclusion in Ezra 6 before the other elements are embarked upon, but the two other elements are somewhat interwoven. Thus the theme-element of obedience to the law first becomes apparent in Ezra 7-10, and then in Nehemiah 8-10, and finally in Nehemiah 13, while the theme-element of the restoration of the city is interwoven with it in Nehemiah 1-7 and again in Nehemiah 11-12. An analysis of the shape of the books of Ezra-Nehemiah as if they were one single and simple story is therefore inappropriate.

3. *The pledge and the reforms: relative priority*

3.1   I readily agree that Eskenazi has the better of me in her discussion of the relative positions of Nehemiah 10 and Nehemiah 13 (§§8.52-8.85). For in my commentary (199-200) I considered only the question of the historical relationship of the events narrated in those two chapters, and I failed to draw conclusions about the significance of their literary placement. On the strictly historical issue, I still feel confident that the pledge of Nehemiah 10 must have been a result of the provisional and sometimes hasty reforms of Nehemiah in Nehemiah 13, and Eskenazi does not dispute this view. But she rightly asks the further question: but what does it mean that Nehemiah 10 precedes Nehemiah 13 in the text?

3.2   Her answer is that the present arrangement of the materials "ascribes the reforms to the community as a whole, making Nehemiah's activities essentially the administering of communally ordained regulations" (§8.85). The measures that Nehemiah "energetically imposes" in ch. 13 are "obligations [that] have been assumed by the community in the earlier pledge" of ch. 10 (§8.82).

3.3   This is a good answer, and one that fits well with the evident stress in Ezra–Nehemiah on the movement of authority from individual leaders to the community as a whole. It is not, however, the only answer that can be given. Williamson (383), for example, believes that the presence of ch. 13 derives from an editor sympathetic to Nehemiah's work, who "felt obliged to include these additions to the [Nehemiah] memoir in order to ensure that Nehemiah's contribution to the cultic reforms was not overlooked; indeed, he gave them a certain prominence by concluding his work with them." So does the focus in the end come to rest upon Nehemiah or upon the people?

3.4   Whatever answer we are tempted to give is further complicated by a textual item which Eskenazi refers to but does not make much of. It is the chronological notation "before this" (לפני מזה) in Neh 13:4. Obviously the narrative intends us to understand that these reforms of Nehemiah took place before the activities of the "ideal community" narrated in 12:44-13:3. But how long before? Before the dedication of the wall (12:27-43)? Before the resettlement of inhabitants of Jerusalem (11:1-2)? Before the pledge-making (9:38-10:39)?

3.41   The chronological indicators throughout the book of Nehemiah are in fact very tantalizing. The narrative begins in "the twentieth year" (1:1). We presume that is of Artaxerxes, noting that in 2:1 we are explicitly in "the twentieth year of King Artaxerxes." But already we are confused, because the events of ch. 2, which logically follow the events of ch. 1, are dated to the *first* month of that year whereas the events of ch. 1 were dated to the *ninth* month (further details: Clines: 136-37; Williamson: 169-70). The next chronological indication we have is that Nehemiah will be governor of Judah from the 20th to the 32nd year of Artaxerxes (5:14), and the next dated event is the finishing of the wall in the sixth month (Elul), no doubt of that same 20th year of Artaxerxes (6:15). Thereafter the seventh month arrives at the beginning of ch. 8, and assemblies are held on the first, the second, the eighth, and the twenty-fourth of that month (8:2, 13, 18; 9:1). The "we" who are praying a penitential prayer in ch. 9 are evidently the same people who are immediately thereafter and "because of all this" (9:38) signing their names to the pledge of ch. 10. The next event is the repopulation of Jerusalem (11:1), how much later we do not know; but it cannot be very much later because thereafter we are reading about the dedication of the wall (12:27-43) which cannot have been long postponed after its completion. To our surprise, however, once the events of "that day" (12:44; 13:1) have been dealt with (appointment of storehouse officials and exclusion of foreigners, 12:44-13:3), we find the narrative of a temple scandal that happened "before this" (13:4). So somewhere in the quite tightly organized sequence of the first 12 chapters of Nehemiah we must find space for the events of ch. 13. But that is not the worst of it for the reader; for when we reach vv 6-7 we discover that even though these events of ch. 13 belong chronologically somewhere earlier in the book of Nehemiah, they come—not from the 20th year of Artaxerxes, which has been our framework hitherto, but—from some time after the 32nd (!) year of Artaxerxes. The narrative loops back on itself with all the consistency of a drawing by Escher. These events of ch. 13, from the 32nd year (at the earliest), have nowhere to go.

3.42   One can easily think of several readerly ploys for neutralizing the chronological disorder. For example, we might take refuge in a loose interpretation of "on that day" in 12:44 and 13:1, supposing it to mean rather "in that general period"; indeed, I have claimed myself that the phrase "that day" means "the whole period from Zerubbabel to Nehemiah" (Clines: 234)! The difficulty with that is that it produces no particular event to which the "before this" of 13:4 can refer, and the scandal at the temple can hardly have taken place before the days of Zerubbabel. Alternatively, we might suppose that since ch. 8 does not name the year in which these assemblies of the seventh month were held we might at that point have moved ahead to the 32nd year; in that case the law-reading, the prayer, and the pledge would all have followed the ad hoc responses of Nehemiah to abuses he found prevalent in the province on his return from the royal court for his second tour of duty. The problem here is that in that case the dedication of the wall would have been delayed more than 12 years beyond the actual completion of the building, for no apparent reason.

3.43   In brief, there seems to be no really satisfactory way of resolving the chronological intentions of the text. The reader is left with uncertainty about the relation of Nehemiah's reforms in ch. 13 to everything else in the book. The one thing we know as readers of the book is that the story the book sets out to relate (its *sujet*) *did not* end with the events of ch. 13; we know that they are *before* something else, even if we do not know *what* they are before. The result of this uncertainty, as far as it impinges on Eskenazi's essay, is that the reader *cannot know* that "Nehemiah's activities [are] essentially the administering of communally ordained regulations" (§8.85). So in the end, the literary shape of the book drives us in the same direction as our attempts at historical reconstruction did; as a matter of *historical fact,* it is probable that Nehemiah's reforms preceded the community's pledge, and the chronology intrinsic to the book itself *suggests* the same thing.

3.5   I find that I have been operating in this discussion with a concept of *two* readers, a casual and a curious one. Perhaps there is some technical nomenclature for them and their varying competences, but will it be better just because it is Stanley Fish's or whoever's? The *casual* reader may well think that what is *narrated* later *happens* later, that the structure of Ezra–Nehemiah makes "[Nehemiah's] reforms appear to be the result of that earlier [pledge] document" (§8.85). The *curious* reader, on the other hand, will worry about the little details of the text, try to sort things out, attempt reconstructions of the *sujet* narrated by the *fabula* of the text. Since there are likely to be more casual readers than curious readers of any text, perhaps Eskenazi is in the end right, or right enough, or mostly right, about the *effect* of the relationship of Nehemiah 10 and Nehemiah 13. But it is not an effect on everyone, and it is not an intrinsic property of the text.

4. Writing not an inevitably good thing

4.1   There is in Eskenazi's paper an unmistakable appreciation of, and enthusiasm for, writing, prose-writing, and the influence of writing on actuality. Ezra–Nehemiah is a book written "in and for an age of prose," which is not at all inferior to an age of poetry; rather, Ezra–Nehemiah "sanctifies the prosaic, the concrete, and the common" (§1.2). "In its own prosaic fashion, Ezra–Nehemiah has moved step by step to implement and actualize the vision of a holy people in a holy city. . . . Ezra–Nehemiah's quietistic way supersedes the dazzling splendor of the Davidic monarchy, providing an enduring model, a way of life" (§9.5). The point is well taken and well made. My only question is whether that is all that is to be said about writing in Ezra–Nehemiah.

4.2   My first observation concerns how we know Ezra–Nehemiah is prose, and how we value it once we know it *is* prose. If prose is the only medium we know, we do not know it is prose. M.

Jourdain in Molière's *Le Bourgeois Gentilhomme* is astonished to find that he has been speaking prose for forty years without realizing it (*il y a plus de quarante ans que je dis de la prose sans que j'en susse rien*). Prose is only definable by way of distinction from poetry. So the identity of prose is parasitic on the existence of both modes, and poetry is necessary for the existence of prose. It is very interesting, but also almost inevitable, that Eskenazi's valuation of the significance of prose should stem from a poet's vision: it is the poet Adrienne Rich, and not some prosaic Adrienne Rich, who can see the "prose-bound, rountine remembering" as a "putting together, inch by inch the starry worlds. From all the lost collections." It is the *poem* that "sanctifies the prosaic," just as it is the *poem* that forms the epigraph to Eskenazi's paper. Things are not half so exciting, and meanings are not half so profound, down among "the dailiness of placing stone upon stone" (§1.2); the prosaic knows nothing about itself, certainly nothing about how to "sanctify" itself.

4.3   Secondly, much has been said in Eskenazi's paper about the movement from text to actuality, but not so much, I think, about the ways in which texts can *restrain* actuality. In Ezra 1-6, for example, Eskenazi rightly observes that "documents precipitate and guide the action" (§7.42), and that "what transpires is essentially the actualization of the written word" (§7.43). But the action is quite often inaction. The written not infrequently functions as an inhibitor of action, especially of desirable and desired action. A mere scrap of text from a local official can generate paperwork that will put hundreds of temple builders out of work and prevent the execution even of the plans of *God*.

4.4   Thirdly, texts are not the only initiators of action; for sometimes heroes, prophets even, prove more potent than texts, and even stimulate action that runs contrary to texts. Thus in Ezra 5:1-2, after work on the temple has been abandoned for nearly twenty years (all because of hostile documents, it seems, at least if you are a casual reader of Ezra 4), what prompts the resumption of work is no document but the prophesying of Haggai and Zechariah and the "arising" of Zerubbabel and Jeshua. So "text-free" is this phase of the temple building that even when the Jews are invited to produce the documentary authority they have for their building (5:3), they have no recourse to it, *even though it exists*.

4.41   Even when it seems that it is "the written text which carries weight" (§3.2), there are often other factors equally weighty. There can be little doubt, for instance, that it is the edict of Cyrus that begins the action of the books of Ezra–Nehemiah, but the edict does not stand by itself. Quite apart from the fact that Cyrus would not be making his proclamation at all without the Lord's "stirring up" his spirit (Ezra 1:1), the narrative insists that Cyrus' decree would have been a dead letter without the further intervention of God: the only Jews who returned to the land were those "whose spirit God had stirred to go up to rebuild the house of the LORD" (1:5). In the finishing of the building, likewise, there is indeed the written "decree" of Cyrus and Darius, but also the unwritten "decree" (never actually formulated as a decree) of the God of Israel (6:14).

4.42   Or again, the impulse to rebuild the city walls comes not from some imperial decree, but from the oral report of visitors from Jerusalem (Neh 1:1-3), which prompts Nehemiah not to write a memo to the king, not even to approach him with a formal request, but simply to wear a pained expression as he serves the king his wine (2:1-2). Authorization for the rebuilding of the city does not come—to be precise—in the form of documents, and not even as explicit permission. The way really important things are done by really important people is the way it happens in Nehemiah 2: the courtier asks primarily for leave of absence from the court, so that he can visit, with due filial piety, the city of his fathers' sepulchres, and almost coincidentally rebuild the city in his spare time. The king cares nothing about the cost, the logistics, or the politics of rebuilding a city in an outlying province, and does not even stop to inquire what may be the name of this derelict city; his only concern is "How long will you be gone, and when will you return?" Everything is dealt with on a personal basis, the "queen sitting beside him" obviously being dragged into the narrative to emphasize the cosy domesticity—if not to drop the hint that it will be she rather than he who most misses Nehemiah. Only after the real authorization has been given do the scribes get busy with the paperwork, preparing a passport for Nehemiah—to ensure he is treated regally enough by each of the provincial governors he encounters—and requisition orders for building timber for the city. We are not really surprised to discover, much later, that what was really happening in that innocent and sentimental exchange between Nehemiah and the king was that Nehemiah was being appointed governor of the sub-province of Judah, where he is still comfortably installed twelve years later, picking up the tab out of his own pocket, to be sure, but plainly having the wherewithal to feed 150 retainers plus sundry visiting dignitaries (5:14-18). If documents were what made Nehemiah's world go round, there would have been a lot less high living at the governor's place in Jerusalem.

4.5   Fourthly, texts take longer to produce than actuality can sometimes afford to wait—or be bothered to. The Jews can blithely carry on with their building for all the time it takes for "a report [to] reach Darius and then answer be returned by letter concerning it" (5:5). And the "open letter" of Sanballat charging Nehemiah with treason (Neh 6:5-7), together with Tobiah's poison pen letters sent to frighten Nehemiah off his city wall building (6:19), are texts that never need answering and become totally inefficacious once the 52 days are up and Nehemiah's wall is completed. The daily placing of stone on stone continues while the mail is on its way.

4.6   Fifthly, texts do not only precipitate action; they can also be true or false, and their truth or falsity will always have some effect on the reader, if not on the action. At one end of the scale of veracity are the prophecy of Jeremiah (Ezra 1:1) and the authorizing decrees of the Persian kings, of Cyrus in Ezra 1 or Artaxerxes in Ezra 8, for example. At the other end of the scale is the (presumably) totally untrue letter of the Persian governor of Samaria that Nehemiah's wall-building is the first sign of a rebellion of the Jews and that Nehemiah has set up prophets in Jerusalem to proclaim him king (Neh 6:5-7). In between are texts that contain both truth and falsehood, as with the letter of Rehum and Shimshai to Artaxerxes (Ezra 4:8-16). This letter says, truly enough, that Jerusalem is notorious in history as a rebellious city and "that was why this city was laid waste" (4:15); but it also claims that "if this city is rebuilt and the walls finished, they will not pay tribute, custom, or toll, and the royal revenue will be impaired" (4:13).

4.61   The effect of this last letter on the action is the same whether it is true or false: the king responds with a prohibition on further work on the temple. The truth in it that can be tested, from search in the records, lends verisimilitude to the falsity in it that cannot be tested. Readers, on the other hand, unless perhaps they are Persian kings receiving the letter of Rehum and Shimshai, are not inclined to believe everything they read. Even if they are disposed to believe everything the *narrator* tells them, they begin to operate in a critical mode again when the narrator quotes someone else, especially if the someone else is not a compatriot. So readers tend to have a different relationship to texts than they have to the text. Texts within the text are open to the hermeneutic of suspicion, even if the text as a whole is beyond suspicion. But this of course spells trouble for the text as a whole. For once a space is opened for the hermeneutic of suspicion, who can tell where it will stop? Can we be so sure, for example, that Sanballat's charge against Nehemiah was totally without foundation?

4.7   Sixthly, living in a world where texts generate actions can seriously damage one's health. It seems perfectly reasonable to have a written list of Pilgrim Fathers (as in Ezra 2), but in the end the existence of such a list does almost as much harm to the people whose ancestors are recorded there as to those whose aren't (the reader is invited to consider whether she would prefer to be, or not to be, a Daughter of the American Revolution). But Ezra 2 authorizes us to consider the cruelty of such lists from the standpoint of those excluded. Six hundred fifty-two heads of families "could not prove" their genealogy (2:59-60), and if that perhaps meant only that they could not prove it orally, Ezra 2 puts their incapacity into writing; it is tough when you have a text against you. It is much worse for the priests, of course; for although they desperately "sought their registration among those enrolled in the genealogies . . . they were not found there, and so they were excluded from the priesthood as unclean." Uncleanness is bad enough, but of course exclusion from the priesthood means as well loss of a livelihood. Not too surprisingly (since living by documents is something of a Persian custom), it is the "Governor" (תרשׁאתא), a Persian official or else a Jew acting as a Persian official, who spells out what that exclusion means: "they were not to partake of the most holy food" (2:63). From the standpoint of the defrocked priests, the period of their exclusion, "until there should be a priest to consult Urim and Thummim," must have seemed pretty eschatological (where *were* Urim and Thummim those days?), and the Talmudic interpretation of the phrase would have sounded exactly right: "until the dead rise and the Messiah, the son of David, comes" (b Soṭah 48b). To discover later in Ezra that one at least of these excluded priestly families had indeed, despite the continuing absence of Urim and Thummim, managed to prove its ancestry (Meremoth ben Uriah of the Hakkoz family is a recognized priest in 8:33) makes things worse, not better. For it means that they *were* legitimate priests all along but had documents against them: first their genealogical documents had gone missing, whereupon the document incorporated in Ezra 2 had put that fact in writing.

4.71 Having the list of Pilgrim Fathers survive the best part of a century into the age of Nehemiah proves to be not an unmixed blessing for those families whose names are enrolled in it. For while it may save some time for Nehemiah to have a genealogical list available for his census (Ezra 2 being reproduced in Neh 7), what it will mean for those mentioned in it is that one tenth of them will be compulsorily resettled from their homes throughout Judea to the newly rebuilt Jerusalem. While "the people blessed all the men who willingly offered to live in Jerusalem," as the euphemism had it for having oneself willy-nilly chosen by lot to repeople the city (11:2), we may be sure that the last thing their families were thinking of was *blessing* them! Lists are usually compiled for the benefit of the compiler rather than the people on them (let the recipient of junk mail understand); being named in someone else's document presages trouble.

4.72 It is true that having documentary authorization for what one is doing can save a lot of difficulty. If one does not happen to like one's neighbors, for example, one can always fend off their kindly offers of assistance by pointing out that their names are not mentioned in one's building permit. No doubt when Zerubbabel and Jeshua administered their classic rebuff to the "people of the land" everything was more complicated than anyone was making out. But for them to say, "You have nothing to do with us in building a house to our God; but we alone will build to the LORD, the God of Israel, as King Cyrus the king of Persia has commanded us" (Ezra 4:3), is to take their stand on a textual technicality and to sweep under the carpet an important human relations problem which was to keep recurring throughout the narrative of Ezra–Nehemiah. Cyrus would not have been offended in the least, and his will would not have been one whit threatened, if the people of the land *had* co-operated in the temple building. But, with a document in their hand, a royal document to boot (the repeated word

"king" shows how they are thinking), the Jews fall to behaving like
petty bureaucrats. For the right people in the right place, and
especially if the Lord is stirring people's spirits at the same time,
a document can be a great energizer; but if one is at all a legalist
a document one can wave at others can destroy both creativity
and civility. Could this perhaps be true of larger documents also,
like, let us suppose, Ezra–Nehemiah itself?

WORKS CONSULTED

Clines, D. J. A.
   1984   *Ezra, Nehemiah, Esther.* New Century Bible. Grand
               Rapids: Eerdmans.
Williamson, H. G. M.
   1985   *Ezra, Nehemiah.* Word Biblical Commentary. Waco:
               Word Books.

SWALLOWING HARD:
REFLECTIONS ON EZEKIEL'S DUMBNESS

Ellen Frances Davis
Union Theological Seminary, New York

ABSTRACT

Ezekiel's prophetic career coincided with two critical developments in Israel: first, consolidation of the sacred traditions into a scriptural corpus, and second, urgent debate about interpreting present events in the light of those traditions. It is the contention of this study that the distinctive character of Ezekiel's oracles and the representation of his historical role may be seen as reflecting those developments. A modified theory of written discourse is adduced: it is proposed that Ezekiel's patterns of thought and public speech were shaped by habits of reading and writing, and that through him Israelite prophecy for the first time received its primary impress in a consciously literary mode. Ezekiel's eating of the scroll and subsequent dumbness are interpreted as figures for the new conditions and constraints imposed upon communication by the move toward textualization of the prophetic tradition.

1.1 The starting point for this study is the observation that the book of Ezekiel has proved peculiarly resistant to the advances of historical critical method. That approach is probably best represented in recent scholarship by Zimmerli, whose careful analysis has undoubtedly yielded a better understanding of the complex process of transmission and reinterpretation lying behind the present text. Nonetheless, many features of the book (e.g., its geographic and historical background, the forms of prophetic speech, and the nature of Ezekiel's social role) remain without satisfactory explanation. The present study focuses on one unresolved difficulty, the phenomenon of Ezekiel's dumbness. This problem will serve to illustrate some of the directions which further critical study of the book might fruitfully pursue.

1.2   It is one of the ironies of critical scholarship that the phenomenon of Ezekiel's dumbness remains among the most explained and least illumined issues in the book. The need for some explanation is obvious: divine imposition of dumbness (3:26) appears to stand in direct contradiction to both the preceding charge to speak God's word to the Israelites (2:4; 3:4,11) and the evidence of the subsequent oracles (against Judah/Jerusalem, through 24:27, and the foreign nations, 25:1–32:31) that Ezekiel fulfilled that charge. Yet the text itself acknowledges no contradiction. Despite his considerable verbal activity during the period of restriction, Ezekiel reaffirms that with the arrival of the messenger announcing the fall of Jerusalem, "my mouth was opened and I was no longer dumb" (33:22).

1.3   Attempts to resolve the difficulty can be outlined in terms of a few basic arguments. A number of early critical treatments followed the suggestion of Klostermann that the dumbness was an intermittent physical condition associated with psychological disturbance. The pathological explanation was generally superseded by Fohrer's symbolical view: Ezekiel's silence is a sign that God has (temporarily) ceased to address the refractory exiles with warnings and calls to repentance. Fohrer argues further that the inference of a seven-year silence beginning immediately after the prophet's call is the result of an editorial transfer of the passage (from ch. 24?) intended to give it greater prominence; the dumbness actually began only with the siege of the city. Zimmerli adopts a more extreme variant of this position, arguing that the dumbness is a wholly secondary development within the prophet's school of disciples. Greenberg offers a sort of hybrid of the symbolical and the psychological views: the dumbness represents God's rejection of the people and reflects also the prophet's reaction to the people's hostility to his message, an "extreme despondency (whereby) . . . he lost the power of normal human contact" (121).

1.4   More promising are recent attempts to treat the dumbness in light of the book's larger structure and its representation of the prophetic office (e.g., Lamparter, Komlosh). Especially noteworthy is Wilson's proposal that the dumbness functions within the call narrative as a figure for divine curtailment of the prophetic office: unlike his predecessors, Ezekiel is not to serve as Israel's mediator (איש מוכיח, 3:26) with God:

> The implication of 3:26 is that in the dialogue which Yahweh carries on with his people through the prophet, communication can now move in only one direction: from Yahweh to the people. . . . The people in turn may either hear or refuse to hear, but they may not turn the divine oracle into a dialogue (101).

Yet, ultimately, Wilson does not uphold a primary connection between the prophet's call and his dumbness. The motive for editorial insertion of 3:22-27, with the consequent narrowing of the prophetic office, is apologetic: if Ezekiel had intervened for Israel, the disaster of destruction and exile would not have happened; therefore, he must have been legitimately prevented from performing his expected task of mediation.

1.5   These various treatments all fail to some degree to account for the biblical text, in which there is no qualification of the dumbness as intermittent (*pace* Klostermann, Lamparter, Greenberg) or dependent upon the people's prior rejection of the prophet (*pace* Komlosh, Greenberg). Moreover, those who read the dumbness wholly as an editorial device do so at the expense of the text's synchronic intelligibility (so Fohrer, Zimmerli) or at least do not recognize an essential link between Ezekiel's dumbness and the larger representation of his prophetic ministry.

1.6   It is the thesis of this study that such a connection can be demonstrated (along the lines indicated by Wilson) and furthermore, anchored, not merely in an apologetic intention of the editors, but in the whole structure of the book as it attests to a significant development in the conception of the prophetic office and, indeed, in the status of the divine word itself. Specifically, it will be argued that the phenomenon of Ezekiel's dumbness witnesses to a critical move in the process by which the word of God became Scripture, namely, the move toward textualization of Israel's sacred traditions. It will be further suggested that, while this move was a historical one, understanding its hermeneutical implications requires more than a purely historical-critical or literary method. The approach pursued here draws upon recent studies which contribute to an understanding of how discourse is affected by the practice of writing.

2.1   One need not look beyond the call narrative to see that Ezekiel's prophetic career is represented as a critical juncture in the history of revelation. The first act of obedience demanded of the prophet is consumption of a meal which is repellent both in form and content: Ezekiel must eat the written word of judgment against Israel (2:8–3:3). He is not, of course, the first prophet to "swallow" the word of God as part of his equipment for service (cf. Jer 15:16). Jeremiah's use of the metaphor suggests already a certain objectification of the revealed word within the prophetic tradition. It is a found thing (in what form and by whom is not specified), which the prophet takes into himself, only to learn how quickly that word escapes his control (17:15) and proves to be a source, no longer of delight, but of anguish (20:8-9) and bitter dispute (28:1-11). Moreover, that ingested word eventually passes out of Jeremiah in a form hitherto unknown for prophecy. It becomes a scroll (ch. 36), a written tradition resistant to destruction (36:27-32), a collection of oracles capable of maintaining its existence and asserting its authority independent of the speaker.

2.2   The book of Jeremiah is important evidence that prophetic speech was coming to be associated, not just with a vivid moment of revelation, but also with a tradition of fixed words. At the same time, through the process of inscription, the revealed word was being gradually detached from the circumstances of its original utterance and freed from dependence on personal contact between the prophet and his audience. Nonetheless, the figure of the found, ingested, and ultimately textualized word is here overshadowed by other figures—notably, those of fire and hammer (5:14; 20:9; 23:29)—more consistent with Jeremiah's highly personalized account of his struggle with the immediate, irresistible power of the divine word.

2.3   The metaphor of ingestion has progressed greatly by the time of its reappearance in Ezekiel. Now it stands prominently in the prophet's call, dominating all further understanding of his career. This time verbal consumption is not a casual, voluntary gesture; it is commanded as the first act of the prophet, the precondition for public service. These words are not merely found; their authenticity and authority are unmistakable, for they come directly from the hand of God. But most strikingly, there is no longer any ambiguity about the form in which the prophet receives the edible revelation. It comes to Ezekiel already *as a text*. This is the form in which he must claim his inheritance and the basis on which he must make his own contribution to the tradition of faithful witness.

2.4   The progress toward textualization of the divine word did not occur entirely as an internal development within figurative speech or the conception of prophetic experience. It was a concrete historical development which profoundly affected exilic and postexilic culture and faith. The first evidence of Israel's recognizing an obligation to order its life by God's word as mediated through authoritative texts dates from the end of the seventh century (cf. 2 Kgs 22:8–23:3). The exilic community probably produced new or greatly revised editions of the Torah, the Deuteronomistic History, and the early Prophets. It should, therefore, not be surprising to discover that the exilic prophet's ministry was from the start affected by the increasingly textual character of the tradition which he received and passed on, with the new constraints and opportunities which that development produced for the communicators of God's word.

3.1   Central to virtually all contemporary discussion of language and texts is the assertion of an irreducible quality of written discourse which cannot be explained entirely by analogy to speech. The most significant effect of writing, in contrast to speech, is the freeing of the text from the immediate situation of dialogue. Living speech is anchored in circumstantial reality: speaker and hearer are present to one another within a particular historical situation which constitutes their common frame of reference. The meaning of speech is taken to be the immediate intention of the speaker, and the words are assisted in conveying that intention to an identifiable and more-or-less personally selected audience by means of intonation, gesture, even props. While it is, of course, true that the possibility of ambiguity and misunderstanding exists, the dialogical situation minimizes this by affording the opportunity for questioning and challenge by the audience, for clarification and self-correction by the speaker. Ricoeur notes that, at the limit, the "ideal sense" of what is said comes so close to the "real reference," i.e., that which is spoken about, that speaking becomes an act of showing (1981: 148).

3.2   In the written text, however, the bond between "speaker" and "hearer," as also between sense and reference within a given set of historical circumstances, is, if not broken, then at least greatly attenuated. For reading a text is much more than another way of listening to a speaker. "The emancipation of the text from the oral situation entails a veritable upheaval in the relations between language and the world, as well as in the relation between language and the various subjectivities concerned (that of the author and that of the reader)" (Ricoeur 1981: 147). No longer is the meaning of the discourse determined primarily by the intention of its originator, who is not present with the text to support or explain its meaning. The phenomenon of writing reveals a new dialectic of discourse whose partners are the text—whereby the author is "instituted" and so "stands in the space of meaning traced and inscribed by writing" (Ricoeur 1981: 149)—and its readers. There is, however, a measure of inequality to their partnership, for only the text "speaks." Written discourse makes no allowance for retort, defenses, or correction from its readers. Yet the text's identity is established only through its partners, who assert their right to an opinion through the act of reading; "it is the response of the audience which makes the text important and therefore significant" (Ricoeur 1976: 31).

3.3   In contrast to the "objectivist" stance maintained by New Criticism and structuralism, recent critical theories, including Ricoeur's, stress that the text means something always and only *to someone*. As for what it means—here the work of interpretation begins. The autonomy of the written text from a fixed frame of reference, its potential for addressing readers whose own frames of reference are incalculably diverse, and, further, its freedom "to enter into relation with all other texts, which come to take the place of the circumstantial reality referred to by living speech" (Ricoeur 1981: 148-49)—these are the characteristics which create the possibility of multiple meanings and generate out of the cessation of dialogue the dynamics of interpretation.

3.4   Paradoxically, the inscription of discourse ensures both its preservation and the perpetuation of uncertainty about its meaning. Hermeneutics only becomes a vital issue when the meaning of the tradition is no longer regarded as patently clear. Those living within "the naiveté of the first certainty" about the tradition are not self-conscious interpreters. For them, the tradition's meaning is obvious and proceeds directly from a past perceived to be in direct continuity with the present. The problem of interpretation becomes acute only in the situation of cultural exile: when we have become aware of our alienation from the past, when the first naiveté has been lost, and we must struggle toward a recovery of meaning and a revitalization of the tradition in a situation for which it was (apparently) never intended.

4.1   The biblical text offers ample witness that it was quite literally the experience of exile which precipitated Israel's central hermeneutical crisis. The challenge was enormous: to maintain the validity of the nation's constitutive traditions—the promises of land and blessing to the patriarchs, the covenantal bond established through Moses, the assurance of an eternal kingship to David's line—in the face of a disaster that seemed to mock them all. It is surely no coincidence that the exilic community greatly intensified the efforts of reconceptualization, writing, and editing of the traditions which eventually yielded a scriptural canon deeply marked with the scars of exile.

4.2   It is also no accident that the question of true and false prophecy became urgent in Judah in the period following the first Babylonian deportation (597). Both the prophets of salvation and the prophets of deeper doom appealed to the same traditions to substantiate their claims (Jer 28; Ezek 33:24-29; cf. Isa 51:2-31). And it was the increasing fixity of those traditions as the standard of judgment for all subsequent revelation and interpretation that brought the hermeneutical crisis to a head. The tradition could not be refuted or circumvented; any prophet who addressed Israel had to reckon with its authority. Sanders has shown that the difference here between true and false prophecy, between a correct reading of the tradition and a tragically wrong one, was a matter of hermeneutics: knowing that the canonical tradition speaks different messages in different contexts. The word of God is heard at the juncture between the static tradition and the current situation. It is the work of the interpreter to trace the line of their intersection: "The mid-term between canon's stability and its adaptability is hermeneutics" (29).

4.3   Ezekiel's prophetic career, then, coincides with two critical developments in Israel: first, the marked advance toward textualization of the sacred traditions and second, the urgent and bitter debate about interpreting present events in the light of those traditions. It is proposed here that the distinctive character of his prophecy was fundamentally shaped by those developments, that both the structure of Ezekiel's own oracles and his disposition toward the received tradition reflect the increasing textualization of the word of God in Israel. A theory of written discourse is adduced because it illumines precisely those features of the text that proved so recalcitrant to historical critical inquiry (cf. §1.1).

4.3.1   It should be noted that, with respect to the inscription of discourse, no absolute distinction can be drawn between Ezekiel and the other classical prophets, all of whom participated in a culture that was progressively converting and expanding its oral traditions into a literary corpus. By the eighth century, writing was a feature of prophecy, not only for transmission and publication at scribal hands (Isa 8:16; Jer 36), but also apparently as a means of illustration and emphasis within the original act of pronouncement (Isa 8:1; 30:8; Hab 2:2; cf. Jer 17:1). Yet Ezekiel differed from his predecessors in the extent to which he exploited the potential inherent in writing as a vehicle for prophecy, and therefore he stands as an important liminal figure as Israel developed from a primarily oral culture into one in which writing played an increasingly formative role. It is suggested here that Ezekiel's was a literate mind, i.e., his patterns of thought and expression were shaped by habits of reading and writing, and that through him Israelite prophecy for the first time received its *primary* impress from the conditions and opportunities for communication created by writing.

4.3.2   It is clear, moreover, that a theory of written discourse formulated in terms of the relation which obtains between modern writers and readers is not wholly suited to represent Ezekiel's situation. Especially apt in this regard are the observations of Ong and Goody concerning the nature and social effects of the move from primary orality to increasingly widespread and diverse uses of writing. Noting the remarkable persistence of oral habits of thought and expression in cultures long dependent upon written composition, Ong claims that such habits disappeared in English prose only with the Romantic Movement of the nineteenth century (1982: 26). Orality and literacy are not dichotomous elements but two poles of a continuum, all along which texts can be located in varying adjustments to both extremes.

5.1   Ezekiel addressed a society whose habits, channels, and, doubtless, ideology of communication were still oriented largely toward orality. Therefore it is not surprising that he made extensive, even exaggerated use of devices associated with oral prophecy: repetition, highly visual images, traditional formulaic language (e.g., the legal language of ch. 18). It is a mark of Ezekiel's genius how far he was able to incorporate such features into a new prophetic idiom, accommodating his language to a changing discourse situation, while yet producing a form of speech which could be recognized and assimilated by the people.

5.2   The fact that Ezekiel, living in Babylon, immediately begins addressing his oracles to Judah and Jerusalem (5:7-17; 6:2-14) has occasioned much speculation concerning the book's editorial restructuring, including relocation of the prophet. Noteworthy in this connection is the text's essential freedom from the immediacy of a dialogue situation. It is the nature of texts to address audiences which are not present to the author. In a culture in which the word of God was increasingly promulgated as text, it is plausible, even likely, that a new idiom should have developed for its proclamation. Moreover, the exigencies of the political situation had changed, and with them the demands on the prophet. Now and henceforth, Israel was a geographically divided community. If Ezekiel was truly to address the whole people over whom he had been appointed as watchman, then he had to find a way of bridging the distance, of confirming in his own proclamation that Israel was one, even in dispersion.[1] Writing afforded him that opportunity. Dwelling among the exiles, Ezekiel could speak directly to

---

[1] This is an instance of what Goody terms the formation of "secondary group relationships" (1977: 15). It should be noted that Greenberg upholds the integrity of the text on the grounds of the essential unity of the exilic and Jerusalem communities. He offers a consistently knowledgeable and sensitive treatment of the text as a coherent, if not always smooth, work of literature. Particularly valuable is his emphasis on the complex interweaving of thematic and stylistic patterns. It is likely that more thorough application of such methods as are suggested in this study would confirm many of his insights about the structure of the book and at certain points yield a more precise understanding of the circumstances of its production and the achievement of its effects.

the people of Jerusalem because God's word was already perceived as escaping the confines of the present circumstances. The prophet who had swallowed the scroll now adapted his speech to the form of a permanent record.

5.3 A further way in which Ezekiel seems to flout scholarly expectations is in his departure from the conventions of prophetic speech. The terse poetic genres usually associated with the economy of oral discourse have all but disappeared. Far more common in Ezekiel than in the other prophets are various developed narrative forms: divine speeches enjoining sign-acts (e.g., 4:1-5:4), elaborate vision reports (1:1-3:15; 8:1-11:25; 37:1-14; 40:1-48:35), extended metaphors in which historical referents show through the figure (chs. 16, 23), allegory and explication (ch. 17), didactic/casuistic formulations concerning judgment and repentance (chs. 18; 33:1-9), a recitation which turns the salvation history on its head (ch. 20). Hölscher was, of course, the outstanding proponent of the pure-poetry principle, according to which ninety percent of the book can be dismissed as secondary, and even Zimmerli often employs a much modified notion of original formal purity as the basis for identifying editorial additions. It has generally been conceded, however, that the historical Ezekiel made significant alterations in the forms of prophetic speech, and the inconclusiveness of the poetry/prose distinction is indicated by the fact that commentators so often resort to the term "heightened prose." It may be that Ezekiel's style can more profitably be considered in terms of another category, that of rhetoric. It would seem that the systematic elaboration of verbal forms is one mark of the transition to greater dependence upon writing. Goody defines rhetoric as "a formalization of oratory, brought about by the increased precision, the heightened consciousness of structural organization, that writing can bring," and asserts that increased awareness of possibilities for dividing the flow of speech and directing attention to the meaning of particular words involves changing speech patterns "into something which is not simply an 'oral residue' but a literary or proto-literary creation" (1977: 115-16).

5.4 The ways in which Ezekiel modifies the established conventions of prophecy are all the more noticeable because of the extent of his dependence on earlier tradition. The form-critical and tradition-historical work of Zimmerli has impressively demonstrated the close and detailed connections, including both motifs and speech forms, between Ezekiel and the Holiness Code. Even more evident is Ezekiel's reliance on but also eclecticism with respect to the prophetic tradition. Like Isaiah but in more elaborate form, he combines his narrative of a personal call (cf. Jer 1) with a vision of the heavenly council (cf. 1 Kgs 22). More than any other writing prophet, Ezekiel revitalizes the concepts of preclassical prophecy: i.e., the hand of God falling upon the prophet at the onset of a trance with exceptional physical or sensory results (Ezek 1:3; 3:22; 8:1; 33:22; 37:1; 40:1; cf. 1 Kgs 18:46; 2 Kgs 3:15); the phenomenon of far-sightedness (chs. 8–11; cf. 2 Kgs 26); "Spirit" or (more rarely) "the Spirit of God/YHWH" operating almost as an independent force upon the prophet (3:12,14; 8:3; 11:1,24; 43:5; cf. 2 Kgs 2:16).

5.4.1   Most numerous are the points of contact with the Jeremianic tradition. In connection with the argument presented here, it is striking that the images Ezekiel picks up (and further develops) from his older contemporary in several instances represent aspects of the prophetic office: not only ingestion of the divine word but also the unheeded watchman (Jer 6:17; Ezek 3:17-21; 33:1-9), the fortified prophet (Jer 1:18 and 15:20; used as a metaphor, Ezek 3:8-9, as a sign-act, ch. 4). A related phenomenon is Ezekiel's transformation of metaphorical figures from other texts into sign acts or fully articulated visions: Isaiah's "razor hired across the river" (7:20) is realized in Ezekiel's shaving (5:1); the parched, scattered bones of the psalms (53:6; 102:4; 141:7) come alive in the vision in the valley (ch. 37).

5.4.2   Although none of these need be the result of written dependence, the accumulation of intertextual evidence suggests a significant degree of fixity and detailed "cross-referencing" within the tradition. Other prophets engage in direct and often heated exchange with various of their contemporaries—kings and priests, disciples, and rival prophets—but Ezekiel appears primarily in conversation with the tradition. Like a creative archivist, he desires not only to preserve the treasures of the past but to make them available and meaningful in the present. Even his disputation speeches are aimed at the tradition, purging it of its useless elements (12:22-28; 18:2-4) and correcting disastrous misinterpretations (33:24-29). There are further indications that Ezekiel is conscious of producing a component of the tradition. The fre-

quent intratextual echoes within the book, which Zimmerli too
readily assigns to editorial reworking, could also be seen as marks
of original shaping in a consciously literary pattern.

5.5 Despite his evident dependence on the tradition in representation of the prophetic role, the way in which Ezekiel himself
appears is quite singular. The lack of historical specificity which
characterizes the prophetic discourse extends also to the person of
the prophet, so that "Ezekiel's personality is hidden by stylized
forms and traditions more deeply than any other of the great
prophetic figures" (Zimmerli, I: 18). In sharp contrast to Jeremiah's passionate explosions, Ezekiel's detached account of his
(no less painful) experience gives no suggestion of subjectivity:
the prophet reports only divine speeches and visions, arranged on
the sparest narrative frame. There is here none of the tension
engendered by Jeremiah's evident struggle with the word he was
compelled to proclaim; Ezekiel is what he ate, his identity wholly
subsumed by the incorporated word. Indeed, the only "personality" which emerges throughout the book, the only voice which
is heard distinctly, is God's deepened by many echoes from the
tradition of divine speech to Israel. Viewed from this radically
theocentric perspective, in contrast to the dominance of the con-
text-laden message, the role of the prophet shrinks drastically.
What becomes all the more clear is the authority of the text.

6.1 Against this background, it is now possible to discover in the
call narrative how Ezekiel's career is shaped from the beginning
by the concept of the word of God as text. Wilson has pointed to
the narrowing of the prophetic office as evidenced in the watchman image and the restrictions on Ezekiel's movement and
speech. But the narrowness of Ezekiel's function relative to his
predecessors is actually apparent from the first moment of God's
address, when he is appointed specifically and solely for messenger speech (2:4; cf. 3:11). Immediately after he swallows the
scroll, the command seems to be reinforced. Greenberg interprets
the unusual phrase ב- דבר (3:4) thus: "'speak in a particular form.'
. . . Here the nuance (absent in the commonplace *dibber ʾet* of
2:7) seems to be verbatim repetition of the message—an aspect of
absolute obedience" (68). But the inference of the odd usage
would seem to be, not that Ezekiel is more obedient than the other
prophets in speaking God's word, but that the requirement of
obedience has changed. Jeremiah's call to prophetic service was

demanding precisely in its breadth: "to pluck up and to pull
down, to obliterate and to destroy, to build and to plant" (1:10).
Further specification of his call comes in the form of images of
confrontation. Jeremiah is called out onto the contested ground
between God and Israel, to wage his campaign of destruction and
restoration with words (1:17). That role leads Jeremiah not only to
exploit the full range of traditional prophetic speech forms in
castigating the people and calling them to repent but also to
frame his own psalmic laments as the anguished bearer of the
devastating word. It would seem that this is the very opposite of
the compulsion laid upon Ezekiel. His call leads, not to urgent
appeal, but to confinement and dumbness. There is no need for
a new prophetic message; the words for this situation have already been proclaimed (by Jeremiah?[2]) and inscribed: words of
lamentation and moaning and woe (2:10). God's judgment on
Jerusalem is now a matter of record. Obedience for Ezekiel does
not mean, as it did for Jeremiah, speaking as the living mouth of
God, testing his own fresh utterances for their worth (Jer 15:19).
Ezekiel must rather fall "dumb" and let the scroll that he has
swallowed speak through him. From now until the fall of the city,
there are no genuinely new oracles; this is the time for performance of the word which has been decreed (12:28; cf. Jer 1:12).[3]

6.2 Wilson's study further advances the notion that the move
toward textuality coincides with the limiting of oral freedom. The
ban on serving as איש מוכיח (3:26) establishes a one-way commu-
nications situation that constrains the people as well as the prophet. No longer do they have a legitimate channel, in the person of
Ezekiel, for seeking special revelations (14:7; 20:3,31) or making
their appeal to God. This may be seen as an instance of what
Ricoeur calls the fundamental inequality of the audience *vis-à-vis*
the text. The author (who, with respect to the scroll of judgment,
must be considered to be God) is not available to explain or
emend. What has been written is fixed. Even the prophet who
swallowed the scroll did not thereby gain control over it. On

---

[2] The inference here is only that there is conscious continuity between the two
prophetic traditions and not that the scroll which Ezekiel eats is specifically intended to be understood as Jeremiah's.

[3] In connection with Greenberg's interpretation of the phrase דבר-ב, it is interesting that verbatim reproduction of lengthy discourse seems to be highly val-
ued and, to a great extent, possible only in literate societies, whereas oral cultures
tend to favor thematic recitation (Ong, 1967: 22-35; 1982: 57-68).

the contrary, during the period of dumbness, Ezekiel is merely the vehicle of the inalterable text.

6.3   With Ezekiel, the goal of prophecy undergoes a profound shift. No longer is it aimed at opening the ears of the people, at repentance and avoidance of disaster (cf. Jer 25:3-7; 26:2-6; 36:2-3. That possibility is foreclosed; the disaster is decreed, and now the function of the prophet is simply to make known to Israel the author of that judgment and the just grounds for its execution (cf. 16:2; 20:4). The divine recognition formula ("that you/they may know that I am YHWH") which recurs continually throughout the book and the related formula, "that they may know there has been a prophet in their midst" (2:5; 33:33), show how completely the role of the prophet and the course of history are determined by that primary intention of God.

6.4   It might even be said that the prophetic representation of history changes with Ezekiel. If, as Wolff has asserted, the prophets understood history as "the goal-directed conversation of the Lord of the future with Israel" (341), then it must be acknowledged that the conversation is suspended in Ezekiel. And with that suspension comes a new perception of the basis of historical continuity. It is not based upon "the obligatory, continual, free conversation of God with Israel" (Wolff: 343). That conversation has broken down, and God is under no compulsion to renew it. Rather, the unity of history is now clearly seen to derive solely from the absolute sovereignty of God, the constancy of purpose which is manifested in judgment and destruction as well as salvation (16:59-63). Other prophets jeered at the illusion that Israel's privileged status meant exemption from judgment (Amos 9:7), but Ezekiel shatters altogether the notion of inalienable privilege. Jerusalem, which has behaved worse than its neighbors (16:47-52), will be restored only when they are, and any pre-eminence which God may confer upon that city will be an expression of God's freedom, not a fulfillment of any binding covenant obligation from the past (16:61-62; cf. 20:37, which suggests that apostate Israel is currently out of covenantal relationship altogether).

6.5   Ezekiel takes a significant step in moving prophetic discourse out of the realm of private conversation between God and Israel and into the arena of universal history. That transition is facilitated—perhaps in a sense required—by the parallel movement toward textuality, with its implication of the restriction of dialogue. It is, indeed, by this double movement away from particularism and toward text that prophecy saves itself from oblivion. Paradoxically, as the mediating function of the prophet declines in significance, the potential actually increases for the prophetic word to gain a hearing. The divine disregard for whether or not the word is heeded at the time of proclamation—expressed, significantly, on either side of the scroll-swallowing incident (2:7; 3:12)—may be understood in this connection. Preserved as text, God's word has a means of overcoming both the human limitations of the prophet through whom it is given and the deafness of his contemporaries. It can wait until such time as it may be heard again. Moreover, it acquires a deeper meaning when seen in conjunction with revelations given at other times. The consciously intertextual and intratextual character of Ezekiel's proclamation draws attention to its place within a larger tradition, whereby the prophetic word gains in authority and persuasiveness (cf. Jer 36:2-3).

6.6   But if the prophet's role shrank as God's word hardened into text, the space around the revealed word did not long remain vacant. A new group of intermediaries arose: the סופרים, the scribes whose responsibility it was to preserve and also to interpret (the two acts never remained entirely separate) the textual tradition. And Ricoeur's theory of written discourse indicates that it could not have been otherwise, for inscription necessitates interpretation. Without the specifications afforded by a speaker and an immediately apparent "spoken about," the meaning of written discourse is frustratingly, temptingly open. The text invites, indeed, demands interpretation; it needs to be "appropriated," anchored in a reader's frame of reference. It needs to mean something to someone.

6.7   This scribal work was far from pedestrian. The task of explication was, in fact, almost as arcane as that of the prophets themselves.

> Nothing was obvious. God's deeds, that is, the accounts of them, had to be "scrutinized [derushim] in their every detail" (Ps 111:2). Those who were to do the interpreting were very much the successors of the prophets—the new bearers

of the divine word—and like prophets depended on something like divine inspiration in order to receive God's word
(Kugel, 136-37).

The evolution of Scripture by no means ended the hermeneutical
debate in Israel. Rather, by ensuring the permanence of the tradition, inscription guaranteed also the perpetuation of debate
about its interpretation. The question of true and false prophecy
seems to have ended with Ezekiel, though without the clear artic-
ulation of any principle by which the two could be distinguished
(except, of course, in retrospect). But the argument about how to
understand and apply ancient traditions in current situations
raged on, no longer among true and false prophets, but among
better and worse interpreters of various stripes. The clamorous
conflict of interpretations never, however, drowned out the voice
of the text. It was rather a form of listening. The prophetic word
of judgment, which originally assailed deaf ears, gained a full
hearing—perhaps for the first time—as a text.

7.1   The test of any interpretation must finally be whether it illumines works in their entirety. It has been argued here that the
connection between Ezekiel's call, particularly the swallowing of
the scroll, and his dumbness is a primary relation to be understood
in terms of the emergence of Scripture in Israel and the effect of
that development on the prophet's historical ministry. If that is
indeed the case, then the interpretation must be found compatible
with the whole structure of the text. Particularly significant in this
regard is the book's inference that Ezekiel's dumbness was total
(in the sense that it applied) but temporary. Therefore it must be
possible to show that there is some absolute difference between
the ways the prophet functioned before and after the lifting of the
restriction.

7.2   A clue to the essential role which the figure of dumbness
plays in the representation of Ezekiel's prophetic career is the fact
that later references to it occur at key junctures in the text. An
anticipation of its termination concludes the long series of denun-
ciations and threats against Judah and Jerusalem (24:27), and the
restriction is finally lifted when news of the city's fall reaches
Babylon (33:22). Now at last, when the word of destruction has
been performed, there is a chance for a new word to be spoken,
perhaps to be heard. And indeed, there is a change of tone at this

point in the text. The whole force of the first twenty-four chapters is to convict Israel of the extent of its sin and the righteousness of God's judgment. Although there is no possibility that the judgment will be reversed, nontheless it is necessary that Israel be brought to recognition of itself (especially through the lurid portraits of chs. 16 and 23) and of God ("that you/they may know that I am YHWH"). Only this recognition, as humiliating as the destruction itself, can serve as the basis of a renewed relationship with God (6:8-10; 16:62-63; 20:43-44).

7.2.1 The outcry of the people—"Our transgressions and our sins are upon us and in them we are rotting away; how then shall we live?" (33:10)—is the first indication that Israel is beginning to understand how desperate is its situation. Now that the turning has come, visions and symbolic acts and evocative imagery yield to argumentation: the oracles in ch. 33 are directed wholly toward demolishing the corrupt tenets of popular theology (33:17, 24-29) and showing clearly wherein lie the seat of responsibility and the possibility of restoration (cf. ch. 18). Ezekiel is still engaged more in diatribe than in dialogue. Nonetheless, seen in close conjunction with the dramatic oracles and visions of restoration which follow (chs. 36-48), his speech here does mark a change. If a productive two-way conversation is not yet possible (although it must be conceded that the strongly theocentric perspective of the book is not well-suited to representing such a dialogue, had it occurred), then at least the pre-condition has been met: through fulfillment of the word of doom, the people learn "that there has been a prophet in their midst" (33:33). Now at last God opens the prophet's mouth[4] and fills it with new words.

7.3 It must be stressed that the change in the prophet's way of speaking is not primarily a response to the people's greater receptivity. The opening of his mouth, like the dumbness, proceeds entirely from God's initiative. The crucial point here is that Ezekiel speaks differently—prophesies, in a sense, for the first time—because this is genuinely new revelation. He is no longer constrained by the scroll he swallowed, because the limits of that text

---

[4] Greenberg's rendering of the phrase פה פתחון, literally "opening of the mouth" (of the redeemed Israel, 16:63, and of Ezekiel, 29:21), as "a claim to be heard"—based on its Mishnaic meanings, "an occasion for complaint, a pretext for accusation"—supports this interpretation (121).

have been exceeded. The word of judgment has been fulfilled, the "laments and moaning and woe" have all been uttered, and now a new word is needed. The regnant theological system asserting the eternalness of David's covenant has been razed along with his city. Standing in that void, Ezekiel has a creative ministry to perform. He must speak the first word of hope to the exiles after the disaster; he must articulate the visions on which the future can be built.

7.4   Historical criticism has moved us irrevocably beyond the once prevalent view of Ezekiel's prophecy as virtually a single literary unit. Zimmerli's notion of *Nachinterpretation* (successive development of kernel elements through modification and expansion in a "school of the prophet") has enhanced our understanding of the diachronic development of the material and is in important respects compatible with the approach taken here. Particularly interesting from the standpoint of this study is how that concept traces the stimulus for elaboration to the nature of the kernel elements themselves. Even at the first level of the tradition, those elements demonstrate an important characteristic of texts: they seek interpretation and provide guidelines for their interpreters. This book offers especially rich examples of the way in which biblical hermeneutics begins within Scripture itself.

7.5   It is noteworthy that Zimmerli considers the process of written development to have begun with Ezekiel himself:

> That the prophet himself knew something of school instruction, which is phenomenologically very different from the older prophetic preaching in public, is made very clear by passages such as chs. 18, 33:1-9,10-20. Thus besides the oral proclamation of rhythmically composed sayings, which continued the manner of preaching of the earlier prophets, we must reckon that the prophet himself undertook the secondary work of learned commentary upon and further elaboration of his prophecies, i.e. with a kind of "school activity" (I, 71).

As critical scholarship places the merger of oral "prophecy" and written "commentary" or "elaboration" ever earlier, now within Ezekiel's own career, it becomes difficult to make any firm separation between those aspects of his activity.

8.1   The clear implication of this study is that the fundamentally literary quality of Ezekiel's historical role is still not adequately appreciated. There is need for a more precise assessment of the cultural forces that shaped his proclamation from its inception in a form peculiarly suited to amplification without loss of coherence and, ultimately, to inclusion within the prophetic canon (cf. Childs: 361). It is likely that methods not commonly applied to biblical interpretation will prove helpful. This effort to locate in the book some of the dynamics inherent to literate discourse is a probe in that direction.[5]

8.2   Pursuit of such investigations should supplement the insights gained through historical criticism, while also providing certain correctives. The elegant architecture of the book grows more impressive with further study. Our investigations must be conducted with regard for the literary integrity of the text at every level, beginning with the earliest stages of composition. We are likely to render satisfactory interpretations only by proceeding on the assumption that the text was always intelligible in its synchronic dimensions, however its meanings may have been enriched and changed through diachronic evolution. It is wise to credit those who produced the text with the concern that it should be read.

WORKS CONSULTED

Childs, Brevard S.
>   1979   *Introduction to the Old Testament as Scripture*. Philadelphia: Fortress.

Fohrer, Georg
>   1955   *Ezechiel*, Tübingen: J. C. B. Mohr.

Goody, Jack
>   1968   *Literacy in Traditional Societies*. Cambridge: Cambridge University Press.
>   1977   *Domestication of the Savage Mind*. Cambridge: Cambridge University Press.

[5] My dissertation, "Swallowing the Scroll: Textuality and the Dynamics of Discourse in Ezekiel" (Yale University, 1987) offers a fuller treatment of issues raised here.

Greenberg, Moshe
1983   *Ezekiel 1-20*. Anchor Bible, 22. Garden City, NY: Doubleday.

Hirsch, E. D., Jr.
1977   *The Philosophy of Composition*. Chicago: University of Chicago Press.

Hölscher, Gustav
1924   *Hesekiel, der Dichter und das Buch. BZAW*, 39. Giessen: Töpelmann.

Klostermann, A.
1893   "Ezechiel und das Heiligkeitsgesetz." Pp. 368-418 in *Der Pentateuch*. Leipzig: Deichert.

Komlosh, Yehuda
1973   "The Silence of Ezekiel at the Beginning of His Prophecy." Pp. 279-283 in *Zer Ligevurot* (Shazar Jubilee Volume). Jerusalem: Israel Society for Biblical Research [Hebrew].

Kugel, James
1983   "Two Introductions to Midrash." *Prooftexts* 3: 131-55.

Lamparter, Helmut
1968   *Zum Wächter Bestellt: Der Prophet Hesekiel*. Stuttgart: Calwer Verlag.

Ong, Walter
1967   *The Presence of the Word*. New Haven: Yale University Press.
1982   *Orality and Literacy: The Technologizing of the Word*. New York: Methuen.

Ricoeur, Paul
1974   *The Conflict of Interpretations: Essays in Hermeneutics*. Evanston: Northwestern University Press.
1976   *Interpretation Theory: Discourse and the Surplus of Meaning*. Fort Worth: Texas Christian University.
1981   *Hermeneutics and the Human Sciences*. Cambridge: Cambridge University Press.

Sanders, James
1977   "Hermeneutics in True and False Prophecy." Pp. 21-41 in *Canon and Authority*. Ed. G. W. Coats and B. O. Long. Philadelphia: Fortress.

Urbach, Ephraim E.
    1946   "When Did Prophecy Cease?" *Tarbiz* 17:1–11 [Hebrew].

Wevers, John W.
    1969   *Ezekiel*. Century Bible. London: Thomas Nelson and Sons.

Wilson, Robert R.
    1972   "An Interpretation of Ezekiel's Dumbness." *VT* 22: 91–104.

Wolff, Hans Walther
    1963   "The Understanding of History in the Old Testament Prophets." Pp. 336–355 in *Essays in Old Testament Hermeneutics*. Ed. Claus Westermann. Atlanta: John Knox Press.

Zimmerli, Walther
    1979   *Ezekiel*. Hermeneia. Philadelphia: Fortress.

WRITE OR TRUE?
A Response to Ellen Frances Davis

Katheryn Pfisterer Darr
Boston University School of Theology

1.1   Throughout the approximately twenty-four centuries of its existence, the book of Ezekiel has confronted interpreters with notoriously difficult problems. Early rabbis struggled to reconcile its legal prescriptions with those contained in the Torah of Moses, and some of them concluded that reading the beginning and end of Ezekiel was potentially too dangerous to be undertaken by anyone younger than thirty years. As modern critical approaches to Scripture came of age, questions of interpretation brought challenges to (aspects of) the widely held view that the book of Ezekiel was primarily the product of a sixth-century B.C.E. prophet/priest who proclaimed God's word in Babylon and who collected and arranged his oracles in what came to be their canonical form. While some scholars were content to deny substantial sections of the scroll to Ezekiel, others argued that such a person never existed at all. The location of his ministry was identified as Jerusalem, Babylon, or both; and the prophet himself was diagnosed as suffering from mental illness and subjected to Freudian analysis.

1.2   One of the most serious difficulties posed by the book, however, concerned the nature and extent of Ezekiel's muteness, which Yhwh imposes seven days after his call vision (3:26) and relieves shortly before the arrival in Babylon of a messenger bearing the news of Jerusalem's demise (33:22; see also 24:26). Despite numerous creative solutions, the dilemma remains: How do we reconcile divinely imposed muteness with the textual witness that Ezekiel fulfilled his call to proclaim God's word by pronouncing judgment against both Judah/Jerusalem (through ch. 24) and foreign nations and rulers (chs. 25–32)? In "Swallowing Hard: Reflections on Ezekiel's Dumbness," Ellen Davis suggests what is in some respects a new solution to this baffling problem.

2.1   Davis rejects attempts to explain Ezek 3:22-27 as an editorial
insertion, be it motivated by the desire to defend Ezekiel's failure
to intervene on Israel's behalf (Wilson: 104) or by his disciples'
wish to introduce early in the book a fuller description of God's
dealings with the prophet (Zimmerli: 161). Dismissed, as well, are
efforts to attribute Ezekiel's muteness to (intermittent) psychological disturbance or symbolic act. Instead, Davis urges interpreters both to recognize the primary relationship between
Ezekiel's swallowing of a divinely authored scroll and his muteness, and to take seriously the "synchronic intelligibility" (1.5) of
the text at every stage of its development. She concedes that Ezekiel's failure to carry out all aspects of the prophetic office is
addressed in 3:22-27, for he is forbidden to act as a channel for
persons seeking to inquire of, or make appeal to, God. His ingestion of the scroll and subsequent muteness, however, also shed
light upon the structure of the work as a whole and function as
"figures for the new conditions and constraints imposed upon communication by the move toward textualization of the prophetic
tradition" (Abstract). Hence, Ezekiel's muteness bears witness to
the "process by which the word of God became Scripture" (1.6).

2.2   Once we recognize the influence of written discourse upon
Ezekiel and his oracles, certain features of the text left unex-
plained by historical-critical investigation can more fully be understood. For example, Ezekiel's remarkably objective account of
his experience conforms to the "lack of historical specificity" (5.5)
which characterizes written literature (and which gives rise to the
need for hermeneutics). Divinely imposed limitations upon Ezekiel's role as prophet serve to underscore the authority of the
scroll he consumes, while his tendency to address distant audiences reflects the restriction of dialogue which is characteristic of
textuality.

3.1   The above remarks touch upon, but cannot summarize fully,
the many intriguing and insightful suggestions set forth by Davis
in the course of her complex argument. "Swallowing Hard" has
much to offer the student of Ezekiel, not least its insistence that
we both recognize a coherent connection between consumption
of the scroll, muteness, and the structure of the entire work, and
take seriously the implications of the often repeated dictum that
Jews living in the exilic and postexilic periods engaged in significant literary activity.

3.2 To be sure, some readers will find themselves in disagreement with Davis at various points. For example, I am not convinced that hermeneutics becomes a vital issue only when speaker and hearer no longer are in direct contact with one another (3.1, 3.4). On the contrary, Israel's literature bears ample witness that prophetic proclamations (for example) could be, and were, heard and interpreted in quite diverse ways by different individuals/ groups, depending in part upon their experience, vested interests, situation in society, and so on. Or again, I discern no evidence to support the assertion that "Jerusalem, which has behaved worse than its neighbors (16:47-52), will be restored only when they are" (6.4). Rather, the descriptions of marvelous future conditions which we discover in the book of Ezekiel are exclusive, rather than inclusive, of lands and peoples outside the land of Israel (Darr). Finally, I find Davis's characterization of Ezekiel's account of his experience as "detached" (5.5) difficult to reconcile with passages like 9:8 and 11:13. However, such points of disagreement are not central to the author's main thesis; and we shall not dwell upon them in this response.

3.3 More important, in my view, are two issues which appear crucial to Davis's interpretation of the function and significance of Ezekiel's muteness, and which raise recurring questions as I read her argument. First, she fails to make clear exactly what she perceives to be the relationship between Ezekiel, writing, and written literature, be it his own oracles or the traditions upon which he draws. Second, her proposition that the scroll-swallowing episode and Ezekiel's subsequent muteness function as figures for the movement toward textuality occurring in his day is not persuasive. Is it not more likely that these phenomena address another, problematic aspect of life in that period—the need to distinguish between true and false prophecy?

4.1 Were Ezekiel's oracles composed in written form, or do his originally oral compositions simply reflect the influence of reading and writing upon the prophet? This question is crucial to Davis's argument. Yet throughout much of her article, she fails to state clearly how, and to what extent, Ezekiel should be viewed as a "writing" prophet in dialogue with "fixed" (written?) traditions. Indeed, many of her remarks concerning this point seem intentionally vague.

4.2   As a result, it is difficult to determine *precisely* what she means when, for example, Davis asserts that through Ezekiel, "Israelite prophecy for the first time received its *primary impress in a consciously literary mode*" (Abstract; see also 4.3.1; emphases mine). Does she wish to convince us that Ezekiel composed his prophecies in the form of texts—a conclusion strongly suggested when, for example, she states that "writing" afforded him the opportunity to advance his claim that "Israel was one, even in dispersion" (5.2)? Or, are we rather to conclude that Ezekiel constructed his oral pronouncements according to a "consciously literary pattern" in order to bridge the gap between oral and written types of discourse, a position urged especially in 5.1 ("It is a mark of Ezekiel's genius how far he was able to incorporate such features into a new prophetic idiom, accommodating his language to a changing discourse situation, while yet producing a form of speech which could be recognized and assimilated by the people.")?

4.3   Careful reading of Davis's argument eventually leads to the view that she has opted for the more modest of these two interpretive options, i.e., illuminating "how [Ezekiel's] discourse is affected by the practice of writing" (1.6). It is true that along the way, Davis hints at more ambitious claims (as the above statement, quoted from 5.1, suggests). Finally, however, she must retreat from attempts to prove that Ezekiel was, from the outset, a "writing" prophet. Davis knows, and concedes at more than one point, that no clearly defined cleft separates oral and written communication ("Orality and literacy are not dichotomous elements but two poles of a continuum, all along which texts can be located in varying adjustments to both extremes," 4.3.2). Although she devotes considerable space to identifying certain characteristics of literary (that is, written) discourse—notably those reflecting the "restriction of dialogue" which is the nature of texts—and then arguing that these same characteristics also appear in Ezekiel's oracles, such observations do not inevitably lead to the conclusion that all of Ezekiel's prophecies were originally written compositions. (At any rate, the fact that certain rhetorical features are shared by both oral and written communication deserves greater prominence than it receives in "Swallowing Hard.")

4.4   Yet even Davis's more modest proposal that Ezekiel merely exploited the "conditions and opportunities for communication created by writing" (4.3.1) rests, at points, upon questionable observations. Certain features of Ezekielian oracles ostensibly affected by the movement toward textualization about which she speaks are better explained in other ways. For example, the observation that "It is the nature of texts to address audiences which are not present to the author" (5.2) is not particularly helpful for understanding why Ezekiel, residing in Babylon, directed oracles to those who remained in Judah/Jerusalem. Far more illuminating is the recognition that the prophet addressed distant groups (foreign nations and rulers, as well as Jerusalemites) because the fate of these groups was of concern to the Babylonian exiles, who were, in fact, his intended audience. Neither am I convinced that the first twenty-four chapters of Ezekiel share "the autonomy of the written text from a fixed frame of reference" (3.3). Far from lacking "historical specificity" (5.5), many of Ezekiel's prophecies are exceedingly situation-rooted—carefully located in time and place.

4.5 Hence, even if we grant that Ezekiel's prophecies bear certain literary characteristics—an opinion shared by many scholars (see, for example, von Rad: 222-23), we must nonetheless conclude that Davis's attempts to delineate those characteristics are not so persuasive as first they appear to be. That being the case, however, we are left with a question: If the increasing influence of writing has not left so profound a mark upon the book of Ezekiel as Davis suggests, can her interpretation of the function of the prophet's subsequent muteness bear the weight that her thesis places upon it?

4.6 Finally, I believe that Davis errs when she argues that in the first section of the book (through ch. 24), Ezekiel's own personality and role recede because oral freedom is giving way to the "authority of the *text*" (5.5; emphasis mine). Should the *form* in which the prophet receives revelation be regarded as the most striking aspect of the scroll-swallowing episode, as Davis claims (see especially 2.3)? Against this view, I suggest that what are emphasized are the divine origin and authority of the lamentations, mourning, and woe inscribed upon the scroll that Ezekiel ingests.

5.1 Hebrew Scripture testifies that ancient Israel struggled to discern God's authentic word in the midst of prophetic conflict.

Out of this struggle emerged certain criteria designed to help the community distinguish between true and false prophets (e.g., Deut 13:2-6 [ET 1-5]; 18:15-22; see Crenshaw: 49-61). No single criterion proved adequate in every situation, however; even the test of fulfillment or nonfulfillment of prophecy required the advantage of hindsight.

5.2   The books of Jeremiah and Ezekiel contain considerable evidence that during the years preceding 586 B.C.E., prophetic conflict increased. Both *shalom*-speaking prophets and prophets of doom claimed to speak in Yhwh's name; and the former, understandably, enjoyed popular support. Without incontrovertible proof of the truth of their words, Jeremiah and Ezekiel were forced to hurl derogations at their opponents. So, for example, Jeremiah urged that prophets of weal be regarded with extraordinary suspicion (28:8-9) and he accused those who predicted a quick return from exile of lying (28:15; 29:8-9, 21, 23, 31-32). Such deceits, he charged, were conceived by the prophets themselves; and Yhwh disavowed responsibility for their messages, insisting that "I did not send them" (29:9; see also 28:15), "I did not command them" (29:23), and "he has talked rebellion against Yhwh" (29:32). Ezekiel, too, contended with peace-speaking prophets, likening them to foxes among ruins (13:4) and accusing them of speaking "out of their own minds" (13:2) since "the Lord has not sent them" (13:6).

5.3   At the same time, both prophets insisted that their own oracles, including predictions concerning a long-lived exile and the destruction of Jerusalem, were authentic messages from God. In recounting his call, Jeremiah claimed that his words were entrusted to him when God's hand touched his mouth (1:9; see also 15:16). His assertion echoes God's promise, ostensibly spoken through Moses, to raise up authentic prophets in Israel's midst: "I shall put my words in his mouth, and he will speak to them all that I command him" (Deut 18:18). It carries, as well, the implicit assurance that Jeremiah's message is free of his own "subjective judgments" and is, in fact, "divine in origin" (Eichrodt: 62).

5.4   Ezekiel, too, speaks of having ingested Yhwh's words. In fact, as Davis notes (2.3), with the latter prophet the ingestion metaphor has developed beyond Jeremiah's figurative expression of it, since Ezekiel is ordered actually to eat the text extended to him. Yet the significance of this scroll-swallowing episode should not be contrasted too strongly with that of Jeremiah's call experience. Like his fellow prophet, Ezekiel recounts his commissioning in a manner which emphasizes God's responsibility for the message he must proclaim, thereby setting himself apart from those prophets who conceive their own messages and deliver them for self-serving reasons. "Eat this scroll, and go, speak to the house of Israel," Yhwh commands (3:1). Several verses later, the divine origin of his proclamations again is underscored, for Ezekiel is ordered to repeat God's words verbatim (Greenberg: 68). He is not free to add extraneous elements of his own. Henceforth, his words will be the words of a scroll bearing content he did not author and over which he has no control.

5.5 In my view, the Ezekielian emphasis upon the prophet's (literal) ingestion of the divine word functions as part of his defense against charges of false, indeed, seditious prophecy. In Greenberg's words (77), the prophet's personal responsibility for his message is thereby attenuated:

> Ezekiel's denunciations are exclusively reports of what God said. The prophet's task is reduced to the conveyance of God's message; he has no further responsibility toward his audience and is answerable only to God for delivering his message. . . .

This agenda resurfaces in 3:17, where we read that the prophet is to warn the people only when he receives a word from Yhwh's mouth, and again in 3:26-27, where he is denied the ability to function as an איש מוכיח on Israel's behalf or, indeed, to speak at all except when Yhwh speaks to (through) him. However, its influence does not end there. Rather, I suggest that efforts to defend the prophet as an authentic bearer of the divine word continue in divine assurances that fulfillment of Ezekiel's prophecies will bring popular recognition not only of Yhwh's power and sovereignty (e.g., 6:10; 12:16), but also of Ezekiel's true status ("When this comes—and come it will!—then they will know that a prophet has been among them" [e.g., 33:33]).

5.6 Of course, Davis recognizes that the appearance of the ingestion metaphor in Ezekiel is not unrelated to questions of origination and authority (see especially 2.3), although she insists that

the written form in which Ezekiel receives his message is of foremost importance. Neither does she ignore the crisis occasioned by
prophetic conflict during the years leading to Jerusalem's demise
in 586 B.C.E.. Her discussion of that phenomenon (4.2), informed
by the work of Sanders, emphasizes the role of hermeneutics in
distinguishing between true and false prophecy. Davis's remarks
about prophetic conflict, however, like the biblical criterion of
fulfillment or nonfulfillment of prophecy, benefit greatly from the
advantage of hindsight. Certainly the prophets themselves, as
well as those texts which address the need to distinguish between
true and false prophecy, did not speak to the problem in this way.
Rather, they focused upon the motivations underlying the behavior of Israel's intermediaries (Ezek 13:18-19), proclamations made
in the names of other deities (Deut 18:20), the authenticity of
claims to speak words entrusted to them by Yhwh (Ezek 13:2-3),
forms of revelation (Jer 23:25-28), and, of course, the actualization
of prophecies in history.

5.7   Such were the criteria upon which Jeremiah and Ezekiel
based their indictments of prophets whom they opposed, and in
light of which they sought to confirm their own status as true
spokespersons of God. So, for example, we read in Ezek 24:27 and
33:22 (see also 29:21) that with the fall of Jerusalem, the prophet's
mouth will be opened, i.e., the fulfillment of his prophecies of
judgment will demonstrate Ezekiel's authenticity (while discred-
iting his opponents). As Greenberg (121) has said, " . . . this terrible concurrence of events with his reiterated prophecies of
doom vindicated him, gave him at once the credit he had lacked
for seven years—gave him 'a claim to be heard,' 'an opening of the
mouth.'" His authenticity confirmed, the prophet moves into a
new phase in his prophetic career—the proclamation of Israel's
restoration—and there is no need to emphasize the divine origination of his words through the description of yet another scroll
extended to him by the hand of God.

6.1   Finally, we note that the form in which Ezekiel receives
Yhwh's words of lamentation, mourning, and woe is not unrelated
to the issue of prophetic conflict, as Davis herself observes. While
it may well be true that Ezekiel's experience reflects the movement of Israel's traditions, including its prophetic traditions, toward textualization (Zimmerli: 137), one of the implications of
this movement is that the divine word becomes "a written tradi-

tion resistant to destruction" (2.1). Inscribed, bound, and sealed (see also Jer 32:10; Isa 8:16), the text of God's words which the prophet ingests communicates unshakable certainty that no word shall be left unfulfilled.

WORKS CONSULTED

Blenkinsopp, Joseph
1983   *A History of Prophecy in Israel.* Philadelphia: Westminster.

Crenshaw, James L.
1971   *Prophetic Conflict.* BZAW, 124. Berlin: Walter de Gruyter.

Darr, Katheryn Pfisterer
1987   "The Wall Around Paradise: Ezekielian Ideas about the Future." *VT* 37: 271–279.

Eichrodt, Walther
1970   *Ezekiel.* Old Testament Library. Trans. Cosslett Quin. Philadelphia: Westminster. [*Der Prophet Hesekiel.* ATD 22/1. Göttingen: Vandenhoeck & Ruprecht, 1965].

Greenberg, Moshe
1983   *Ezekiel 1–20.* Anchor Bible, 22. Garden City: Doubleday.

von Rad, Gerhard
1965   *Old Testament Theology,* vol. II. Trans. D. M. G. Stalker. New York: Harper & Row. [*Theologie des Alten Testaments*: Band II, *Die Theologie der prophetischen Überlieferungen Israels.* Munich: Chr. Kaiser, 1960].

Sanders, James
1977   "Hermeneutics in True and False Prophecy." Pp. 21–41 in *Canon and Authority.* Eds. G. W. Coats and B. O. Long. Philadelphia: Fortress.

Wilson, Robert R.
1963   "An Interpretation of Ezekiel's Dumbness." *VT* 22: 91–104.

Zimmerli, Walter
1979   *Ezekiel 1.* Hermeneia. Philadelphia: Fortress. [*Ezechiel 1, 1. Teilband.* BKAT XIII/1. Neukirchen, 1969].